RELATIONSHIP
RESCUE

Also by the author:

Love Smart
Family First
The Seven Keys to Weight Loss Freedom
The Ultimate Weight Solution Food Guide
The Ultimate Weight Solution Cookbook
The Ultimate Weight Solution
Self Matters
Life Strategies

RELATIONSHIP RESCUE

**A Seven-Step Strategy for
Reconnecting with Your Partner**

PHILLIP C. MCGRAW, PH. D.

New York

Visit Dr. McGraw's website at:
www.drphil.com

Copyright © 2000 Phillip C. McGraw, Ph.D.

Mass Market ISBN: 0-7868-9110-6
ISBN-13: 978-0-7868-9110-8

Original book design by Lisa Stokes

FIRST MASS MARKET EDITION

10 9 8 7 6 5 4 3 2 1

This book is dedicated with love and gratitude
to my wife, Robin,
who never stopped being a wife even though
she became a mother,

to my sons,
Jay and Jordan,
who continue to inspire me to want to "do it right,"

and in loving memory of my father,
"Dr. Joe" (alias the "old man"),
a man of deep passion and emotion who overcame huge
odds to positively impact so very many.

CONTENTS

──────── ACKNOWLEDGMENTS

I thank and acknowledge Oprah Winfrey for her continuing friendship and belief in and support of my work. I thank her for her vision for this world and for sharing with me the platform of her show, which embodies her commitment to bring a few moments of sanity and constructiveness into the days of those who watch. She remains the clearest and most compelling voice in America, and has changed the fiber of our world by living with integrity and courage.

I thank my wife, Robin, and my sons, Jay and Jordan, for believing in "Dad," and sacrificing personally while I hibernated and worked. All three showed nothing but enthusiasm and excitement for the project, never once complaining or resenting the intrusion. A special thanks to Jordan for his constant visits to the study and his lurking on the balcony above. "Thanks, Peteski." My family lifts me up and loves me without condition. I thank them and continue to count on them as my soft place to fall. If a man's worth is reflected in the life and spirit of his wife and family, I am truly a wealthy and blessed man.

Thanks to Skip Hollandsworth for his passionate and energetic editing of this manuscript. Skip was unbelievably hardheaded, argumentative, and relentlessly committed to improving me and my manuscript. He accomplished both objectives. His humor, his all-nighters, and his tireless talent for unraveling and untangling were such important ingredients to this book. Thanks, Skip, for your great spirit and friendship to me. You've made a huge difference and are a true professional in every sense of the word.

Jonathan Leach once again brought his unique writing and organizational talents to this project, particularly in the most difficult and pivotal point of the book. Thanks, Jonathan, for your willingness to help, even though you did not really have the time. You were there when I needed you, and I am grateful.

Thanks as always to Gary Dobbs, my lifelong friend, partner, and godfather to my children. He is always in my balcony, as I am in his.

Thanks to Bill Dawson, the "Tulia Flash," first for his genuine friendship and second for his legal guidance. Bill is on the short list of those who never say no. Thanks again to Scott Madsen who is always on the short list.

Thanks once again to Tami Galloway and Melodi Gregg, who, happily, worked tirelessly in preparing this manuscript. Their spirits were always bright, even in the wee hours of the morning and on weekends when they could've been a million other places. I could not have done it without them.

Once again, thanks also to the thousands and thousands of seminar participants who taught me year after year what makes real-world relationships work or not. I hope that my work in general, and my writing in particular, shows that I was the real student and clearly was the one who "got the training."

Thanks again to Bob Miller and Leslie Wells at Hyperion. I have never spoken to Bob and Leslie without coming away feeling better about myself for the experience. These are people who believe in the integrity of a book, or they do not publish it. They bring out the best in me by challenging me to rise to their level.

Lastly, but certainly not least, I thank all of those who have supported my television work and *Life Strategies*. It has meant so much to hear from all of you about the changes in your lives.

GET REAL: RECONNECTING WITH YOUR CORE

If your relationship is in trouble, big trouble or small, I'm going to tell you straight-up how to fix it. I'm not going to try to be cute or glib, and I'm not going to hit you with a lot of clever buzzwords. I'm not going to use a bunch of psychobabble or the *en vogue* theory *du jour*. I'm going to give you the straightforward, no-nonsense answers that work—answers that have always worked, but have just been buried in a deluge of pop-psych nonsense.

But there is a serious and outcome-determinative precondition that you have to meet if you expect to successfully rescue your relationship and reconnect with your partner. *You* have to get real about *you*. And when I say real, I mean one hundred percent, drop-dead, no-kidding real. No defensiveness, no denial—total honesty. Get argumentative, be rigid, be defensive and hardheaded, and you will lose for sure. While the focus of this book is rescuing your relationship and reconnecting with your partner, the vehicle to achieving that is you. Not you and your partner, but you. Reconnecting with your partner cannot and will not happen if you do not reconnect with yourself first.

I promise you, you can change your partner from daylight to dark, you can dump your partner and trade up to a better one, but it won't make a damn bit of difference unless and until you decide to clean house inside yourself first. This journey does not begin with you and your partner; it begins with you. You have to take your power back and become the kind of person who commands quality, inspires respect, and settles for nothing less than an active and abiding love. That change begins from the inside out as you get back in touch with who you are and as you decide what to do with your love, your life, and your vision. Your clarity and your purpose must become crystal clear. The fix, the rescue, depends on you. To proceed with any other mind-set is to guarantee failure, miserable failure. That's why I have to begin by getting you right with you. I know you aren't being true and right with yourself, or you wouldn't be in relationship trouble and you wouldn't be holding this book.

In fact, if you are in a relationship that has gone awry, a relationship that is laced with pain, confusion, or emptiness, then by definition I know you have lost touch with your own personal power, your own dignity, your own standards, and your own self-esteem. You've allowed yourself to accommodate pain and disappointment and self-destructive attitudes. You have rationalized away many of your hopes and dreams, you've settled for so many things you did not want, you've allowed apathy to set in, and along the way you've probably let your partner mistreat you over the years. But most important, you've mistreated yourself. You've blamed your partner or other circumstances for your place in life rather than making the effort to find the true answers within you. You've lost touch with that part of you that I call your core of consciousness—that place where you are absolutely defined, the place within you where your greatest strengths, instincts, values, talents, and wisdom are centered. Think back; there was a time and a place when you knew who you were and knew what you wanted. You believed in yourself, and your life was full of hope and optimism. You were in touch with your core of consciousness. You were centered on this God-given core that uniquely defined you. And you can be centered on this core again.

This is not silly self-help talk. This may well be the most important concept you'll ever seek to master. I've studied successful people my entire life. I always wondered why these people create wonderful, rewarding relationships and lives when others just as talented muddle through with mediocrity. We all know people who get all the breaks and opportunities, yet who still can't do anything with their lives. And we know others who seemingly come out of nowhere to defy the odds and overcome immense challenges to carve their niche in the world. What I've discovered with stark and undeniable clarity is that the ones who do well are so in touch with their individual core of consciousness, so aware of their self-worth and their sense of personal value, that they not only treat themselves with enormous self-respect but they inspire others to treat them with equal respect. They live with an empowering inner clarity, one that gives them the unshakable confidence that they and they alone can determine the quality of their life. They have tapped into their core of consciousness, claimed their right to a fulfilling life, and have refused to accept less from themselves or anyone else.

The truth is not always easy to hear, but it always remains the truth—and I'm not going to let you hide from it and, in so doing, cheat yourself. So listen to me: if you don't scrape away all of life's layers of distortion, negative input, and doubt-inducing messages, and get back in touch with your own core of consciousness, then no matter what else you learn, you will have such low standards that you will continue sabotaging your relationship. You will remain mired in pain, guilt, anger, and confusion. You can bet on it.

That's why I'm coming after you first. You must reclaim your own power and strength so that you can build something extraordinary for yourself. The power I'm talking about is not the kind of power that will make you more domineering over your partner. It will not give you more control over your partner; nor will it allow you to win more arguments.

This is not about power to take things from people so that you have more for yourself. It's about the power to give and to lift up those around you. What I'm talking about is the power that comes from depth and conviction—the power to inspire, the power to create, the power to experience your life and relationship at a totally different level. It is the quiet, calm power of dignity and worth. When you tap into your own core of consciousness, and you start creating your own experience, you will notice that the world, including your partner, will start to relate to you differently. As Emerson once wrote, "What lies behind us and what lies in front of us pales in comparison to what lies within us."

So that is your precondition. As you go forward into this book, you must contemplate everything that's presented with an eye toward how it can get you back in touch with yourself—how it can get you back to that core of strength that has been there since you were born. As you read, think about how you will put honor and nobility back into your heart and mind so that you can begin to engage the world from a position of strength instead of weakness. Commit right now to requiring more of yourself, for yourself, in every area of your life. With every page you read, I want your head to lift, I want your chin and your chest to come out, not as an act of arrogance but as a message of determination. Tapping into your core of consciousness, rediscovering your inner strength and drive for greatness, can be the single most significant act of your life, and your greatest gift to your relationship partner.

ONE

IT'S YOUR TIME;
IT'S YOUR TURN

It has been fifteen years since I sat with Carol and Larry in my psychology office. They were a pretty typical couple—typical because they were having relationship problems. Like so many other couples, they were once absolutely certain that their deep love and optimism would make their relationship last. They had come together because they wanted to, because the idea of a life together felt so right, because they believed their union was the one thing that would complete them. They approached their relationship seriously, made sacrifices, and promised they would offer up their hearts and souls to each other.

And now here they were, trying to understand why the very thing that they once thought would make them so happy had left them feeling trapped, overwhelmed by an unspeakable feeling of disappointment. They were hurting, second-guessing themselves, wondering how something could go stagnant and painful so quickly. Carol swallowed, touching her throat with her fingers as tears slid down her cheeks. Larry stared out the window, his shoulders sagging, his chin propped on his fingers. Their relationship had become defined by a quiet desperation, punctuated by angry silences, which alternated with animated attacks on each other's character—and in a last-ditch effort they had dutifully sought out professional help. "I am so tired of feeling alone," Carol told me. "I feel like I want to scream or hit something, but I don't know what and I don't know why. We used to be so fresh and so alive—and now our love has become cold and bitter and lifeless. Is this it, is this all there is?"

I started talking, giving Larry and Carol the same platitudes, the same conventional wisdom, that I and every other therapist in the country had been doling out for years. You're going to have to commit to solving your problems, I said. You need to communicate better, see things through your partner's eyes, try to resolve each and every one of your differences, remember your marriage vows. Just as I had been taught, I was acting warm and genuine as I trotted out all the usual reponses. But suddenly all I could hear myself saying was blah, blah, blah. Blah, blah, blah, blah. As I sat there, I asked myself, "Has anybody noticed over the last fifty years that this crap doesn't work? Has it occurred to anyone that the vast majority of these couples aren't getting any better?"

Here were these two people, searching for answers, and I realized I was telling them things about "the nature of relationships" that weren't going to make a damn bit of difference. My profession's advice was all well and good if life was an ivory tower or if our clients lived in some sitcom-like Ozzie and Harriet existence. But it did little for those relating in the real world with real problems, real children, real financial demands, real competition for affection, real stress. The vast majority of relationship advice offered in our society not only did not work, it didn't even come close to working. That was true then and it is true now. Research shows that over two-thirds of couples, married or otherwise, who attend relationship counseling are worse or at least no better after one year. The divorce rate in America refuses to drop below fifty percent, and twenty percent of us will divorce not once but twice in our lifetime. Clearly, pleasant and generic instructions on how to "communicate" better or theoretical musings that give you great "insights" about relationships just weren't going to cut it fifteen years ago and won't cut it now.

That day with Carol and Larry was a turning point in my life. I decided that if I continued imparting the conventional wisdom, I would be cheating them and everyone like them out of any chance they had to turn their relationship around. I resolved right then and there that I was going to get real about why relationships were failing in America and what needed to be done to turn the tide. People needed a solid, practical way to reframe their lives and their lifestyles in order to create a healthy relationship rather than live in such a way as to maintain and support a bad one. It didn't matter that I had more degrees than a thermometer. I decided that I was going to have to be willing to get my hands dirty in the ugly side of life, stop dispensing easy advice, and meet the Carols and Larrys of the world where they were in their lives as well as in their relationships.

That's what this book is all about. I'm going to tell you what I believe is the truth about what you have to do to meet your needs and the needs of your partner, and exactly how to rebuild the foundation of your life so that you can have a fulfilling relationship.

What I am going to tell you will not have a thing to do with textbook communication theories like "active listening" or "relating with empathy." I'm not going to cry with you, and I'm not going to gently hold your hand. I'm not going to try to make you and your partner feel better by having you write mushy love letters to one another and then put roses on your pillows at the end of the night. If you are looking for something to read that will act like a quick salve on your emotional wounds, then I recommend you give this book to someone else—because I want to shake you back to your very core, to wake you up, and then help you start designing a memorable life and a memorable relationship.

I admit, I am pretty much an in-your-face, tell-it-like-it-is sort of person. And I want you to know that this book is not going to make things easy for you. This book is designed as a clarion call—an unapologetic command that you strip away all your defenses and fears, that you break through the clutter of your past, that you raise your standards of personal excellence, and that you stay diligently on course so that you may get what you want in your life. My mission is to help peel away the layers of confusion and distorted thinking that have dominated your relationship, peel away the false world you have constructed, put you back in touch with your inner core of consciousness, and help you find the answers that work.

And I recognize that means that a whole lot of you need a lot of answers. Relationships in general, and marriages and families in particular, continue to disintegrate before our eyes. Families are losing their focus, and domestic violence, abuse, and emotional dysfunctions have gone vertical. The epidemic is like a train careening at an ever-increasing speed down a steep hill—and if you're reading this book, that means you, too, are probably on that train and could very well be barreling toward disaster.

I know you had no intention of getting on this train. All you wanted to do was love somebody and be loved right back. You believed a relationship was the one thing that would complete you. You weren't an idiot, you weren't some masochist who looked for a relationship so that you could suffer, and you sure weren't lazy. Nonetheless, here you are. And we both know that no matter how much willpower you have to keep hanging in there, there is a line out there that, if pushed across, you will say, "That's enough, I won't take this another minute." You know yourself well enough to realize that if you cross that line, it will be the beginning of the end. You know your dignity and your heart can take only so much, and if it is violated one too many times, then you will finally dig your heels in and this deal will be over in a flash.

That line may still be looming way out in your future somewhere, or at this very moment you might be walking that line like a tightrope. But I'm here to tell you that I want to keep you from crossing that line. You may not know how or why your relationship got into such a mess, but I do know. I know what you're going through, and I know how it all happened to you. What I'm about to say may sound arrogant, and if it does, I am sorry for being so blunt. But after having been to hell and back with thousands of couples in a variety of settings, I've gotten street smart. I know how to get your relationship under control and back on the right track. And if you stay with me through this book, I'll show you what you've been missing, and I'll lead you to clear answers, starting with this one: you are not inadequate or incompetent when it comes to a relationship. The brutal and sad fact is that the deck has been stacked overwhelmingly against you.

IT'S A WONDER YOU'VE MADE IT THIS FAR

If you know anything about me through my recent writings or my television work, then you know I am the last person on earth ever to tell you that you are a victim or that there is somewhere besides yourself to look to as the cause of this or any other situation that now defines your life. But the very society that has taught you that it is good and right and natural to share your life with another person, the same society that in large part defines and measures success by how you manage your relationships and your family, never bothered to teach you how you are supposed to do that.

Think about it: the requirements for a driver's license are tenfold the requirements for a marriage license—to drive, you at least have to take a test to demonstrate some level of knowledge and competency before you are turned loose. Yet our collective society is willing to turn you loose with someone else's life for two bucks and a signature down at the courthouse. You probably got your only lessons about being in a relationship by watching your parents. The problem with that is they no doubt had less instruction and knew less about relationships than you do. You went to school and learned how to read and write, add and subtract, but you never went to a class that taught you how to understand your emotions. At no time did you ever receive any systematic education about what to expect in a relationship or how to behave in one. No one ever taught you how to relate. No one ever taught you how to select a good mate. No one ever taught you how to be a husband or a wife. And no one ever taught you what to do when things went wrong. If you think about it, no one even taught you how to define what "wrong" was.

As a result, you probably chose your mate for the wrong reasons and then proceeded into your relationship with ill-defined skills, goals, and expectations. And then came the double whammy: when you went looking for help, most of those in the "helping professions," with their textbook therapies and psychological theories, seemed to have absolutely no understanding of how to help you. It is amazing to me how this country is overflowing with marital therapists, psychiatrists and psychologists, counselors, healers, advice columnists, and self-help authors—and their approach to relationships is usually so embarrassing that I want to turn my head in shame.

It's time for the double-talk and fuzzy thinking to stop. In this journey, the one through the pages of this book, you won't be relying on theory and bad information. You will be relying on techniques and realities for creating and managing a healthy relationship. Instead of resorting to another round of expensive therapy or reading some warm and fuzzy euphemisms that could very well keep you from doing those things that can genuinely help you, you're going to learn the truth—and the truth is that your relationship is in trouble because *you* set it up that way.

Read that sentence again: your relationship is in trouble because *you* set it up that way. And let me be real clear,

I'm not saying that you set it up that way because you were in a bad mood once in a while. You didn't set it up that way because of something really outrageous that you did one time five months or five years ago. You set it up that way by actively, consistently, and efficiently designing, programming, and choreographing your entire lifestyle to generate and then support a bad relationship. You have chosen to live in a way in which no other result could occur.

I will say this over and over before you finish this book: it is not possible for you to have a seriously defective long-term relationship unless you have generated and adopted a lifestyle to sustain it. Every single person in every walk of life has a lifestyle that supports who and what he or she is. If you are a healthy, vibrant, efficient, and productive person who is in touch with your core of consciousness, then I know without question that you have a lifestyle that supports that manner of living. If you are an emotionally pained and relationally troubled person who has lost touch with your core of consciousness, I know that you have a lifestyle that supports that too. You cannot have a bad relationship unless your lifestyle is characterized by stress, pressure, distraction, and a harried and chaotic existence. Moreover, if you are living in a dysfunctional relationship with another person, it's because you have a dysfunctional relationship with yourself.

I'm not blaming you; I'm just telling you how it is. A bad relationship cannot exist if it is not fed and nurtured in some way. If you think I am wrong, just look out your window. If you see weeds in your yard or in the field next door, they didn't just happen. Some way, somehow that weed had to get started. And what's more, it had to be fed and nurtured in some way. It didn't grow in concrete; somehow the environment had to support its very existence or it could not be.

I'm not saying you necessarily chose any environment or lifestyle consciously, and I'm not saying that you generated your dysfunctional relationship on purpose. But I'm telling you that the reality of your relationship along with your overall lifestyle and your relationship with yourself are one hundred percent inextricably intertwined. If you have not designed and carried out your life to create or allow distance instead of intimacy, combativeness instead of co-operation, blame and rejection instead of accountability and acceptance, you cannot maintain the erosion and pain that you are now experiencing. Problems don't flourish in isolation. They have to have help and nurturance.

As an example, simply compare the lifestyle of someone who is chronically and morbidly overweight with the lifestyle of someone who is fit, energetic, and of normal weight. I will promise you that both of these people have designed their worlds to sustain what they have become. The overweight person will use food differently. You will find that he or she lives to eat, while a person of normal weight eats to live. This is a painful truth, but it is the truth. When it comes to your relationship, you have chosen to live patterns of thought, feeling, and behavior that have generated something that is not giving you what you want. You are living to suffer instead of loving to live. That has to change, and it has to change first before anything else will begin to fall into place.

I have no doubt that many of you at this very moment are saying, "Wait a second, Dr. Phil. All your talk about getting me straight is just great, but you have no idea what a jerk my partner can be. You have no idea what manner of hell my partner brings into my life. I'm fine about making my life better, but what about my partner? Why all this total focus on me? I'm just one-half of this deal!"

Trust me, I do know what you may well be living with, and I promise you, your partner will get his or her turn in the barrel. But in all likelihood, your partner isn't sitting right beside you reading this book. You're the only one reading it. My only input, my only influence, is with you, so that is who I am focusing on, and if you are smart you will do the same. But I do know it takes two to tango, and if you are able to change yourself, if you are able to create a different lifestyle and environment in which your relationship takes place, if you are able to regain your own power and reclaim your right to dignity and respect, then your partner is going to be seriously affected.

You can't control your partner. You can't make changes for your partner. You can't tell your partner what to do. But you can inspire your partner. You can give your partner a whole new set of behaviors and new set of stimuli to respond to. If you drop out of the destructive mind-set and vicious circle of mutually frustrating interactions that are causing your relationship to implode, if you drop out of the fight and start living a new way, it's going to be real difficult for your partner to continue spewing and seeking venom. You can stop sabotaging yourself and your relationship, and you can start inspiring the kind of reactions you want from your partner. In the face of such constructive input, he or she can't fight alone, argue alone, or continue to be offended. Your partner can pout for a while, perhaps withdraw and be suspicious for a while, but eventually he or she is going to feel pretty stupid sitting over in the corner while you seem to be getting so very much happier and so much more optimistic and at peace with yourself.

RESCUING YOUR RELATIONSHIP MEANS RESCUING YOU

Besides, what's the alternative—to allow your current lifestyle to persist, a lifestyle that with each passing day broadens the gap between you and your hopes and dreams? This isn't brain-surgery or quantum physics here—what you are doing, how you are living, is not working. Plain and simple, it is not working. If you do not push yourself to find out what it is in your lifestyle that isn't working, what it is about your lifestyle that has created and supports this negative relationship, you will continue to suffer. You will continue to work on the wrong things that have nothing to do with the status of your relationship at the expense of that which most certainly determines its success or failure. You will try to believe that it's okay to forget some of your dreams, telling yourself that at least you are "secure" and "comfortable." You'll find yourself relying more and more upon the language of losers, telling yourself that you know you "should" do something about your plight and that you'd like to change but that you just aren't sure where to start. When you choose the behavior, you choose the consequences, so you must start choosing differently right here, right now, by being open to this book and everything in it.

So now you know where we're headed. If you are going to rescue your relationship, the first lifeline we have to throw is to you so that you can pull yourself out of your emotional swamp. By changing how you treat yourself, you alter the most important element of the entire equation. It means altering the environment in which your relationship exists and changing the priorities that dictate your time and energy. You must redesign the backdrop or context in which your relationship occurs. Until you begin to live with dignity, respect, and emotional integrity, you will not have that quality and level of interaction with anyone else. As I like to say, you cannot give away what you do not have. If you don't have a pure and healthy love and regard for yourself, how can you possibly give that to anyone else? And if you can't give it to anyone else, then how can you possibly expect to have it reciprocated?

I am not suggesting that you become someone you are not. I am suggesting that you become the best of who you are. Right here, right now, you can stop hurting, and you can start changing your life. You may feel like you are lost in a maze from which there is no real exit, no route that leads back to your core of consciousness and all of the strength and wisdom that resides there. Well, I'm all about creating a route and an exit for you whenever and wherever you want it. I'm no longer caught up in ivory tower ideology. All I want to do is create good results. I'm prepared to kick a hole in the wall of the pain-ridden, unhappy maze you've gotten yourself into, and provide you clear access to action-oriented answers and instructions on what you must do to have what you want.

But as I said, I need your help. You have to be willing to admit that when it comes to conducting a relationship, whatever you are thinking and feeling and doing is not working. You have to be willing to move your position on some very deep beliefs and long-held emotions and behavioral patterns. When I say "move your position," I mean that you must be willing to utterly change the way you think, feel, and act in relationship to yourself and your partner. This can be harder than you could ever imagine. I am asking you to give up your security blankets and free-fall. I am asking you to hit the erase button on ideas that you may have been holding for ten, twenty, thirty, or forty years. I am asking you to wipe the slate clean and start over in your thinking. Bottom line, I am asking you to believe once again that you are a qualified person who deserves a quality relationship. Getting back in touch with your core of consciousness will remind and convince you that there is nothing wrong with you that justifies your having less than a rewarding relationship in which you can live, love, and laugh every day of your life.

Are you ready to embrace a new kind of thinking, a new belief system, a new way of looking at yourself and your partner? To see if you're ready to move forward in this book, answer the following questions.

QUESTION
Can you forget what you think you know about managing relationships?

QUESTION
Can you decide to measure the quality of your relationship based on results instead of intentions or promises?

QUESTION
Can you decide that you would rather be happy than right?

QUESTION
Can you stop playing the blame game and recognize that it is a new day?

QUESTION
> *Can you be willing to move your position on how you approach and engage your partner?*

QUESTION
> *Can you be willing to get real and be honest with yourself, about yourself, no matter how painful it is?*

QUESTION
> *Can you stop the denial and be completely, totally honest about the state of your current relationship?*

I know that right now it may be difficult for many of you to honestly answer yes to all of those questions. Either way, don't give up, at least not until I tell you two very important things.

BUCKING THE TREND: YOU CAN MAKE YOUR RELATIONSHIP WORK

First: it is not too late. If you do not allow yourself to believe and accept that, you will think your way out of this relationship before we have the chance to save it. You may think your relationship has failed, you may feel like you have tried everything, you may feel tired, deflated, and defeated, but I'm telling you, you have to get that thought out of your head or you are dead in the water with an anvil tied around your ankle. No matter how many times you've been hurt—no matter how many times you've been disappointed, no matter how many times you've believed it could be different only to be blindsided again—you have to be willing to give yourself one more chance. Even if you have hurt so long and so badly that you aren't at all sure if you care whether your relationship survives; even if you're not sure you can ever subject yourself to any more pain from a relationship; even if you do not feel motivated or very hopeful, you can start getting out of your ditch if you will just say to yourself, "I *wish* I felt good about my relationship again." That's all we need. If all you can muster in your mind and heart is to say, "I wish I felt good about this relationship again, and I wish I felt lovingly toward this person again because I know that at least at one time in my life, those emotions felt good," then that is enough of an ember for us to fan into a flame.

Second: you are not alone. You might feel bewildered and demoralized right now, engulfed by the loneliness that comes with a deteriorating relationship. You may feel intimidated and overwhelmed by what may seem like insurmountable problems or hurts that tend to run so very, very deep. But I want you to know that from now on, you have a partner. You have a partner who is willing to walk with you through this intimidating maze of emotion and who is willing to interact without judgment or criticism, but with the willingness and courage to tell you the truth. I am going to be that partner for you. I have now counseled thousands of people and taught tens of thousands in seminars, helping them create and maintain the key relationships in their lives. I have learned what you know and, more important, what you don't know about sharing your life with another person. I have designed this approach to meet you at whatever point you find yourself in your relationship and give you the power to make changes—power that can come only from learning the absolute naked, unvarnished truth. Indeed, once you learn the real truth about how you got into this mess, and then once you learn what you can do to get rid of the mess, you will shudder to think you almost walked away. You are closer to success than you could ever imagine if you just have the courage to get real with yourself.

We will not proceed in a random fashion. The strategy for rescuing your relationship involves seven major steps. First, we will focus on defining and diagnosing where your relationship is now, because you will never be able to change what you do not acknowledge. Only if you are able to define specifically, precisely what is wrong with you—as well as what is wrong in your relationship—will you be able to set reasonable goals for change. I'm talking about taking your understanding about yourself and your relationship to a whole new level. It is one thing to say, "It hurts; I don't like the way I feel; something is missing." It's another thing to get to what is structurally, behaviorally, philosophically, and emotionally not working. Only when you figure out what the problem is can you match a solution to it. You will be amazed at the power this knowledge gives you as you pursue the rescue of this relationship.

Second, we must rid you of wrong thinking. As I stated earlier, you haven't suffered just an absence of information; you have suffered a poisoning of your thinking by an infusion of wrong information. This wrong information— the "myths" that abound about relationships—have sent you down the wrong road, pursuing the wrong alternatives to poorly defined problems. If you have misdiagnosed the problem as we just discussed, and then unknowingly embraced faulty thinking in these popularized myths, you're living a life where you are resorting to the wrong treatment for the wrong problems.

Third, it will be important to blow the whistle on your

own negative attitudes and behaviors and the specific ways you do irreparable harm to your own relationship—in other words, how you interact in ways that are in direct opposition to the healthy self that is defined in your core of consciousness. You can't get defensive here and start complaining about your partner, because I promise you that based on results, you are going to find plenty to fix in yourself before you ever get to focus on your partner. You either get it or you don't, and only when you start "getting" how and why your relationship is not what you want will you be able to start shaping it into what you do want. The fact that you are the focus should be great news because you can control you!

Only then, after understanding the full extent of your wrong thinking and bad attitudes and actions and the powerful impact they have on your relationship, can you move to the fourth step, which is to internalize a set of what I call "Personal Relationship Values" that will become the new foundation for your relational life. It's these Personal Relationship Values that lead you back to your core, emotionally tune you in to the best parts of yourself, and behaviorally set you up to give your partner positive things to respond to.

Then comes the fifth step, in which you will be taught one of the most basic and powerful formulas active at the core of human functioning: the specific formula for a successful relationship.

RED ALERT: The formula will do you no good until you've mastered the first four steps. Without completing the first four steps, you are likely to blow your chance to apply the formula effectively. Be patient enough to prepare for success.

The will to win is eclipsed by the will to prepare to win. So don't jump ahead and try to work the formula. You will get there soon enough, and if you do the work, you will arrive ready.

In our sixth step, we begin the reconnection process. Many of you have allowed the connection with your partner to remain broken for many years. For others, it is simply weakening, and distance is beginning to creep in. Either way, whether preventative or remedial, this will be the time to reopen negotiations, to work through a series of critical steps in order to learn how to deal with your own needs and your partner's needs in a way that sets you up for success.

One of my mantras is that you have to name it before you can claim it. You have to decide what you really want out of your relationship, what you want from yourself and your partner—and we will learn how to do that. As part of that reconnection process, you will go through a highly structured and powerful fourteen-day program where you and your partner begin to enact your new life—where the process of reconnection actually takes place before your eyes.

Finally, in our seventh step, you will learn how to manage your relationship once you have reconnected with your partner. Let's be honest. Neither you nor your partner were born yesterday. You have lots of emotional baggage, and we will spend considerable time on how to make sure that emotional baggage gets jettisoned so you can have a fresh start and a new chance in your relationship. And to make sure you are prepared for what lies ahead in the real world, I will give you another chapter that deals with the issues that define day-to-day life in a relationship, including topics as intimate as sex and as volatile as fighting and physical abuse.

RELATIONSHIP: PROJECT STATUS

To accomplish these seven steps, you must do one thing, starting right now. You must put your relationship on what I like to call Project Status. This means that you must consciously decide to actively, purposefully work on improving your situation each and every day. I don't mean that you need to "want to" or "intend to" work on it. I mean *do it*, every single day. Discipline yourself to do the work. You make time for other things in your life every day—you're able to take out the trash every day, you're able to get the children to school every day, you're able to get to your job every day—and your work on your relationship should be no different. You are going to have to set aside time each day to get this relationship recharged and to do the specific things that are assigned over the course of this book. You will get out of this project what you put into this project. It may mean that you must consciously reschedule or forgo other activities in order to make the time needed to work on the relationship. It may mean that you change your long-term schedule in terms of everything from weekends to vacations to allow you to deal with the relationship's demands. Putting your relationship on Project Status means that it becomes of great conscious importance to you.

Putting your relationship on Project Status also means you must be committed for the long haul. A tried and true formula fits the need here: Be—Do—Have. Be committed, do what it takes, and you will have what you want. Don't decide to work on your relationship for some preset period of time. You have to commit to work on this "until." You have to work on this until you have what you want, not until some arbitrary time limit expires. I suspect that it took you a good while to get things this screwed up, so give yourself equal time to get the relationship right.

Throughout this journey there will be setbacks, there will be pain, there will be disappointment, but there also will be change. Stay committed to facilitating that change. You have to be committed to the long-term development of an entirely new lifestyle of thought, feeling, and action. It is not enough to have some sort of "desire" or "hope" that you will develop a better relationship. You must be willing to reach down and find that long-hidden hunger for excellence that lurks somewhere inside you, and then you must be willing to unleash it.

You must take a stand that you are going to defy the odds, defy your own insecurities, and defy the conventional wisdom that has failed you so miserably. Set this personal standard for yourself from the very beginning. Adopt a philosophy of passion that says, "I will not quit. I will not allow my hopes and dreams to be pushed aside." Never forget, this life is your only shot. This is no dress rehearsal. You must be willing to reach for what you want and reach right now. And if you are willing to settle for less, then that is exactly what you will get.

Finally, to be in Project Status means that you don't forget about the importance of your relationship with yourself. You must demand nothing less than the best of yourself and for yourself. You must tell yourself that it is not wrong to want it all. It is not wrong to demand dignity, love, honor, and romance in your life. You must decide that you are worthy of everything that you want. You must decide that peace, joy, and abundance in a relationship is not just for other people. It is for you. It is not selfish to want it, it is not naive to want it, and it is not immature to expect it. What *is* immature is to sell out and settle for less than what you really want.

It is not wrong to want, expect, demand, and aspire to a relationship in which you are treated with honor, dignity, and respect. It is not unrealistic to believe that your mate can and should be your soft place to fall. It is not a pipe dream to believe that God has provided for you another person in this world whom you can trust with your most intimate and vulnerable secrets and needs.

I am not suggesting that blind optimism or denial about the risks is the right approach. I am not telling you to pretend that there are not problems, or that they will go away. I am asking you to exercise the belief within yourself that you can do this, and that your relationship can be much better. I have often said, "Sometimes we make the right decision, and sometimes we have to make the decision right." If you want the information, tools, and specific plan of action you need to make that decision right—to genuinely create change in your own life, rescue your relationship, and turn it around—then keep reading. You will find in these pages the no-nonsense but powerful strategy that can get you and your partner reconnected.

You might not like hearing about all of it. You might not like having to blow up a bunch of deceptive but highly destructive myths about what makes a relationship work, and you might not like having to confront the truth about yourself—but I predict that you will love the outcome. You will love that you will be able to reprogram yourself for success rather than failure, that you will be able to go from an individual hoping for a future to an individual making your future happen. And then both you and your partner can begin working to get what you want, to stop the pain that both of you are feeling, and to create more peace, love, and the deepest of joy in your relationship.

TWO

DEFINING THE PROBLEM

Whenever people tell me their relationship is not working, the first question I ask is, "What specifically is the matter?" Usually, my question is met with . . . Silence! "Tell me where you are in your relationship," I'll say. Again, silence. Some of you are able to tell me about some "incidents" that have taken place between you and your spouse and describe the pain you are feeling, but you can't or you don't know how to articulate the underlying problem that's causing the friction.

Sorry, but that won't cut it. You need to get real and extremely clear about where you are in your relationship and why. You need to know your relationship's assets and liabilities, the things that work well and the things that don't. You need to understand exactly how your relationship is evolving or deteriorating, whether it's stagnant or drifting or even spinning out of control. There is an old adage that says, "Half of the solution to any problem lies in defining the problem." Simply put, we need to know specifically just how good or bad your relationship is, and what makes it that way. You cannot change or heal what you do not acknowledge.

Most important, you need to find out what you personally have done, both positively and negatively, to put your relationship in the position you now find it. How have you contributed to it, and how have you contaminated it? When you say something doesn't feel right about the relationship, do you know specifically what that "something" is, or are you guessing and making knee-jerk reactions as opposed to following a strategy defined by clarity? Is it your lack of communication, your tendency to fight, your fear of intimacy, a general emptiness, or any of a number of other problems? Are you sure that the anxiety or concern you're feeling is about the relationship, or might it be about something else entirely?

Make no mistake: the sick relationship is like any other ailment that is subject to diagnosis. If you make a wrong diagnosis, you not only treat the wrong thing; you ignore the real problem because you already think you are on track.

The worst thing you can do is to draw faulty conclusions about the cause-and-effect aspects of the problems in your relationship. To rescue your relationship, your job is not only to thoroughly and accurately diagnose what it is that needs to change, but then implement the correct intervention strategies that will make that change happen. This does not have to be an overwhelmingly complex process. You don't have to have professional training to make such a diagnosis—in fact, it is better that you don't. But it does require you to be excruciatingly honest about this relationship and the part that you play in it. You cannot kid yourself, and you cannot sugar-coat what's happened to you. If your relationship is absolutely off in a ditch, you must admit it. If your relationship is emotionally bankrupt because you and your partner are completely drained, admit it. If you are married but are living an "emotional divorce," admit it. If this relationship is killing you and your self-worth and value, admit it. If you have become hardened and callused by the pain, admit that too.

Please, don't tell yourself, "Well, we need to do a little bit better," when the truth of the matter is that you'd better do a whole lot better. Either get real or get ready for a whole lot more of the same in your relationship. Is the problem caused by one of you dumping on the other for frustrations about life that have nothing to do with your relationship? Have the two of you been parents for so long that you've forgotten what it means to be friends and lovers? Have you forgotten how to pay attention to each other? Do you no longer have sex in your marriage? What's happened to the intimacy? Are you cold and distant to your partner because of something that happened ten years ago? Are you a double-income couple with no time for each other? Is there tension because of a past affair on the part of one partner?

I told you that this would not be one of those books that you get to just sit and read. So get out your pen and paper. You must play an active role from start to finish. Like any coach, I can go only as far as the sideline. You are the one who is on the scene, and therefore you are the agent of change. You must engage your mind, your heart, and your soul so you can get in touch with your own feelings.

PERSONAL CONCEPTS PROFILE

Start with the following questionnaire, which is designed to stimulate your thinking about your current relationship and how it has affected you. We will use these insights and this information as we move forward in creating clarity about what's going on in your relationship. This questionnaire presents the beginnings of forty-two sentences. You are to finish each sentence with an honest and spontaneous thought. Do not spend a great amount of time contemplating any one item. Your first reaction will probably be the most revealing.

RED ALERT: Let me tell you before we even begin our first exercise that you must be brutally candid in all of your responses. You and I both know that you can manipulate this process by giving a bunch of goody-two-shoes, socially desirable responses. Resist the temptation to put down a "right" answer. No one need see these responses but you. If you soft-pedal now, you are cheating yourself and your partner later.

To help maintain your confidentiality and for ease of responding, I recommend that you use a journal to record your thoughts. Thinking about answers in your head versus writing them down on paper is distinctly different. By writing out your answers, you are forced in the direction of coherency and completeness, which is particularly important now that you will be pulling together a number of different thoughts, feelings, and responses. Being able to reflect back on certain thoughts that you have preserved in writing will also be invaluable as we move forward. A journal provides some of the objectivity that you need when you are evaluating yourself.

Make sure, however, that your journal is for your eyes only. In fact, protect the privacy and confidentiality of your journal at every turn. It is important that you feel free and uninhibited in your writings. Nothing less will give you the clarity you need to make the changes and create the relationship that you want.

1. I tend to deny _____
2. I am happiest when _____
3. Sometimes I _____
4. What makes me angry is _____
5. I wish _____
6. I hate it when _____
7. When I get angry I _____
8. I would give anything if my partner would _____
9. Sometimes _____
10. I would be more lovable if _____
    _____
11. My mother and father _____
12. If only I had _____
13. My best quality is _____
14. Sometimes at night _____
15. When I was a child _____
16. My worst trait is _____
17. My life really changed when _____
18. If my relationship ends it will be because _____
    _____
19. My partner hates it when I _____
20. When I am alone I _____
21. My partner gets angry when _____
22. My partner's greatest fear is _____
23. It hurts me when my partner _____

24. I feel the most lonely when _____

25. I am afraid _____

26. I love _____

27. We used to laugh more because _____

_____

28. It would be best if _____

29. Friends _____

30. I feel like a phony when _____

31. I can't forgive _____

32. Together we _____

33. What surprises me is _____

34. I believe _____

35. Other people think _____

36. Men _____

37. Women _____

38. I regret _____

39. It doesn't pay to _____

40. It helps when we _____

41. If only _____

42. We never seem to _____

• • •

Whether you realize it or not, your answers to these questions have provided you with some important revelations about your attitudes and some equally important patterns or trends in your behavior. Based on your forty-two responses, now answer the following questions:

1. Look at your responses to items 4, 6, 7, 16, 17, 24, 25, 31. What do these answers tell you about anger in your life and your relationship? Write a two-paragraph answer in your journal.

2. Look at your responses to items 1, 2, 14, 25, 27, 30.

What do these answers tell you about fear in your life? Write at least a two-paragraph answer in your journal.

3. Look at your responses to items 2, 8, 10, 14, 20, 23, 24, 42. What do these answers tell you about the loneliness in your life and relationship? Write at least two paragraphs in your journal.

4. Look at your responses to items 4, 6, 8, 11, 12, 16, 19, 31, 38, 41. What do these answers tell you about blame and forgiveness in your life and relationship? Write at least two paragraphs in your journal.

5. Look at your responses to items 2, 3, 5, 8, 12, 26, 28, 34, 41, 42. What do these answers tell you about the dreams in your life and relationship? Write at least two paragraphs in your journal.

RELATIONSHIP HEALTH PROFILE

Now that you have learned some more about yourself, let's take an overall look at your relationship. The following is a broad questionnaire, a true/false test that includes items relevant to the health of you and your relationship. Again, be honest and go with your first reaction. Do not spend an excessive amount of time debating any one item.

CIRCLE EITHER TRUE OR FALSE FOR EACH ITEM.

1. I am satisfied with my sex life.   TRUE   FALSE
2. My partner doesn't really listen to me.   TRUE   FALSE
3. I trust my partner.   TRUE   FALSE
4. I feel picked on and put down.   TRUE   FALSE
5. I am hopeful about our future.   TRUE   FALSE

6. It is not easy to share my feelings.   **TRUE**   **FALSE**

7. My partner often says, "I love you."   **TRUE**   **FALSE**

8. Sometimes I feel rage.   **TRUE**   **FALSE**

9. I feel appreciated.   **TRUE**   **FALSE**

10. I am out of control.   **TRUE**   **FALSE**

11. My partner is there for me in hard times.   **TRUE**   **FALSE**

12. My partner is harsh in his or her criticism.   **TRUE**   **FALSE**

13. My partner understands me.   **TRUE**   **FALSE**

14. I fear my partner is bored.   **TRUE**   **FALSE**

15. My partner doesn't like to share what's on his or her mind.   **TRUE**   **FALSE**

16. I imagine myself divorced.   **TRUE**   **FALSE**

17. My relationship is what I always dreamed of.   **TRUE**   **FALSE**

18. I know I am right.   **TRUE**   **FALSE**

19. My partner treats me with dignity and respect.   **TRUE**   **FALSE**

20. My partner is a taker.   **TRUE**   **FALSE**

21. We often do fun things together.   **TRUE**   **FALSE**

22. Sometimes I just want to hurt my partner.   **TRUE**   **FALSE**

23. I feel loved.   **TRUE**   **FALSE**

24. I would rather lie than deal with a problem.   **TRUE**   **FALSE**

25. We still have a lot of passion in our relationship.   **TRUE**   **FALSE**

26. I am trapped with no escape.   **TRUE**   **FALSE**

27. My partner thinks I am fun to be with.   **TRUE**   **FALSE**

28. Our relationship has gotten boring.	**TRUE**	**FALSE**
29. We enjoy going out on dates alone.	**TRUE**	**FALSE**
30. My partner is ashamed of me.	**TRUE**	**FALSE**
31. We trust each other a great deal.	**TRUE**	**FALSE**
32. We have become nothing more than roommates.	**TRUE**	**FALSE**
33. I know my partner will never leave me.	**TRUE**	**FALSE**
34. I am no longer proud of my body.	**TRUE**	**FALSE**
35. My partner respects me.	**TRUE**	**FALSE**
36. My partner constantly compares me to others.	**TRUE**	**FALSE**
37. My partner still finds me desirable.	**TRUE**	**FALSE**
38. We just seem to want different things.	**TRUE**	**FALSE**
39. I am allowed to think for myself.	**TRUE**	**FALSE**
40. I feel crowded by my partner.	**TRUE**	**FALSE**
41. I am honest with my partner.	**TRUE**	**FALSE**
42. People have no idea what our relationship is really like.	**TRUE**	**FALSE**
43. My partner is open to suggestions.	**TRUE**	**FALSE**
44. My partner has shut me out.	**TRUE**	**FALSE**
45. My partner is my primary source of emotional support.	**TRUE**	**FALSE**
46. I feel judged and rejected by my partner.	**TRUE**	**FALSE**
47. My partner cares if I am upset or sad.	**TRUE**	**FALSE**
48. My partner treats me like a child.	**TRUE**	**FALSE**
49. My partner puts our relationship ahead of all others.	**TRUE**	**FALSE**
50. I'll never satisfy my partner.	**TRUE**	**FALSE**

51. My partner wants to hear my stories.	**TRUE**	**FALSE**
52. I chose my partner for the wrong reasons.	**TRUE**	**FALSE**
53. I look forward to our time together.	**TRUE**	**FALSE**
54. My partner thinks I am boring in bed.	**TRUE**	**FALSE**
55. My partner is lucky to have me.	**TRUE**	**FALSE**
56. My partner treats me like an employee.	**TRUE**	**FALSE**
57. I win my share of disputes.	**TRUE**	**FALSE**
58. I envy my friends' relationships.	**TRUE**	**FALSE**
59. My partner would protect me if necessary.	**TRUE**	**FALSE**
60. I am suspicious of my partner.	**TRUE**	**FALSE**
61. I feel needed by my partner.	**TRUE**	**FALSE**
62. My partner is jealous of me.	**TRUE**	**FALSE**

Now go back over your test and count all of the even-numbered questions to which you answered True. Write down the total. Now go back and count all of the odd-numbered items to which you answered False. Add that number to your "True total" to get your overall score.

Even-numbered "True" Responses   _____

Odd-numbered "False" Responses   _____

OVERALL TOTAL   _____

This test is designed to give you a quick snapshot of the health of your relationship. If your overall score is above 32, it is likely that your relationship is in extreme danger of failing. If your total score is between 20 and 32, then your relationship is seriously troubled and you may be living an "emotional divorce." If your total score is between 12 and 19, then your relationship is probably about average (which is not great) and certainly needs work. If your score is below 11, then your relationship is well above the norm and may have isolated areas in which you can improve.

GENERAL RELATIONSHIP PROBLEM PROFILE

Look back over the just completed Relationship Health Profile test and write down those areas that scored against the health of your relationship. In other words, write down the subject matter of all the even-numbered items to which you answered True and those odd-numbered items to which you answered False. For example, if you wrote "True" to question 60, write down, "I feel suspicious of my partner." If you wrote down "False" to question 61, then write down, "I don't feel needed by my partner." It will be important to list these in your journal because they too will add to the clarity of your objectives for helping your relationship. We will be using this information extensively in some later profiles you will be generating, so do a good and thorough job.

Now, after studying your list, look at the following list of characteristics that describe a problem relationship, and list them from strongest (one) to weakest (ten) in terms of presence and influence within your relationship. (For example, if you believe that hostility/contempt is the strongest emotion in your relationship, it would generate a rating of 10. If love is the weakest emotion in your current relationship, it would receive a ranking of 1.)

Hostility/contempt	_____
Apathy	_____
Fear	_____
Distrust	_____
Hatred	_____
Love	_____
Loneliness	_____
Guilt/shame	_____
Anger	_____
Frustration	_____

SPECIFIC RELATIONSHIP PROBLEM PROFILE

Now let's get more specific. I have listed some problem areas that could be applied to your relationship. If in fact these are areas where you have identified problems, circle the corresponding number. Then rank the problem areas from one (your worst problem area) to whatever corresponds to your least problem area. In other words, if you believe your biggest problem area involves trust, that would be number one. If your least problem area was sex and you have identified seven relevant areas, then sex would have a ranking of seventh. You don't have to rank everything—just the ones that you think apply most significantly to you. In the space provided, write one sentence that describes the essence or core element of the problem.

Trust	_____
Sex	_____
Money	_____

Family   _____

Time   _____

Children   _____

Lack of intimacy   _____

Communications   _____

Rage   _____

Drugs/alcohol   _____

Harshness   _____

Criticisms   _____

Fear   _____

Infidelity   _____

Boredom   _____

Lack of passion   _____

Jealousy   _____

Division of labor   _____

Communications   _____

THE RELATIONSHIP BEHAVIOR PROFILE: YOUR PARTNER

Here are ten questions that will help organize and guide your thinking about why you feel the way you do about your partner. If some of your answers are the same to each question, that's okay. Use your journal, if you wish, to help you better understand your feelings.

- List five instances of your partner's loving behavior toward you during the last month.
- List five instances of unloving or hateful things your spouse has done to you during the last month.
- List and describe your partner's five best qualities.
- List and describe your partner's five worst qualities.

- List five things which you have asked or scolded or nagged your partner to correct or improve, but which your partner has not corrected or improved.
- List five things that made you fall in love with your partner.
- List five things that today would make you fall out of love with your partner.
- Describe your partner's sexual relationship with you, paying particular attention to your partner's:
  - Pattern of initiation
  - Frequency
  - Quality
  - Problems
- Describe your partner's tendency or lack thereof to focus on you, paying particular attention to:
  - Desire for being physically close
  - Desire to talk with you one-on-one
  - Desire to spend time alone with you
  - Desire to protect you or comfort you during times of need
  - Desire to please you
- Do you look forward to seeing your partner at the end of a day? If not, write in your journal the reasons why. Be as specific as possible. If your partner complains about the way the house looks, write it down. If it's a look on your partner's face, write that down. If it's because you feel you have to invent conversation to make things pleasant between the two of you, write that down too.

THE RELATIONSHIP
BEHAVIOR PROFILE: YOU

That was the easy part. Now here are ten similar questions that you absolutely must answer with total honesty and candor to help organize and guide your assessment about the way you think about yourself, and about the way you and your partner relate. These are questions that you might not think to ask yourself, so consider them carefully. Resolve right now that you are not going to lie to yourself. Propel yourself to deal with the truth about yourself, even if it hurts. Prepare your heart and mind to be open rather than defensive. It is cowardly to blame, and it is cowardly and self-destructive to be in denial. Use your journal, if you wish, to help you understand why you feel the way you do.

1. List five instances of loving behavior toward your partner during the last month.
2. List five instances of unloving or hateful things you have done to your partner during the last month.
3. List and describe your five best qualities.
4. List and describe your five worst qualities.
5. List five things which your partner has asked or scolded or nagged you to correct or improve, but which you have not corrected or improved.
6. List five things that made your partner fall in love with you.
7. List five things that today would make your partner fall out of love with you.
8. Describe your sexual relationship with your partner, paying particular attention to your own:
   • Pattern of initiation

- Frequency
- Quality
- Problems

9. Describe your tendency or lack thereof to focus on your partner, paying particular attention to:
   - Desire for being physically close
   - Desire to talk with your partner one-on-one
   - Desire to spend time alone with your partner
   - Desire to protect or comfort your partner during times of need
   - Desire to please your partner

10. Does your partner look forward to seeing you at the end of a day? If no, write in your journal the reasons why. Be as specific as possible. If you tend to complain to your partner about the day you've had soon after you see your partner, write that down. If you tend to have a stressful look on your face when you see your partner, write that down. If it's because you feel a sense of dread upon the sight of your partner, write that down too.

I hope this test helps you understand that fixing a relationship means a lot more than fixing your partner. In fact, as I will insist over and over throughout this book, there is no need for you to approach this rescue mission from the perspective of straightening your partner out. Trust me, you've got a lot of work to do yourself. This is not about winning out over your partner; this is about winning for the relationship.

You will also hear me frequently say throughout this book that you must approach your relationship with a willingness to own your part of the problem. Whatever your partner repeatedly does in your relationship, he or she does it at least in part because of how you respond. You teach your partner how to treat you—or how to continue treating you—by the way you respond. You either elicit, maintain, or allow the behavior by your own responses. If, for example, your partner takes certain excesses in the relationship or is consistently rude and insensitive, I promise you he or she has learned that such behavior is acceptable because of the way you have responded. You may in fact have actually rewarded your partner for such behavior by giving in, abandoning your position, or by getting so upset that you no longer can express adequately what you feel and believe.

Acknowledging your own problems can be most refreshing when you realize that at last you are getting real about what is going on. I am betting you will find that that willingness to take a non-defensive look at yourself can and will be inspiring to your partner.

YOUR RELATIONSHIP LIFESTYLE PROFILE

Throughout this book I'm also going to ask you to evaluate your own lifestyle and the lifestyle you and your partner have collectively defined and created. You must identify what it is in your lifestyle as a couple that is eliciting, maintaining, or allowing a bad relationship.

You and your partner have mutually defined your relationship. You two have come together, consciously or otherwise, to define this relationship as it is. You negotiated your relationship into its current condition, each of you influencing the other through your feedback and responses.

It may not have been the outcome that you consciously wanted in the negotiation—but that's where you are. And that's where you will stay until you develop a lifestyle that creates healthier behavior.

So let's see where you are in your lifestyle. I cannot overemphasize how important it is to accept this concept of "lifestyle accountability" in order for you to change your current relationship and enjoy a healthy, rewarding relationship in the future. There are no exceptions. The following questions will help you see how your own lifestyle works to hurt your relationship. Once again, if you're not absolutely frank in your answers, you're doing yourself no good.

- Do you and your partner have serious talks? Do you talk mostly about problems?
- Are the two of you generally pessimistic about how things in your life will work out?
- Do you feel you are dominated by your kids? By your work? By housework? By financial debt?
- Do you feel out of shape? Are you overweight? Has your grooming or desire to look good around the house declined?
- Do you find that you have very little energy? Do you sit for extended periods of time watching TV? Do you find it hard to keep your eyes open after supper? Does one of you tend to already be asleep when the other comes to bed?
- Do you go through long periods in which one or both of you are disinterested in sex, affection, or physical contact?
- Are you easily bored with one another?
- If people saw the two of you in public, would they describe you as looking or acting unhappy?

- Are you turning toward others for comfort and entertainment?
- Do the two of you drink more than you used to? Are you doing drugs of any kind?
- Do each of you worry about the other getting the upper hand in the relationship, forcing you two to stay "on your guard" when you're together?
- Do you make sure, when you do something in support of your partner, that he or she knows it and now owes you a favor—and does your partner do the same thing to you?
- Do the two of you not know when to stop when an argument breaks out?
- Do both of you tend to make harsh remarks and personal attacks when arguing?
- Do the two of you often withdraw from one another instead of saying what is really on your minds?
- Are you no longer interested in what interests your partner—and vice versa?
- Do you think that you have behaviors or attitudes that, even though you know they are destructive, you don't wish to change for the good of the relationship? Are there similar behaviors or attitudes in your partner?
- Even when you are your most loving toward your partner, is it hard for you to forget your negative feelings about him or her? Do you think your partner feels the same way about you?
- Have the two of you stopped talking about your future together? What you two might be doing at retirement? What you dream about?

RELATIONSHIP COMMUNICATION TEST

What type of communication pattern have you and your partner developed within your relationship? Take this quick true-false test designed to get you to understand better the ways you relate, or don't relate, to your partner. These questions will also help you realize how comfortable you feel with your partner—the person who is supposed to be the most significant and trusted person in your life. Again, this is for your eyes only. Circle "True" for all of the statements that express at least occasional problems on your part.

1. I often can't seem to find the right words to express what I want to say.   **TRUE   FALSE**

2. I worry that exposing myself to my partner will result in rejection.   **TRUE   FALSE**

3. I often don't talk because I'm afraid my opinion is wrong.   **TRUE   FALSE**

4. Speaking up will only make things worse.   **TRUE   FALSE**

5. I talk too much and don't give my partner a chance to speak.   **TRUE   FALSE**

6. I don't look forward to talking to my partner.   **TRUE   FALSE**

7. Once I get started in an argument, I have trouble stopping.   **TRUE   FALSE**

8. My speech is often defensive.   **TRUE   FALSE**

9. I frequently bring up his or her past failures.   **TRUE   FALSE**

10. My actions don't match what I say.   TRUE   FALSE
11. I don't really listen.   TRUE   FALSE
12. I try to repay anger with anger   TRUE   FALSE
    or insult with insult.
13. I tease my mate too much.   TRUE   FALSE
14. I talk about really important   TRUE   FALSE
    things too rarely.
15. I often lie by omission.   TRUE   FALSE
16. I hate it when my partner brings   TRUE   FALSE
    up a problem.
17. I think it's important to lay out   TRUE   FALSE
    to my partner all of the complaints
    I have about him or her.
18. I state my complaints in a heated   TRUE   FALSE
    manner.
19. I tend to say, "You always" or   TRUE   FALSE
    "You never," when discussing
    my complaints with my partner.
20. I rarely state my complaints   TRUE   FALSE
    to keep from hurting my spouse.
21. I don't like to argue because I   TRUE   FALSE
    feel arguing reflects badly on the
    relationship.
22. I don't like to discuss our negative   TRUE   FALSE
    feelings because it only makes us
    feel worse.
23. I don't feel I should have to bring   TRUE   FALSE
    up what's bothering me because my
    partner should already know.

There is no right or wrong number of true or false answers to this test. You should look over your responses to get a feel for where communication problems or perceptions exist. This will help you answer the next series of questions and assist you in formulating a reconnection strategy in a later chapter.

CHEMISTRY TEST

Here's another way to gauge how your relationship lifestyle is working. Answer the following questions about the chemistry that exists or not between you and your partner. Don't be afraid to tell yourself the truth. As superficial as some of these items may sound, these issues can have a powerful influence on your relationship as a whole.

1. I am no longer physically attracted to my partner.   **TRUE   FALSE**

2. My partner makes me feel sexy.   **TRUE   FALSE**

3. My partner and I no longer kiss and caress.   **TRUE   FALSE**

4. Sex with my partner is energetic and satisfying.   **TRUE   FALSE**

5. My partner and I no longer flirt with each other.   **TRUE   FALSE**

6. My partner and I would rather be together alone than with other people.   **TRUE   FALSE**

7. I no longer look my partner in the eye when we are alone together.   **TRUE   FALSE**

8. If we do not have sex every few days, I really begin to miss it.   **TRUE   FALSE**

9. At various times I resent my partner.   **TRUE   FALSE**

10. I love to give my partner   **TRUE   FALSE**
    physical pleasure.

Any odd-numbered item to which you answered True or even-numbered item to which you answered False scores against your relationship. If your score is higher than three, you obviously have problems with the intimate/sexual aspect of your relationship. Note the items that scored against your relationship so as to use them as objectives in later planning.

THE FIVE TOUGH QUESTIONS

Now let's get to the nitty-gritty. I know, I know, you're asking yourself, "Hey, what have we just been doing?" But these are five very difficult questions that you need to ask yourself to see just how close you are to that danger line that we talked about earlier. Just how dark are your feelings about your relationship, and just how negatively do you think about yourself and your partner? Under no circumstances should you share these answers with your partner. As you're going to learn later on in this book, we tend to overexaggerate our negative feelings when we get in disappointing situations, and we forget to emphasize our positive feelings. But for now, let's get it all out—and get it into your journal. Have the courage to be honest here, even if it is scary to admit certain things through your answers. The only thing worse than having a relationship in trouble is to have a relationship in trouble and be in denial about it. As is the case with so many problems, early and appropriate intervention can be the key to the ultimate outcome.

1. Considering that at least one definition of love is that the security and well-being of your partner is as significant to you as your own security and well-being, then would you say that, based on results, you behave in a way that reflects that you are in love with your partner? Why?

2. Using that same definition, is your partner in love with you? Why?

3. Knowing what you now do about your relationship, would you still get involved with the same person if you had to do it all over again? Why?

4. When comparing yourself to other people in relationships, do you feel that you have been cheated or have settled too cheap? Why?

5. If you could break off your relationship or get a divorce from your partner right now without any inconvenience, legal costs, or embarrassment, without any undue hardship on your children (if you have any), would you do it? Why?

I know that dealing with these issues is about as much fun as getting a root canal, but having done it, you have taken an important step in getting this relationship out of the ditch. By getting real about your relationship, yourself, and your partner, you have identified some dangerous and powerfully destructive forces in your life that you must now contend with. I want to know whether you are in this relationship because you really want to be, or if you are in it today simply because you were in it yesterday. Spending your life with someone because it's just easier not to change is no basis for a healthy relationship—and if you feel this way, then you've got some work to do. But at least you're recognizing and acknowledging how you feel. I am convinced you can deal with anything as long as you know what it is. If you force yourself to deal with the truth, then at least you know where the bottom is, and you know where to go from there. You know what you have to contend with so you can marshal your resources and get up for it. Delusion is no solution.

I suspect that you have never been as brutally honest about yourself, your feelings, and your relationship as you are being now. As a result, I strongly suspect that you may be meeting yourself, and thus your partner's partner, for the first time ever. You could be having mixed emotions right now, but please, don't get down on yourself here. If you have emerged from these tests thinking, "Whoa, my relationship is far, far worse than I thought," just hold on and keep reading. As I told you at the start of this book, you have been given so much misinformation that it's amazing that you have maintained any kind of relationship at all. I want you to get excited about getting real with yourself. You are about to make a huge U-turn in your relationship.

BLOWING UP THE MYTHS

As I told you at the very beginning of this book, one of the biggest reasons you might believe you're a relationship failure when in fact you are not is because you think you and your partner should be following certain "rules" or meeting certain standards in your relationship. These are rules that, at face value, sound pretty logical—and you naturally come to believe that if you're not following them, then you're screwing up.

But that should have been your first warning sign: logic, right! Applying logic to the emotions of love and romance doesn't work. The truth is that those rules are largely myths, generated by well-intended but utterly misinformed counselors, and by equally misguided but maybe not so well-intended authors who might be more interested in selling books than providing aid. (You may decide I'm no better, but that's a chance I'll take by raising the issue.) You've been told, over and over, all the "attributes" that make up a happy couple. You've been bombarded with romanticized images of what it means to be truly in love. You've been led to believe that you and your partner should be a perfectly intertwined unit, floating through life in glorious harmony and bliss.

I'm sorry to say it, but I believe that you and your relationship have been getting jerked around in the worst possible way. It's time to blow the whistle on this false logic. I am about to share with you ten of the most dangerous relationship myths that are commonly taught, believed in, and practiced. When you read them, your initial reaction might be to wonder if I have gone nuts. Some of these myths have been part of your mind-set for so long that you might have difficulty even contemplating the idea that they are false. You may very well think that if the myths I'm going to share aren't true, then they *should* be true. They sound so right, they sound so nice. They sound so logical!

All I can say is that your tendency to hold on to these beliefs just because they are familiar will result in your continued delusion. I classify these long-held beliefs as myths because they simply *do not work*. And I have made this judgment call using one simple criterion: results. Based on results, these myths don't have one whit to do with whether your relationship is successful. Unfortunately, based on those same results, these myths have everything to do with making your relationship unsuccessful. If you buy into these myths, you are setting yourself up for continued and ever-increasing disappointment. If you continue to believe that these myths should be among the guiding principles of your relationship, you're going to feel like a failure, no matter what Herculean efforts you make to pursue and apply them. Wrong information means wrong decisions, and wrong decisions mean wrong results. It's a lot like the old joke: "We're totally lost, but we sure are making good time!"

It is thus critical that you move your position on these ten commonly held beliefs about what makes a healthy relationship so that you do not continue to misdiagnose and mistreat your relationship. Your quest for relational happiness must begin with right thinking—and that means first ridding yourself of wrong thinking—cleansing the "lens" to your core of consciousness so that the truth, your innate wisdom, can shine through. Now is the time to get the myths out of your head and out of your plans so that you can be open to focusing on what does really matter in a relationship.

MYTH #1: A GREAT RELATIONSHIP DEPENDS ON A GREAT MEETING OF THE MINDS

I have rarely encountered a couple in distress who didn't think the answer to their problems was at least in part that they should be more alike, that they should see things through each other's eyes. Oh, yes: empathy. The pabulum cure-all. Sounds logical, doesn't it? Sounds pretty darn lofty and unselfish, right?

The problem is, it's a crock. You're not ever going to see things through your partner's eyes. You will rarely understand and appreciate how and why your partner views the world in his or her particular way. The reason you won't be able to do it is because you are so totally different from your partner. You are genetically, physiologically, psychologically, and historically different. You have been conditioned differently by the world, you have different learning histories, you have different priorities, and you value different things in different ways.

It makes sense on paper to set the goal of seeing things sensitively through your partner's eyes. It makes good conversation in the therapist's office, and a great homework assignment for some distressed couple to go forth and do. Traditional therapy strives diligently to teach men to be more sensitive and less unemotionally logical, and it strives to teach women to operate less off their immediate feelings and to think more logically. I have just one question: Who do these therapists think they are kidding?

Men are going to be men and women are going to be women, and no therapist can change it. And you know what? That's okay. Different is okay.

If you are now thinking that I must be some reactionary old coot who has no sympathy with the evolution of women's and men's roles in society, think again. I think it's great that women can have powerful careers and that men can stay at home changing diapers. But I take issue with those who think a man's and woman's psychological makeup are interchangeable. As one who accepts that there is a master plan that has been orchestrated by a higher power from the beginning of time, I am a strong believer that we are wired up differently, and we are wired up that way for a reason. In the original plan, there was a division of labor in which men were expected to perform certain jobs that did not lend themselves well to emotionality or sensitivity. In this division of labor, women dealt with responsibilities in which sensitivity and discernment were more essential than was brute strength.

Men are not as sensitive and emotional as women are because they are not supposed to be. To try to force these traits and characteristics into the personality of a man is foolhardy. What's more, if you're a woman and you're trying to shoehorn yourself into a man's point of view, you're spinning your wheels. It is not natural for me to see a situation through my wife's eyes, any more than it is natural for her to see it through my eyes. Furthermore, it wouldn't help our relationship if we could. We are different and that is that, and we need to live with it because it isn't going to change.

Obviously, a lot of people don't get this, and that includes many of the therapists offering couples therapy. These folks maybe just haven't been down enough different roads of life and have no clue about real-world relationships. Make no mistake: these therapists understand the psychology of sex differences. They all have had instruction about the magnitude of the disparities. But they seem to forget about those fundamental differences when they start trying to heal broken relationships and have the avant-garde "millennium mind-set." The problem is, the more we attempt to blur roles into a unisex world, the more we are spinning out of control and try to fix "what ain't broke."

This kind of wrong thinking is dangerous because this myth-based advice given to an unsuspecting couple can truly paralyze any constructive actions they might be taking. Dangerous because there is not one chance in a million that either party is going to be able to do it. It doesn't work because of something called instinctual drift.

Instinctual drift is the tendency for all organisms, when under pressure, to resort to and exhibit their *natural* tendencies. It is even true with animals. I never cease to be amazed when I am watching CNN and hear the shock and dismay of some reporter and some forlorn victims who have been attacked by a wild animal that they have "tamed" and raised as a pet. The announcer typically says something like, "A shocking story from Sheboygan today . . . Authorities offered no explanation for the unprovoked attack by this savage animal that turned on its master!"

Every time I hear that, I shake my head and think, "Are you people morons? You take a wild animal that has for centuries survived as a predator, artificially modify its behavior, and then are shocked when the animal reverts to its genetic programming and has his 'master' for lunch!" The animal isn't being "savage"; it is just being what it is. It is doing what is natural for it to do. We humans may be smarter (or not), but we operate much the same.

You might be able to play that forced role for a while, but in the final analysis, you can't be what you are not. That is a psychological truth, and that's okay.

Please understand: I'm not telling you that two people of the opposite sex should not try to be compatible. Although our primary characteristics might be different, we can secondarily have certain traits and tendencies that are "somewhat" in the direction of the opposite sex. But please get rid of this idea that your personal relationship is going to be worse off than those of your friends if you and your partner don't seem to have both male and female perspectives and characteristics. The male in your relationship just may not be in touch with his "feminine side," and the female may have absolutely no interest or inclination to "muscle up" and defend the cave.

We will talk later about how we can meet out partners where they are naturally in their hearts and minds. We also will talk about accepting our differences rather than making them sources of conflict. As I hope to show you later, a relationship is far more enjoyable when you're with someone who enriches your life, not simply reflects it. I believe that before this journey is over, you will become thankful for the differences that may now be sources of frustration.

MYTH #2: A GREAT RELATIONSHIP DEMANDS A GREAT ROMANCE

This, you're asking yourself, is a myth? How can this be, because didn't I just say in Chapter 1 that you should get what you deserve, which includes great love and romance? How can it be a myth to want romance?

I'm talking here about expecting unrealistic, Hollywood romance. Believe me, your life with your partner should include plenty of romance. There are many times when you and your partner need to make an effort to be romantic, to go out on real dates as you did when you first met, to fill your life with candlelight dinners and weekends away from the kids.

But don't kid yourself. As jarring as this sounds, the truth is that being in love is not like falling in love. So many times I have listened to people in relationships say, "Well, Dr. McGraw, I just don't feel like I'm in love anymore." They tell me the spark is gone in their relationship. After I question them for a while, I start to understand what that person is really saying: "I don't feel the way I did when I was first falling in love." What this person is genuinely missing is that dizzy feeling of infatuation that takes place at the very start of the relationship.

This is what I mean when I say most people don't know how to measure success in a relationship. Most people have a distorted view of what love is. Just because feelings change doesn't mean that those feelings have to be less rewarding. Isn't it possible that there are a number of emotions and ways of experiencing them that, though different, are all equally rewarding? What once was dizzying and exciting and thus very positive can very well become deep and secure— which is also very positive.

The infatuation stage is, I admit, an addictive experience. There is nothing like the thrill of the chase, the initial courtship, the feeling that you have found someone who is the salvation for all else that is lacking in your life. Falling in love not only brings out a surging sense of desire, it makes you believe you can surmount all your limitations. You think your days of loneliness have come to an end for good. You are convinced you have found the person whom you can talk to all night long about whatever is on your mind.

Over the years I've talked to young couples who have met and fallen head over heels in love with one another, and they're thinking about marriage, and they genuinely believe that "love" will get them past any future pitfalls or disasters in their relationship. I remember talking to a woman about a man to whom she was recently engaged, and she was honest enough to bring up several problems that were bothering her—not the least of which were his inability to hold a job and his abuse of alcohol. I said, "So why are you sure you want to marry him?"

"Dr. McGraw, I can't help it. I'm in love with him."

Clearly, she didn't have a clue what love was. She was in heat, mesmerized by the tingle that is so common to "phase one" infatuation, oblivious to the fact that his dysfunctions would cheat her out of depth and security in "phase two." The myth too many people believe is that the ecstatic emotion that one feels when first falling for someone new is real love. It is only the first stage of love, and it is humanly impossible to remain in that stage. Inevitably, with all couples, that initial wild passion transmutes into a deep and abiding commitment—still exciting, still rewarding, but not always so dizzying. The answer is not saying to yourself that you aren't in love like you used to be. The answer is not ending that relationship so that you can start the chase all over again with a new mate, springboarding from one emotional high to another. The answer, as you will learn by the time you finish this book, is learning how to move to the next stages of love. When you do that, you will discover a deeper, richer experience with your partner than you ever could have imagined. Emotions change, but that doesn't mean that they are less intense or less meaningful than the tingling excitement of the early days.

If you have been deluded by this myth and therefore judge your relationship against the sizzle of the early days or the Hollywood version of a dramatic love, you could unfairly label a genuinely quality relationship as being substandard. In real life you can't hear Whitney Houston singing in the background; you don't go to dinner every night in tuxedos and evening gowns. Unlike the characters in the afternoon soaps, you have to go to work, you do gain weight, you do get tired, and you do have to pump your own gas and get that gunky stuff out of the bottom of the garbage disposal while your partner feeds the dog.

You're living in the real world here. Great romance can be caring and checking on where your partner is if it's getting a little late. Great romance can be as simple as sharing the newspaper in the morning, sharing a biggie fry at the Burger Doodle, and making love a couple of times a week, even though neither one of you would be caught dead in a thong. Great relationships and great romance?

It's all in the yardstick that you use to measure. It's all in defining what "great" means in the real world.

MYTH #3: A GREAT RELATIONSHIP REQUIRES GREAT PROBLEM-SOLVING

Let's return for a moment to our hypothetical therapist's office. You and your partner have scheduled a session to discuss the fact that the two of you have been fighting over certain issues, and none of them are getting resolved. Dr. Expert tells you that you and your partner must learn "conflict resolution" and problem-solving skills. He says that you need to develop these "skills" so that the two of you can calmly reach "common ground."

The message you'll get in that office will be very clear: if you and your partner can't learn to solve your differences, you won't have a good relationship because it will be riddled with conflict and confrontation. Wrong! That's completely naive and fanciful thinking. The myth that so many fall for is that couples can't be happy if they cannot resolve their serious disagreements. In the twenty-five years that I have been doing work in the field of human behavior, I have seen few if any genuine relationship conflicts ever get resolved. I know that sounds strange, but I'm telling you it's true. Some simple, everyday "no-brainers" get resolved, but most of the key issues that create real conflict within a relationship never get resolved.

Reflect back on your relationship, and I'll bet you'll have to agree with what I am saying, even though it differs from what relationship "experts" tell you. There are things that you and your partner disagree about, have always disagreed about, and will always disagree about. Maybe the disagreement is about sex, the way to raise or discipline the children, how to allocate money, how to show affection. Whatever the particular subject matter is, I will guarantee you that you now and forever will have certain basic issues over which you disagree. You will not resolve them because they cannot be resolved without one of you sacrificing your true beliefs or breaking from your core of consciousness.

Let's turn to an old, familiar example. A woman often thinks the man shouldn't use too harsh a tone of voice with the children. He in turn thinks she's too easy on them. She says he's punishing them. He says she's spoiling and enabling them.

Isn't it fascinating that generation after generation this same conflict emerges between a man and wife, and in fact continues to be a point of differentiation and conflict even after the children are grown? The debate continues, but it now just shifts to the grandchildren.

Why do such recurrent themes keep coming up in arguments between males and females? Because they never get solved—and it's a waste of time to think you can figure out a way to solve them, or that you can persuade your partner that your opinion is for some reason more valuable than his or hers. My mother and father fought for fifty-three years about whether she should be more social and support him in his various efforts to entertain customers, clients, or colleagues. He thought she should be there. She disagreed entirely. He thought she'd like entertaining if she gave it more of a chance. She said she had given it a chance, and she hated entertaining.

They never resolved the issue, and neither one ever embraced the other's position. You could have put them in all the conflict-resolution and problem-solving training that has ever been created, and they were just not going to find common ground on that issue.

Some couples, because they cannot agree on a core issue, interpret that lack of agreement as a purely personal rejection, and they stay bent out of shape about it forevermore. Because they are believing the myth that they should be great problem-solvers to have a happy marriage, they carry that emotional pain forward and may well start telling themselves that there's something wrong with the relationship—which is in fact just fine.

Other couples—healthier couples, in my opinion—simply agree to disagree. They don't let the arguments get too personal, nor do they resort to insults or counterattacks because they feel so frustrated. Realistic partners achieve what psychologists call "emotional closure." They don't achieve closure on the issue, but they do achieve closure on the emotions. They give themselves permission to disagree without having to declare that one party is right and the other party is wrong. They eventually relax and go on with their lives. They decide to *reconnect* at a feeling level rather than *disconnecting* at an issue level.

We will talk more about this ability to place the relationship above the conflict later, but suffice it to say that efforts to reconnect give you a much more rewarding outcome than vainly trying to lead a life together devoid of conflict.

MYTH #4: A GREAT RELATIONSHIP REQUIRES COMMON INTERESTS THAT BOND YOU TOGETHER FOREVER

Here we come to a myth that sends people down the road into astonishingly ridiculous situations in which they often return bewildered or unhappy or even hostile. I know the "hostile" part all too well—for I too at one point believed in the myth that my relationship would be better if Robin and I did some activity together, if we developed a common interest.

I wasn't satisfied with the fact that we had all sorts of smaller common experiences that interested us. I thought we needed one big thing to do together. So I came up with the idea: Tennis! I probably play tennis three hundred days a year. My wife, while not nearly as avid a tennis player as I, is an accomplished player who enjoys the game and appreciates the camaraderie. Frankly, I don't play for camaraderie. I play to compete, and everyone I play with plays to compete. The group of guys that I regularly play with would just as soon hit you right between the eyes with a short lob as look at you. My wife, on the other hand, gets a different kind of reward from the game. She loves the exercise, the time that she spends with friends, and the challenge of learning to hit the ball better and better each time she plays.

About ten years ago, based on this very myth, we signed up as a team in a mixed-doubles league. Common interest, right? Shared quality time, right? Good for the relationship, right? As I said, that was ten years ago, and I am not sure we are over it yet. She made me so mad I could have killed her. I made her so mad I think she did try to kill me. By the end of the first set of the first match on the first night, we were not even speaking. She could not believe I was being so mean. I apparently slammed the ball too close to the lady on the other side. I wasn't friendly when we changed sides of the court (they all wanted to have a tea party). I allegedly rolled my eyes and sighed when she missed a ball.

She, on the other hand, wanted to chat during points. Not just with me, but with the people on the other side. If the ball wasn't hit right to her, she wasn't about to run for it, I assume because she didn't want to mess up her hair.

You've no doubt attempted some major project with your partner as well, thinking it would make the two of you closer. I'll never forget a woman friend of mine who tried fly fishing one morning with her husband. After an hour of listening to him complain to her about how she wasn't standing in the right place or casting to the correct part of the river, she dropped her rod and said, "It's six a.m., it's cold, you're rude, and I'm going home. In case you haven't heard, you can buy fish at the supermarket in the middle of the afternoon."

Perhaps you and your partner have a great common interest that makes the two of you happy. That's fine. All power to you. But the greater myth is that if you don't have one, you must find one in order to make the relationship more fulfilling. That's just not true—not true at all. I have encountered thousands of older couples who have been married happily for years and years. They love their time together, they love being great companions, but they also respect each other's idiosyncrasies and don't feel they have to engage in lots of activities together.

It's not what you do, it's how you do it. If forcing yourselves into common activities creates stress, tension, and conflict, then don't do it. Simply don't do it. It's wrong to think that there is something amiss in your relationship if you don't have common interests and activities. I promise, you have a number of significant commonalities that you may not think about. You live together, you sleep together, you eat together, and if you're married with children, you parent together. You may worship together, spend holidays together, and even ride to work together. If it doesn't work for you to take a ceramics class together, just don't do it. The important thing is that you not label yourself as deficient or having a less committed love because you don't share common activities.

MYTH #5: A GREAT RELATIONSHIP IS A PEACEFUL ONE

Once again, wrong! So many people are terrified of volatility because they think arguing is a sign of weakness or relationship breakdown. The reality is that arguing in a relationship is neither good nor bad. Indeed, let me turn this myth on its head. If arguing is done in accordance with some very simple rules of engagement, it can actually help the quality and longevity of the relationship in a number of ways. For some couples, such fighting provides a much needed release of tension. For others, it brings about a certain peace and trust because they know they can release their thoughts and feelings without being abandoned or rejected or humiliated.

I am not saying that arguments are something that you should strive for, but research simply does not support the notion that couples who fight fail in their relationships. In fact, there are as many relationship failures associated with the suppression of conflict and the denial associated with it as there are failures associated with volatile and vocal confrontations.

As children we learned early about the importance of being considerate of another person. We were taught lessons in manners and self-restraint. Oh, God, you're probably thinking, Dr. Phil is about to tell me that politeness is a myth. Wrong again. I reserve a special respect for partners who are polite and full of goodwill toward each other. But think about it. After all we've already discussed about the vast physiological and psychological differences between two people, is it really natural for a couple always to be marvelously thoughtful of each other, never disagree, show little impatience, and rarely get peeved? Is it really natural to avoid getting nose-to-nose on occasion with the one you love the most? Is it a sign of strength if you don't get flat-out pissed off once in a while?

Don't worry about how many times you argue: that's not the determining factor in your relationship stability and quality. Instead, it is determined by the nature of the way you argue, and by how you deal with the argument once it has run its course.

If, for example, you are the type of combatant in a relationship who quickly abandons issues of disagreement and instead attacks the worth of the person with whom you are arguing, you are being a destructive force in your relationship. If you are the type who gets into arguments with your partner because the arguments are, in effect, more stimulating than the day-to-day life of being together, you are being equally destructive. And if your rage and impulses are so unchecked that you pursue a scorched-earth, take-no-prisoners approach, then you are taking on the quality of viciousness, which is an absolute killer in a relationship.

Similarly, if you are the type of combatant who never achieves emotional closure at the end of an argument and instead "gunny sacks" your emotions, only to have them come bubbling out later, this is equally destructive. You must get emotional closure at the end of your arguments; otherwise, you are very likely to react in some cumulative fashion the next time there is a confrontation and create a huge disruption in the relationship.

Don't confuse cumulative reaction with overreaction. Both are destructive interactions and are often mislabeled. Overreaction refers to a disproportionate reaction to an isolated event. It's analogous to the old expression of killing a mosquito with a shotgun. It just seems all out of proportion or scale, particularly from the mosquito's point of view.

Cumulative reaction, while just as explosive, is actually the exact opposite of overreaction. Cumulative reaction occurs when you have failed to get closure in prior confrontations, related or unrelated, because you denied yourself the right to participate healthfully in a confrontation with your partner. If in ten previous situations you have bitten your tongue rather than making an appropriately assertive response, you have stored all of that emotional energy inside. You are now like a pressure cooker with the vent valve closed up. This energy—whether anger, resentment, bitterness, or some other painful feeling—eventually has to go somewhere. In the cumulative reaction, it finally comes bubbling to the top, and the energy from all ten situations comes flooding forth, overwhelming your partner and making you sound like someone who has gone insane over the most trite and insignificant point.

We will have a detailed discussion about how to fight and argue without being destructive, and how to keep from making it a personal attack (or taking it as a personal attack) in later chapters. You must also learn how to properly put your relationship back together after a confrontation and how to let your partner off the hook rather than browbeating them into submission. Similarly, you will need to learn how to make your escape with your ego and feelings intact if you are the one that was wrong, or are the object of dogmatic browbeating by your partner.

Again, let me be very clear about what I mean when I say "emotional closure." I do not mean that you solve the problem. I mean that you get your mind and heart in balance and allow your partner to do the same. That will never happen if you buy into the next myth. Take a look.

MYTH #6: A GREAT RELATIONSHIP LETS YOU VENT ALL YOUR FEELINGS

Because we live in an era where we are constantly exhorted to get in touch with our inner this or that and then let it all come out in one great rush of emotion, it certainly makes sense that we should follow this dictate in relationships. We should just get everything off our chests, unload any thought or feeling that crosses our minds, hold nothing back, all in the name of openness.

The problem is that, based on results, totally uncensored venting of your feelings often just does not work. We all have an infinite array of thoughts and feelings about our partners, a lot to which we have given a voice because it seemed like "a good idea at the time." But upon reflection, the thoughts shouldn't have been communicated for a number of reasons—not the least of which is that you didn't really mean it. Think about the number of times that you have blurted out something in the heat of the moment about your partner's weaknesses. Let's be honest: it felt sort of good to let loose like that, to finally feel like you had the upper hand. But what good did it do? None. For a moment you felt the exhilaration of rage—and you quite possibly damaged your relationship, and sometimes the damage can be permanent.

I have seen many a relationship destroyed because one or both partners simply could not forgive something that was said in the process of venting. Even if you were willing to give your front seat in hell to take something back, you can't. Indeed, I would wager that you can think of things right now that you said months or even years ago that, true or not, hurt your partner very deeply and have not been forgotten.

Perhaps you've heard the story about the Baptist revival in which a zealous pastor was encouraging everyone to bare their souls by unloading their guilt in front of the congregation. An old farmer stood up in the front, moved by the invitation to confess, and exclaimed, "Reverend, I've drunken whiskey," to which the reverend said, "Tell it all, brother, tell it all." The old man felt great and said, "Reverend, I have chased women and been to houses of ill-repute," to which the reverend excitedly responded, "Tell it all, brother, tell it all." The congregation clapped wildly to encourage this brave man who, finding never-before-felt courage, shouted, "I've been to the barn and had sex with the animals."

Immediately, a hush fell over the congregation. After a long silence, the reverend looked down from the pulpit and said in a hushed tone, "Brother, I don't believe I'd have told that."

The point is clear. Before you say something that could be disastrous, you must give yourself breathing room, you must (perhaps literally) bite your tongue, you must allow yourself time to deliberate. This is absolutely critical to the future of your relationship. I'm not telling you to hide truths and be dishonest. But I am telling you that in order to meet the criteria of being open and honest, you need to be sure how you genuinely feel, you need to know if what you're about to say is going to be said in the most appropriate manner, and that may take more deliberation than is available in the heat of the moment. If what you have to say is going to potentially turn into a "life sentence"—either for yourself or your partner—you'd better think about it and think about it hard.

I also want to point out that venting is not only verbal. Oftentimes, deeds do in fact speak louder than words and are as much of a communication as any words you could ever speak. Slamming a door in your partner's face, walking out at a critical time, throwing a drink in your partner's face, shutting out your partner, or failing to be there when he or she needs you can all communicate powerfully destructive messages.

What's more, you need to be doubly careful of the way you vent when you feel you have been wronged by your partner and you want that partner to know it. How you respond can cost you a lot of credibility and completely take the focus off whatever your partner may have done to hurt you. I have dealt with hundreds of couples over the years in which one partner would commit some serious transgression, only to be totally overshadowed by the outrageous reaction of their partner. When these couples were present in my office or one of my seminars, the focus would invariably be on the outrageous reaction rather than the original act. Suddenly the situation became even worse for the original victim because they had reacted so outrageously that he or she essentially let the partner who started it all off the hook, giving him or her a free pass.

There is no better example than George and Karen. This couple, purportedly very much in love, attended one of my seminars on relationships. They had been referred to the seminar by Karen's attorney, an excellent, high-profile divorce lawyer of national repute, but one who preferred to see relationships healed rather than dismantled. Living and working in Manhattan, both George and Karen had active and rewarding careers as a product of their hard work and mutual support. Yet they were in the midst of a divorce because Karen, although unable to prove it, was convinced that George was unfaithful on an increasingly regular basis.

In fact, just before attending the seminar and one month into a voluntary separation, Karen, after some creative investigative work, became convinced that George was away for the weekend with "some little slut-dog-whore." Totally enraged and decidedly self-righteous, she talked her way past the doorman at his new separate apartment building and gained access to his penthouse. Once inside, she found a butcher knife in the kitchen and methodically hacked a hole in the heart of every shirt, suit, and sweater hanging in his closet. She then used the knife to cut the crotch out of every pair of pants he owned. I won't insult your intelligence by explaining the symbolism of either of these acts. Let's just say Karen was beyond crabby—way beyond.

Not nearly done, she used green spray paint to deface a quarter of a million dollars in paintings and sculptures. She threw all of his stereo equipment into the bathtub, covered it with laundry soap and bleach, and filled the bathtub with water. She then nailed a short and clear note to his door: "Good morning, George. I hope she was worth it, you no-good, rotten son of a bitch. May you burn and rot in hell for what you've done to me. I hate you! Your loving wife, Karen."

Now, the truth of the matter is, George may very well have been on a love tryst that weekend, but nobody ever got around to talking very much about that. Everyone wanted to talk about Karen. She turned out to be very embarrassed and ashamed of her actions. She knew she had lost credibility in the eyes of even the most casual observers. Meanwhile, George saw his chance to play the self-righteous victim because of what this lunatic had done to him. He was very happy to let everyone in the seminar pat him on the back and tell him just how awfully he had been treated.

I hope you can see that in addition to Karen having sent a really bad message to her partner about what she was capable of doing—a message that she can never take back—she let him emerge as a sympathetic figure. Even though he had great responsibility for what happened, he was cleared! Because of Karen's venting, she allowed him to escape accountability. Don't be a sucker and get baited into going off the deep end in the name of some misguided self-actualized self-expression.

MYTH #7: A GREAT RELATIONSHIP HAS NOTHING TO DO WITH SEX

Don't you believe it for a minute. Sex provides an important time-out from the stresses and strains of a fast-paced world and adds a quality of closeness that is extremely important. Sex is a needed exercise in vulnerability wherein you allow your partner to get close. In fact, it can be pretty darn good exercise, period. It is in most circumstances a mutual act of giving and receiving and sharing a symbolic act of trust. For most couples it is perhaps one of a very short list of things that distinguishes their particular relationship as different from others.

I'm not saying sex is everything. If you have a good sexual relationship, it registers about ten percent on the "important scale"—meaning it makes up about ten percent of what's important in the relationship. But if you do not have a good sexual relationship, that registers about ninety percent on the "important scale." A good sexual relationship can make you feel more relaxed, accepted, and more involved with your partner. But if your life together is devoid of sex, then the issue becomes a gigantic focus of the relationship.

Sex can be of enormous symbolic importance: it can be the greatest single factor of disappointment in a relationship. It can lead to feelings of deep anxiety (a woman, for instance, believing she is not pleasing or desirable to her husband), inadequacy (a man not feeling he can perform at the expected or an inspiring level at the right time), and ultimately rejection and resentment. Once the sexual problems get to that level, any number of destructive behaviors can begin to emerge between you and your partner. One of you might think the other is trying to punish you by withholding sex, and so you decide to fight back—which causes, of course, even more destructive behaviors. Feelings of rejection by one or both partners in a relationship can be crippling and painful. Because sex is so intimate, so personal, feelings of rejection in this particular area are magnified a hundredfold, as compared to your partner rejecting an idea or concept, a much less emotionally charged category.

Later, I will take up in more detail—and I mean a lot of detail—how to overcome sexual problems and reinstall sexual activity at a healthy level. For now, however, all I ask you to do is get this ridiculous myth out of your head. I don't care how old you are; I don't care how compromised your health may be; or how worried you are about being discovered. The belief that sex is not important in a relationship is a dangerous and intimacy-eroding myth. Couples who eliminate this important element of intimacy from their relationship make a grievous error in judgment. Take that sexuality away, and you may degrade the relationship to one devoid of uniqueness.

Sexual urges and needs are natural, appropriate, and important to act upon. When I say that, I'm not just restricting myself to the act of intercourse. I'm talking about sex as a physically intimate experience, combined with a mental and emotional connection. In this context, I define sex as all forms of private (and to some extent public) touching, caressing, holding, and any other means of providing physical comfort. I hardly believe you must return to the heated sexual stage that you might have had when the two of you first met—please refer to Myth #1—but there must be a sexual bond between the two of you, a kind of chemistry that makes you two recognize that you are more than friends who share a life. You are mates.

MYTH #8: A GREAT RELATIONSHIP CANNOT SURVIVE A FLAWED PARTNER

Most therapists will wrongly tell you that if you have "craziness" or even serious weirdness in the character makeup of one or both partners, a healthy relationship is impossible. Of course, they *are* selling therapy. I have heard an alarming number of therapists and authors take the position that you cannot relate to "craziness."

I know of many marriages that came to a quick end because, as one of the parties would later say, "The guy (or gal) I married turned out to be really, really crazy." "He (she) was a nutcase." "I don't know what happened. After the wedding, he (she) started acting really bizarre."

When you really stop and think about it, I'm not sure that we even have a very good handle on what "normal" is. Everybody you know has some characteristic that is different. Even though that characteristic may not be what you, or even they, might choose in a perfect world, it should not be allowed to frighten or dominate your thinking about who they are. And that applies to your relationship. As long as the quirks or nuances are not abusive to you or blatantly destructive to your partner, you can certainly learn to live with them.

My father and I shared a clinical practice for some years, and once worked jointly with a family that included a husband and wife and three teenage daughters. To be completely honest, the mom was schizophrenic. She would routinely hear voices, particularly in the late afternoon before the children got home from school. However, when she wasn't talking to someone that wasn't there, she was sweet, kind, and highly talented in many areas.

I'll admit, this is not exactly the kind of thing I would consciously look for in a mate. But, unlike most psychotics, the woman basically functioned pretty well, and took excellent care of her family. She was absolutely devoted to her husband and children. Her hallucinations were fairly benign and non-disruptive to the family and home. Still, this was behavior that was worthy of change, and Carol Ann herself wanted to be better. Her husband, Don, attended therapy sessions one hundred percent of the time that he was asked and was one hundred percent behind his wife. With his support, Carol Ann did ultimately make some progress.

I say "some progress" because, in one of our later sessions when she had reportedly not heard a voice for fourteen days in a row, the longest period of silence ever, she added a few details that concerned me. When I asked her if she was hearing any voices, she said that she was not. When I asked her if she completely and fully understood that they were hallucinations and not someone trying to possess or control her, she also answered in the affirmative, but added that just to be on the safe side, she had cut every wire in her home's intercom system. She did so based on the theory that if they did decide to start talking to her again, they wouldn't be able to do it using these built-in speakers.

Not what I would call a cure, and again not what I would refer to as a desirable characteristic, but the couple and the family found a way to deal with it. That couple has now been married thirty-seven years, and could not be happier in their intercom-less home.

Granted, Carol Ann is on one end of the continuum. At the other end, there are plenty of people who have nuances that some other person might describe as abnormal. Say you have a wife who, after the birth of your children, becomes absolutely paranoid about the children's safety, getting up ten times a night to check on them. Or say you have a husband who becomes so involved in conspiracy theories that he wants to build a bomb shelter in his backyard. Or your partner seems, in certain public surroundings, deplorably shy or goes on crying jags for seemingly no reason at all. It doesn't mean that you can't mesh with them, that you can't get along just fine.

Sometimes, we feel that because something is not mainstream, then it must be toxic to the relationship, and that's not necessarily true. Everyone has quirks and odd personality traits, and they can sometimes seem bizarre. If your partner's quirks and nuances are non-abusive to you and non-destructive to him or her, you can work on them. But at the same time, you can also accommodate them and enjoy a rewarding and fulfilling relationship. Even "craziness" can be made to work.

MYTH #9: THERE IS A RIGHT WAY AND A WRONG WAY TO MAKE YOUR RELATIONSHIP GREAT

Nothing could be further from the truth. There is not some etched-in-stone right way to be in a relationship. There is not a right way to show support or affection. There is not a right way to raise children, relate to your in-laws, handle disputes, or any other challenges involved in a complex relationship.

What is important is that you find ways of being together that work for you. Whether or not it meets some standard that you find in a book or conforms to what your mother and father think you ought to be doing should not be the standard you use in defining your relationship. The litmus test for you should be whether or not what you and your partner are doing is generating the results that you want. It's not important that you follow particular principles. It's important that the two of you are comfortable with the principles that work, and then you write your own rules.

I'll bet you know couples that conform to no known models of relationship theory, yet are healthy and happy. My grandparents on my mother's side are a perfect example. They defied every relationship rule or model I have ever even heard about. These two simple, uneducated, and hardworking people spent their entire life in a small West Texas town with a population of only five thousand. My grandfather ran the local freight warehouse, and my grandmother took in ironing, which she worked on seven days a week. They were dirt-poor, salt of the earth West Texas folks.

I had a great opportunity to watch these two people because I spent summers there as a teenager, living in their home and working at the warehouse loading and unloading freight. They probably didn't speak to each other more than twenty-five words a week. They did not sleep in the same room, and their only common interest was survival. But even then I noticed that they did relate. No matter where we were or what we were doing, they always seemed to arrange things in such a way that they were physically very close and in most cases actually touching in some way. They had a huge dinner table in this giant old house, and even if it was just the two of them eating a meal, they would sit in one little corner of the table actually kind of scrunched up together.

He called her the "old maid" and she called him "Cal." While they said very little to each other, they frequently spoke about their partner to anyone else who would listen. He was six foot nine and she was four foot eleven. Seeing them walk side by side down to the corner, you had to wonder if he even knew she was down there. He told everybody that she was crazy as a "peach orchard bore" because she watched professional wrestling every Saturday night and would get so mad at the wrestlers and referees that she would "cuss 'em a blue streak." She told people he was so old that she had to remind him to breathe.

Not exactly one for the textbooks, but they had been

married sixty-eight years when he passed away. The last time I saw them together, they were totally ignoring each other except that they were holding hands. Maybe the poets and songwriters are right, when they lament "you say the most when you say nothing at all."

Trying to force a couple into some arbitrary mind-set of rightness and wrongness is incredibly artificial and truly impossible. There can be as many different ways to successfully relate as there are different couples. There are different styles of communicating, showing affection, arguing, or problem-solving. One is not better than the other.

Don't get hung up on trying to conform to some made-up set of behaviors concocted by people who have never even met you or your partner, or who at best see you for an hour per week. Focus on what works.

RED ALERT: In addition to avoiding rigidity about your own thoughts, feelings, or behaviors, do not be rigid and judgmental about your partner's thoughts, feelings, and behaviors. There is, for example, not a right way or a wrong way for your partner to love you. If he or she shows love in a way that is different from the way you think it should be displayed, that does not mean that you are right and your partner is wrong. More important, it does not mean that the quality of what your partner is giving you is less than it would be if he or she were thinking, feeling, or behaving in the way that you have arbitrarily decided is right.

Let's say your partner expressed genuine love to you in a foreign language that you could not understand. Conclusion? You could think that your partner had no love and commitment for you. The frustration for your partner in this situation, however, is that this might be the only language he or she speaks. Does the fact that he or she did not choose a mode of expression that is precisely that which you or some therapist has decided is correct make the partner's feelings for you of any lesser quality or value?

I have always been a cat lover, and I remember early in my relationship with my wife, Robin, I sent her a "cat card." There was a drawing on the front of the card showing two cats, from behind, sitting on a fence. One was kind of a masculine-looking, scroungy alley cat and the other was drawn as a fluffy, pretty female cat. Their tails were slightly intertwined. They were looking at the moon. When you opened the card it read simply, "If I had two dead rats, I would give you one." She was probably a little perplexed. I, on the other hand, was intending to send a very clear message. Despite its humor, the card expressed my genuine feelings.

Yes, lots of us could work much harder at expressing our love and devotion to our partners, but we could work equally hard at learning our partner's "foreign language." If we learn our partner's language instead of demanding that they adopt our language, we may find that we have far more of what we want than we think we do. It would be tragic for you to miss quality offerings of love and devotion from your partner because you failed to recognize the value of a really good dead rat.

My best friend, outside of my wife, is Gary Dobbs. Gary has been many things to me in my life, including a spiritual mentor who has helped me greatly to mature in my personal relationship with God. I was lamenting to him one day how frustrated and cheated I felt when I heard credible people telling me that God had spoken to them on some critical issue. I wasn't talking about some knot-head tele-vangelist with enough hair spray and jewelry to shame the Gabor sisters; I was talking about credible, legitimate peo-ple who seemed to enjoy this great connection. I was help-ing Gary put up Christmas lights one night (because he was too chicken to go up the ladder) and I paused, looked at him, and said, "What am I, dog meat? How come God doesn't talk to me?" Gary never even missed a beat as he was untangling the Christmas lights. He said, "I guess the real question is, why won't you hear him?"

Dang, I hate when he is right. But he was right. It wasn't that God wouldn't speak to me; it was that I wouldn't hear him because I had some predetermined notion of exactly how he was supposed to speak to me. Having watched *The Ten Commandments* a half dozen times, I fully expected that if God had something to say to me, he could at least roll out the booming voice, part a few clouds and rivers, and deliver his message. I had rigidly decided that there was a right way for God to communicate with me, and had failed to accept or recognize any other mode of communi-cation.

The incident with Gary also gave me new understanding about my relationships with others—to make sure I didn't sabotage those relationships by living with some precon-ceived notion of how those people should relate to me.

If you approach your partner with rigidity and fail to ac-cept or recognize what may seem like a foreign language or other untraditional means of expression, you may very well cheat yourself out of the peace and joy of having a quality relationship simply because your partner isn't act-ing in accordance with some arbitrary standard you have set. Resist being rigid in your own modes of relating, and resist being judgmental about your partner's modes of relating. Do what works.

MYTH #10: YOUR RELATIONSHIP CAN BECOME GREAT ONLY WHEN YOU GET YOUR PARTNER STRAIGHTENED OUT

Many of you still have this childlike notion that you don't have to take too much responsibility for finding your own happiness. You still believe the fairy tale that falling in love means finding someone who is going to make you live happily ever after.

And when that fairy tale turns out to be untrue, you want to point the finger, to blame, to believe that all the unpleasant things you are experiencing in your relationship are being caused by your partner. Your unhappiness, you believe, is the result of your partner's deeds. Your life would be so much better, you say to yourself, if your partner would just change. As a result, you conclude, there's little you can do until your partner shapes up his or her act.

When I have counseled people in distressed relationships, I have asked them who, if they had the choice, they would most like to influence. Their answer invariably is their mates. You're probably no different. You assume that if you could just modify your partner's thinking, feeling, and behavior, your relationship would be so much better.

That's a myth. The most important person for you to influence is yourself. You are the most important person in this relationship, and you must be the focus of your beginning efforts to change this relationship. You must rediscover your own dignity and self-esteem—your own personal power. You cannot reconnect with your partner if you are not reconnectable.

Understand that I am not saying you are to blame for the problems that may exist in your relationship. But I am saying that you are, at the very least, jointly accountable for the current state of your relationship. If your relationship is not everything that you want it to be, then it's your thinking, your attitudes, and your emotions that need challenging. You have flaws, fallacies, and characteristics that either destructively stimulate your partner, or through which you destructively respond to your partner.

As I have said, you have chosen to live a lifestyle that leads to a bad relationship. You have chosen the thoughts, feelings, and behaviors that are creating the pain in this relationship. You have chosen your thoughts, feelings, and behaviors just as surely as you choose the clothes you wear each day, the car you drive, and where you work.

You have chosen these behaviors, thoughts, and feelings because at some level they work for you. At some level these characteristics or interactive patterns have provided you with a payoff that has reinforced the recurrence of these behaviors. If you find the payoffs, you have found the lifeline that keeps the destructive behaviors alive and recurring. Once you identify the payoffs, you can shut them off and remove them from your life. Once the behavior no longer works for you, once it fails to generate you some payoff, it will cease to occur.

I once encountered a crystal-clear example of this concept of payoffs with a newly married couple. Apparently, Connie was insanely jealous of Bill and lived with a horrible and gripping fear that he would violate their marriage vow. She felt that he would either leave her or have an affair during his frequent job-related travels. Connie would call and page him incessantly throughout the day to verify his where-abouts and his activities. In one day she called or paged him seventeen different times. Each contact was the same: "Are you with any other women?" "Have you flirted with any-one?" "Do you think they are prettier than I am?" "Do you wish you were with them instead of me?" "You don't love me, do you?" "You think I am ugly and boring and uninter-esting, don't you?"

Bill consistently and patiently reaffirmed his love and commitment to her. He denied the presence of other women, even if they were involved with him in work-related ways. He constantly reassured her in terms of his commitment, fi-delity, and appreciation for her and her attractiveness. This pattern continued on until both were so addictively involved in it that it was destroying their marriage. She could think of nothing else, and he had become a slave to the phone, beep-ers, and constant reassurances. Both professed a desire to stop it. My question was, "If you don't like it, why don't you quit doing it? You are not stupid people; you have the ability to make a choice, so make it and quit whining about it."

Both said they wished that it was that easy, but that try as they might and commit as they would, they constantly returned to the pattern. They both expressed frustration and confusion over why they would consciously do what they didn't want to do.

The answer is probably as obvious to you now as it was to me then. Both Connie and Bill were getting some kind of sick payoff out of this destructive interactive pattern. As our interactions wore on, it became apparent that Connie was terribly insecure personally. (Duh!) But the real revelation to her was that she was feeding on the constant reassurance, placated each time he passed "the test." Every day that she badgered him with this need for reassurance, she would ultimately confront him and tell him, "Why don't you just get it over with and leave me, because you know that is what you are going to do." Each time Bill denied that he had those thoughts, professed his love, and did not leave, he had just passed the test again, thus reassuring her. She was getting an ill-gotten gain of reassurance and recommitment every single day. She became so addicted to the need for this that it controlled her.

For Bill, it was like trying to fill a bottomless pit. Since her problem had nothing to do with him, and everything to do with her own personal insecurity, as well as her lack of willingness to properly diagnose the situation and resolve the problem from the inside out, they were spiraling down at an ever-increasing rate. Bill, who seems like the poor victim in the whole thing, undoubtedly got a sick ego trip from being so "valued, pursued, and worried about." It stroked his ego that his wife was so obsessed with him. But soon, like all addictive behaviors, both Connie and Bill became slaves to their addictive payoffs.

She was going to have to make a decision about whether she wanted to nurse this sick, green-eyed, narcissistic, and self-destructive monster that dominated her every waking hour, or grow up and take the risk of letting herself love and trust. It was also clear to me that if she didn't, Bill would be out of there and out of there soon. Bill had to decide whether to be controlled by the ego trip or mature into a more healthy partnership.

Instead of waiting for your partner to change, you can and will serve yourself much better by looking at yourself instead of your partner. What kind of payoffs are you affording yourself that are keeping these destructive patterns alive? You may find that it is now obvious, or that it is still hidden. Either way, make no mistake: there is a payoff there. You are no exception to the rule because there are no exceptions to the rule.

So you can either stay self-centered and keep blaming your partner, or you can make the choice to be self-directed and start working for real change. You either can fill yourself up with impotent anger at your partner, or you can choose to get busy and stimulate your relationship to get headed in the right direction. You can either let your partner dictate your behavior, or you can own your own thoughts and attitudes, both of which will be chosen with a clear objective in mind.

I guarantee you by the end of this book, you will inspire your partner to behave and think and feel in different ways. But never think you can control your partner. And never think that it's up to your partner to make your life better. You are in charge of yourself.

FOUR

ELIMINATING YOUR
BAD SPIRIT

Believing in myths is not the only way you poison your relationship. There's an even more insidious technique that you use to harm the very thing that's most important to you. That's when you approach your relationship with what I call your "bad spirit."

Every one of us has an irrational and destructive emotional side to our personalities. There is a part of each of us that is immature, selfish, controlling, and power seeking. Not fun to hear about yourself, but it's true and you know it. Just as you can send your relationship down a dead-end road by falling for myths that are misleading and unimportant, you will send your relationship right over the cliff if you start letting your bad spirit—your dark side—sabotage your attempts at intimacy and peace.

If you are being honest with yourself, about yourself, you know, of course, exactly what I am talking about. Unfortunately, it's during relationship interactions—the most emotionally charged part of your life, the place where you have the greatest personal stake—when your bad spirit can leap out of you. In effect, through your own negative attitudes you are unconsciously bringing about everything you most wanted to eliminate. Even the most normal, intelligent people can resort to the most spiteful behavior when dealing with those they claim to love. There can be astonishing hostility and cruelty, childlike defensiveness, pathetically immature reasoning, accusations and counteraccusations, blaming and shaming, exaggerations and denials. When your bad spirit comes roaring out, you are the most disconnected from your core of consciousness that you can get. You have totally moved away from feelings of worth and dignity and cast yourself as a victim.

Most of you find this side of yourselves so distasteful that you cannot face it. You have a stockpile of denials to justify and explain away your terrible behavior. You like to think instead of how you are when things are going well in your relationship and you act mature, giving, flexible, and democratic. But your bad spirit is always there, always lurking, and it's during those times when the waters get rough—when you get frustrated, threatened, and hurt—that you give in to your dark side. Allowing this ugly side of who you are to take control can cause your relationship to fail—not some of the time, but all of the time. Regardless of what else may be right with the relationship, your bad spirit, if left unattended, will poison every fiber of your relationship and seal its fate.

Make sure you hear me. You may be thinking that, well, "I'm not always sunshine and light and I may have some 'sort of' bad spirit," but you take reassurance in the fact that you're not one of those crazy, yelling abusers. Let me assure you that you can be just as destructive with a bad spirit that does not have the dramatic expressions of some you have encountered.

As you're about to learn, there are a variety of ways this bad spirit can express itself. While some of you have a flair for dramatic self-destruction that can sink a relationship overnight just like a gaping hole in the bottom of a boat can sink it in minutes, others self-destruct with a style that is more like a slow leak. That slow leak may not have the same entertainment value to your friends, neighbors, and in-laws who stand gaping when a wild-eyed bad spirit controls the day, but it just as surely and relentlessly drains the life from your relationship. As time passes, you will become more and more controlled by your internal negative attitude. In effect, you will unconsciously bring about everything you most wanted to eliminate—and most likely you won't have a clue as to what's happening.

Because this aspect of yourself can be so devastating, you can't afford to be defensive about it or pretend that it doesn't exist in hopes that it will go away. Nor can you rely on traditional, conventional therapy in which you spend session after session with someone trying to understand where these attitudes came from—doing some analysis, perhaps, of what your mother or father did to you. That can be entertaining mental masturbation, but it is little else.

I can't change whatever happened to you as a child that may have influenced the way you are now behaving—and you can't change it either. The important thing to realize is that you are not a child anymore. You are now an adult, and you have the chance to choose what you think, feel, and do. If you have a tough history, I'm sorry. I really am. I don't mean to make light of or minimize suffering that you may have been through. I've heard stories that were so horrible that they made me physically sick to my stomach. If you are one of those stories, I absolutely hate that for you. But the only thing worse than having terrible things happen to you in one phase of your life is mentally and emotionally carrying those terrible events and feelings into the next phase of your life. If you are one of those who suffered through such an event, you cannot hide behind it or use it as an excuse to justify your dark side. If you do keep hiding, you'll just keep the suffering alive by transplanting it into your current life.

You must be willing to meet your bad spirit face-to-face, recognize how it manifests itself in your behavior, and then quickly get yourself out of that mind-set before it does even greater damage. You will never analyze your bad spirit away; you just need to be ready to knock it back before it starts to consume you. That's the best, most effective therapy that I know. Indeed, I don't want you to run from your bad spirit; I want you to know this self-defeating nature so intimately that if it even tries to stick so much as a little toe into your life, you'll be able to spot it and stop it. I want you to be able to say, "Bingo. There's my stalker. I will not be ambushed. I will not allow those characteristics to come into my life and relationship and sabotage my happiness. It is not going to come between me and my partner."

Going through the next section of this chapter will not be fun, because we are going to look at the most typical ways that this bad spirit shows up in a life and a relationship. But remember, you cannot change what you do not acknowledge. Have the courage to get real about this dark side, and you can take control.

Characteristic #1: You're a Scorekeeper

A healthy relationship is clearly a partnership. Partners co-operate, they support one another, and they depend on one another. They do not compete. Some competitive hard-heads may be thinking, "Competition? I'm possessed by a bad spirit if I feel competitive? Yeah, right!"

When it comes to your relationship, however, that's exactly right. Please understand, I think there's nothing better than great banter between a man and woman. I love watching a couple playing their games of verbal volleyball—teasing one another, swapping funny stories, joking about the other's eccentricities. There's a great spark to their relationship, a feistiness that makes it fun. That's not competition; that's love with a sense of humor and with abundant spirit.

But competition, real competition, between partners can quickly turn a relationship into a battle of one-upmanship that can turn ugly. Competitiveness means "score keeping"—and if you allow your life with your partner to be guided by a tit-for-tat trading of favors and duties, an "I'll do for you if you'll do for me" score keeping, you are in danger of turning what should be a mutually co-operative and supportive relationship into a fight for leverage and the upper hand.

True intimacy and caring is not a game. Nothing short of selfishness is in control when one or both of you are trying to justify privileges or claim entitlements as opposed to focusing on what you can give. In any relationship, you are either a giver or a taker. Takers keep score to justify the taking. When the element of competition is added, your relationship will become a *quid pro quo* tussle dominated by the attitude, "You owe me."

Think about it. Competition by its very nature means that you have an adversary, an enemy. How can you possibly be a winner if it is at the expense of making the person you supposedly love a loser? How can you possibly expect to enjoy harmony in a relationship where one or both of you are fighting for leverage, power, and control? Solid relationships are built on sacrifice and caring, not power and control.

The joy of giving is completely lost when a husband picks out a beautiful dress and gives it to his wife, not as an act of kindness, but just to build up brownie points so that she is in his debt and under his thumb. Or a wife who stays home, baby-sitting the kids so her husband can go fishing with his buddies, not because she wants to give him a relaxing gift but because she wants him to owe her big time. This is not a couple that is attempting to be mutually supportive. These are two people who are each trying to get the upper hand in order to control their partner. It of course never occurs to either person that with genuine caring and giving, their partner would probably volunteer more than could ever be demanded of them.

Oftentimes this score keeping leads to a kind of paranoia in which partners begin to worry about accepting a seeming gift or act of kindness for fear that the ultimate price of this "gift" will be much too high.

In a competitive relationship, there can never be any honest acknowledgment of shortcomings or mistakes made because that would be giving up valuable leverage. Never mind that such an acknowledgment would be honest. Defensiveness, deflection, and resistance to even the most constructive criticisms rules the day, all at the expense of the relationship.

In short, competitiveness between partners is an ill wind that can blow through an otherwise healthy relationship. To keep the upper hand, you soon begin to put your partner down, to inflate your ego, and constantly try to maximize your deeds and minimize those of your partner. Your attitude is always "Hooray for me." If your children do well, it's because of the way you raised them. If you have a beautiful vacation home, it's because you paid for it. You can't ever get to the point, as we talked about in the previous chapter, where you and your partner can agree to disagree and respect each other's positions. Because you're keeping score, it's much more valuable if you can prove your partner wrong.

When this kind of attitude begins to dominate the relationship, you will never come to understand what it means to be loving. You will never focus on the spirit of cooperation and coalition. You'll be running your relationship like a commodities market, trading one thing in hopes of getting another.

Here are some telltale warning signs that you can use to determine whether or not competition has replaced cooperation in your relationship:

- You tend to keep score of things your partner does, such as leisure time, outings with friends, hours with the children, and chores completed.
- You make sure your partner never gets the upper hand and never gets by with a "freebie."
- You bank "points" which are held over your partner's head for leverage.
- You make concessions in a negotiating fashion rather than offering them as a gift of support.

- You seldom if ever do something in support of your partner without making sure that he or she knows it, including a detailed explanation of the imposition it created for you.
- In any type of dispute or confrontation with your partner, you actively seek outside allies in the form of family and friends in an effort to shift the balance of power.
- You insist on having the last word or final act of defiance.

If this spirit of competitiveness has infiltrated your relationship, do not allow yourself to be in denial. Just as with cancer or any other infectious disease, denying the problem will only make it worse. There is something wrong with a partner whose spirit and agenda in interacting with their partner is committed to finding leverage. You and your partner are a team: you're supposed to be mutually supportive. The spirit of competitiveness, however, assures that there is a negativity in the air that can drain the joy, confidence, and productivity from any situation.

Characteristic #2: You're a Fault Finder

There is nothing wrong with legitimate criticism or input in a relationship. There is nothing wrong when one party complains about the actions or attitudes of another—if that complaint is designed to improve the relationship.

But constructive criticism too often gives way to constant fault finding—in which you obsess over the flaws and imperfections rather than find value in your partner. You're almost always telling your partner, in one form or another, what he or she should be doing. When you "should" on your partner, you send the message that you not only disagree with your partner, but that your partner has violated some standard. That is misleading. Your opinion may be your opinion, but as the old saying goes, "Unless someone died and left you in charge, your opinion hardly rises to the level of being a standard."

If you think about it, what you're really doing is taking a sick pleasure in studying someone else's negative inventory. You get used to making criticisms, and once you start it's hard to stop. In fact, no matter what your partner does or how hard he or she tries, it's not enough or it's never as correct as you wish it to be. If your partner had ten things to do and did eight of them to perfection, you would spend ninety percent of your time talking about the two things that did not get done. You will neither focus nor comment on your partner's beautiful dress or suit. Instead, you'll make a comment about a scuff on the shoe. Living with you is like trying to fill a bottomless pit. You are the type who will say to your partner, "We had a great day together except for when you . . ." You have no idea how sick to death your partner can get of your constant criticism. Some of you pick at your partners so relentlessly and so anal-retentively that I think you must have been potty-trained at gunpoint.

Even if you think I am not describing you, take a brutally honest look at yourself here. This is an attitude that can quickly overtake you. Think back to the last time you said something critical to your partner and the last time you said something positive. Which statement did you make with the most passion or intensity? Spend a few seconds right now and make two lists about your partner. In the first list, write down, as quickly as you can, five little things you like about him or her. In the second list, write down five little things that irritate you about your partner. What happened? If you're like most people who take this test, then you were able to come up with the five negative things far quicker than the five positive things.

Now, I'm not here to be your Norman Vincent Peale and tell you that the answer to life is to think positively at all times. But for too many of you, criticizing and blaming and disparaging have become your stock in trade. Because you no doubt feel a lack of satisfaction with your own life, you attempt to "level" your partner. Instead of building your own sense of self-worth, you shoot your partner down to your own perceived low level of functioning. Understand that we are talking about your partner here, the person you are supposed to love and cherish.

Here are some telltale warning signs that you can use to determine whether or not critical perfectionism and a bad case of the "shoulds" dominate your relationship style:

• You seldom if ever let an infraction by your partner slide by, regardless of how trivial.

• You find yourself saying such things to your partner as, "You should have known better." "You should have helped me out when I was stressed." "You should have done what I wanted without me having to ask you."

• You tend to say "always" and "never" when criticizing your partner. "You always do this." "You never help me out in the kitchen." "You always ignore me." The terms "always" and "never" are judgmental and argumentative. They also should be embarrassing to the one using them because such absolute statements are typically insupportable.

• You tend to complain about how you're not getting what you deserve or that life is unfair to you—an attitude that you quickly transfer to your partner, as if he or she is to blame.

• You counterattack with criticism whenever you're being criticized yourself. Your partner, for instance, tells you that you forgot to take out the garbage. Instead of hearing the message, your competitive attitude and critical spirit kicks in and you counterattack; "I can't believe you have the nerve to say that. You never do what you're supposed to. I'm fifty times more reliable than you are. You don't even lock the door at night."

• You are obsessively interested in getting your partner to admit to wrongdoing rather than listening to what your partner has to say.

If you are controlled by this bad spirit and think your critical perfectionism is making your partner a better person, think again. What you are doing is nothing more than making your partner more confused, more anxious, and perhaps more resistant to your legitimate criticisms. And even more important, you're driving your partner away. By constantly pursuing, attacking, and resisting, you are only going through the peaks and valleys of a relationship roller coaster instead of aiming for the peaceful coexistence of people who accept and believe in themselves and each other. If you're criticizing, you're not praising. And if you're criticizing, you are not connecting. You create your own experience; get off your partner's back and you may see your partner moving toward rather than away from you. You will also start realizing that you have a lot of work to do on yourself, and that no amount of criticism of someone else is going to improve you.

Characteristic #3:
You Think It's Your Way or the Highway

This particular bad spirit goes a step beyond competitiveness and criticism. Here, you become self-righteous. You turn unyieldingly rigid. You are obsessed with control. Everything has to be your idea, and everything has to be done your way. No other method than yours, however sufficient it might be, is acceptable.

As a rigid controller, you are intolerant of initiative by others and expect them to be passive puppets to your ideas and wishes. You refuse to recognize or acknowledge contributions by your partner. You are not happy unless you are deciding what to do, how to do it, when to do it, and why it should be done. You always feel justified in everything you do. You set yourself up as the repository of all that is right and good. You cannot and will not admit that you are wrong because you are addicted to rightness. The message to your partner is clear: "I am better than you."

Your objective is not just to dominate, to manage your partner with condescension and intimidation, but to stake out the moral high ground. You seek to set up a hierarchy, a pecking order in which every exchange is designed to elevate you to some pedestal of sanctity. Once again, you're probably saying to yourself that you hardly act this way, but the brutal fact is that so many of you masquerade at some elevated level of confidence and competence, artificially inflating your own ego so that you can delude yourself and your partner into believing that you are superior to everyone else.

Let me state the obvious: you cannot serve two masters.

You cannot act with such self-righteousness and overbearing control, and at the same time believe that you are pursuing what is best for the relationship. Eventually, you will compromise and sacrifice the relationship rather than admit ownership in a problem. I cannot imagine a more self-defeating spirit than this one, for you are putting your own ego above the welfare of the relationship. You will let the relationship go down in flames rather than be honest about your own shortcomings.

Here are some other telltale warning signs that you can use to determine whether or not self-righteousness is the master you serve:

• You are intolerant of your partner's initiatives or ideas.

• You regularly interrupt your partner during conversations so that you can get in what you want to say instead of patiently allowing your partner to finish what he or she has to say.

• You "change the game" on those few occasions when you realize that your partner is making a good point. You might say to your partner, for instance, "You don't have to use that tone of voice." "There is no reason for you to look that way." "Why do you relish trying to hurt me?" Suddenly, you've got the subject turned back at your partner.

• You cannot end a confrontation until your partner acknowledges that you are right.

• If your partner won't admit the rightness of your position, you tend to sulk or act like a martyr, making sure your partner understands that you don't feel appreciated.

• You regularly assume a saintly, pious position with friends and family, telling them about all you have to put up with, about how your partner is impossible to live with.

• You tend to start sentences with guilt-inducing phrases like "If you loved me . . ." or "If you cared for me . . ." or with "I told you so; you should've listened."

I admit that in the heat of anger, the self-righteous desire to occupy the moral high ground can be very seductive. So you must examine yourself with a very critical eye to make sure that you are not sabotaging your relationship in this way. By putting on the cloak of self-righteousness, what you're really doing is keeping yourself from looking at your own faults. By being the first to recognize when your partner breaks the rules of a relationship—or arbitrarily deciding that the rules you have set have been broken—you don't have to confront your own shortcomings.

Characteristic #4:
You Turn into an Attack Dog

This characteristic is so easy to trigger and so hard to undo. How many times have you started out discussing an issue and ended up ripping into your partner with a personal attack? You genuinely believe you are going to stay in control during the discussion, but then you suddenly bail out on the topic or issue and lay waste to the dignity of your partner. And once you get going, you have trouble walking away from the confrontation. Your attacks are totally out of proportion to the business at hand, and you will use any ammunition or any subject matter to undermine the confidence and self-worth of your partner. When you get vicious, you may not even remember or care to remember what you started out to discuss. In the blink of an eye, the interaction becomes open warfare.

It's when viciousness gets out of hand—and it does so more than anyone would anticipate—that we see crimes of passion where a once loved and cherished partner is beaten or even murdered. On the more day-to-day end of the continuum, the viciousness is just verbal, yet the self-worth of your partner and the viability of your relationship fare little if at all better. The message is clear: "I want to hurt you."

Sometimes our viciousness is blatant and easily recognizable. We can spew out the kind of vitriol that would shock anyone within earshot. But sometimes our viciousness comes out in more subtle ways. Sometimes, it is possible to be equally vicious by coldly introduced content. A partner who knows what buttons to push, which accusations will cut the deepest, can be cruelly vicious while never raising his or her voice. For example, imagine a loving, devoted, and dedicated mother who sits worried and guilt-ridden in the emergency room of a hospital while her toddler is getting treated for a painful burn suffered in the kitchen while she spoke on the phone to a friend. It happened in a flash; it was not foreseeable and may well have been non-preventable. Her husband walks in, sits down beside her, puts his head in his hands, and asks, "How could you be so selfish? Are you ever going to quit being so self-absorbed and ignoring our child while you talk incessantly to your stupid friends?" The message is clear. The damage is done, and never a voice was raised. When a partner hears viciousness in the words coming from the person who is supposed to be their greatest ally in the world, it can tear them apart. It isn't just that they disagree; it is a venomous communication of disgust and condemnation.

Once this spirit takes over, relating stops and the -

destruction starts. These interactions can happen in a flash or grind on for hours. Either way, the damage is done. If you have been subjected to this kind of spirit by a parent, partner, or "friend," then you know how difficult it is to trust that person ever again. It takes time and repair, and much good work can return to ground zero with a single episode of vicious behavior.

Here are some other telltale warning signs that you can use to determine whether or not viciousness is poisoning your relationship:

- Your interactions are marked by, at the least, a very harsh tone of voice and often by "in-your-face" shouting.
- Your interactions are marked by such body language as a curled upper lip, a pointed finger in the face, or a deliberate Clint Eastwood type "killer stare" or exaggerated eye rolling.
- Your comments are laden with condescension, such as "Well, you really turned out to be a great catch!"
- Your comments are full of insults and name calling, from "bitch" and "bastard" to "fat" and "ugly."
- Your comments are filled with "you" statements such as: "You make me sick." "You disgust me." "You are stupid and worthless."
- You purposely and pointedly attack your partner's vulnerable areas and values.
- As opposed to an act of overt commission, you withhold from your partner that which you know they want and need to have peace in their life.
- You seek to manage your partner with intimidation, both physical and mental/emotional.

I admit, these kinds of behaviors are often rewarded in the short term by a partner who concedes in order to escape the pain of character assassination. However, in the long run, the target of the abuse—your partner, whom you claim to love—becomes so filled with bitterness and resentment that he or she will ultimately pull away from the relationship, if not physically, then at least in some emotional fashion.

It's difficult to stop this kind of behavior once it gets going, which is why, later in the book, we're going to talk in more detail about how you can give yourself a time-out from these horrible confrontations and get back in control. But for now just remember: your scorched-earth mentality of winning through the destruction of the other person's confidence and self-worth really will create a scar that is as hard to repair and overcome as almost anything else that might occur.

Characteristic #5:
You Are a Passive Warmonger

After reading about the open aggression used by those afflicted with the bad spirit of viciousness, passive aggression might seem a far less harmful characteristic. That's not true. Passive aggression is still aggression. It is still a spirit that expresses itself through an unfair attack on an unsuspecting partner. It's just as obstructionistic; it's just that it is sneaky and underhanded. Those who are controlled by the passive-aggressive spirit are masters at what I call "sabotage with deniability." These toxic partners will work long and hard to obstruct that which they do not desire, but yet do so in such an indirect way as to escape accountability if they are confronted. They always have an excuse, they always have a justification, but yet they do in fact relentlessly obstruct. Trying to trap the passive-aggressive spirit is like trying to nail Jell-O to the wall. You just can't ever quite seem to get it done. You may know it, you may feel it, but you just cannot prove it.

If you turn to passive aggression in a relationship, you are not only a master of gutlessly avoiding accountability, you are also a master tactician at undercutting your partner and all that he or she seeks to achieve. As opposed to critical perfectionism, which engages in confrontational fault-finding, and as opposed to viciousness, which uses the tactics of rage and character assassination, if you are afflicted with this bad spirit, you try to thwart your partner by constantly doing that which you deny you are doing or the exact opposite of what you say you are doing.

Possessed by this spirit, you also conveniently forget to do what you promise you're going to do, or you purposefully screw up what you want your partner to think you are earnestly attempting to do. You don't outwardly reject what's been offered or is said by your partner. Rather, you just don't comply. You complain about it in subtle, whiny ways. You clearly do not want resolution with certain issues, and you seem to thrive on playing the role of a victim. You value that role far more than the peace and harmony that your partner might be seeking to generate.

Make no mistake, if you are possessed of the bad spirit of passive aggression, you are as much of an overbearing controller as the most aggressive, in-your-face person you could imagine. The difference is, you do it insidiously and underhandedly.

Let's say you are passive-aggressive and your partner suggests a vacation. But you don't want to go where your partner wants to go. Instead of saying that, you tell your partner, "That sounds great to me." Then you immediately start putting up barriers. You can't seem to work out the time to travel, you can't seem to get a fairly priced airline ticket, you come back and tell your partner that the hotel is going to cost five times more than you expected. "But I'm still fine with this trip," you say. "If it's okay with you, it's okay with me."

Ultimately, by openly agreeing to do something and then covertly sabotaging it, you are trying to get your partner to submit to your wishes—without having to stand up and tell your partner exactly what those wishes are. If you are passive-aggressive, your greatest moment in life is when your partner says, "Oh, forget I said anything," or "Why don't you go figure out what we should do?" You come out smelling like a rose.

Here are some other telltale symptoms that you can use to determine whether or not passive aggressiveness is undermining your relationship:

- After listening to your partner make a suggestion, you agree with the suggestion, then a few minutes later start talking about why the suggestion will fail rather than how it could succeed.

- You feign confusion when your partner explains even simple rationales for changing something in your relationship that you happen to like.

- You feign ineptness over activities that you don't like to do—painting a room of the house, for instance, or putting a child to bed.

- You time vague and subjectively defined illnesses or come up with competing events to interfere with plans made by your partner that you don't like.

- You often start sentences with the phrase "Yeah, but . . ."

In other words, in your passive way, you aggressively hurt your relationship. Such an attitude is terribly frustrating for your partner, especially when it comes to improving the state of your relationship. You rarely take responsibility for what is happening in your relationship, you never offer a constructive alternative to its problems, and you seemingly hold out for the perfect solution, which of course does not exist. In so doing, you guarantee failure and frustration because the standard you seem to be looking for is so terribly unrealistic.

Characteristic #6:
You Resort to Smoke and Mirrors

Like those who sabotage their lives and relationships with passive aggression, those of you afflicted by this dishonest spirit also lack the courage to get real about what is really driving the pain and problems in your relationship. But as opposed to passive aggression, what you do here is to give your partner overt misdirection signals at almost every turn with regard to how you are feeling or what is important to you.

In this self-defeating menagerie of smoke and mirrors, you contaminate your relationship by hiding the real agenda and instead substitute superficial but safe topics to talk or argue about. You criticize one thing about your partner when you're really upset about another. One partner may nag the other partner, for example, for being too overbearing as a hostess because he feels inadequate socially and is jealous of her social success. You may passionately and vehemently discuss and argue about trivial things which really don't matter to you. One partner may heatedly disagree with the other partner about the meaning of a movie they have just seen as a way to get out his or her irritation at that partner over things totally unrelated to the movie. Or you could seem very excited about doing one thing when it's all a ruse to keep from doing something else. For example, a partner acts inexplicably interested in taking a walk through the neighborhood when in truth he or she is trying to kill time so as not to have to sit quietly with the other partner or have a sexual interaction.

The result is utter emotional confusion. What is real never gets voiced, and what gets voiced is never real. When you deceptively control the perceptions of your partner, you make your partner spend untold energy trying to solve a problem that is nothing more than a decoy—a decoy that is set up because you lack the strength to get real about what matters.

In one of my seminars a couple good-naturedly acted out how they had previously lived this kind of constant hidden agenda. Neither Jim nor Lisa ever truly said what was on their minds. Here's a typical conversation:

Jim: *"How did the day go, honey?"* (Translation: *"I wonder if she's been goofing off again."*)

Lisa: *"It was a really nice day, dear."* (Translation: *"When are you going to quit checking on me?"*)

Jim: *"You sure look nice, honey."* (Translation: *"How much did that outfit cost me?"*)

Lisa: "You're so sweet." (Translation: "I guess he's
        horny.")

Jim: "Any mail today?" (Translation: "I wonder where
        she's hidden the bills.")

Lisa: "It's around here somewhere." (Translation: "Uh-oh,
        I hope he's real horny.")

Those lines are funny, but I encountered a much more stressful example of how the hidden agenda can damage a relationship with another young couple I met also in a seminar several years ago. Newly married, Jason and Debbie had enjoyed a whirlwind courtship that was rich in camaraderie and sexual interaction. Shortly after getting married, Debbie became pregnant, but then suffered a miscarriage in the beginning of her second trimester. Because she'd had difficulty with the pregnancy throughout the entire first trimester, the young couple's sexual activity had ground to a virtual halt for several months. This asexual pattern continued even after the physical recovery associated with the miscarriage. It was clear to even the most casual observer that Jason was hurt by what he interpreted to be a rejection by Debbie.

Yet rather than dealing with his feelings of rejection up front—a subject too risky for Jason's ego—he began to pick at Debbie over every little thing he could find. He vented his frustrations and his resentment through criticism about her low-paying job and her lack of great career ambition. He criticized her housekeeping, her cooking, and her family, but he never spoke the "s" word. Had Jason dealt with the issue of sexual deprivation and his feelings of rejection, he and Debbie might well have been able to work their way through it and find some common ground. But

Jason was unwilling to take the risk. He feared being told by Debbie that he was no longer desirable.

Debbie, of course, didn't know what Jason's real issue was, so she took his criticisms at face value. She found, however, that as soon as she would make a change and fix one problem, he would simply substitute another. A wedge was soon driven between the two that lasted for a very long time.

Operating on a hidden agenda is bad for both partners. It was highly destructive to Debbie because she was being personally criticized over issues that she could not fix. Meanwhile, Jason was hurt by the situation because he would never get resolution of what was really bothering him because it lay buried under a mound of false problems.

These are some warning signs that you can use to determine whether or not the hidden agenda is part of your relationship:

• Your interactions constantly focus on superficial and trivial topics.

• Your interactions that begin to approach the real issues are disrupted by anger, abrupt changes of subject, or withdrawal.

• You tend to talk passionately about the problems of other people that mirror what is really bothering you, but when confronted, you deny its relevance. (For example, Jason might have talked about the sexual problems in a friend's relationship and then denied that he was making a suggestion about his own relationship.)

• You find yourself becoming very defensive if your partner directly asks you if there is anything bothering you.

• You are a master of defensiveness. You always know how to direct attention away from yourself if the questions get too personal. You're so good at self-protection that if someone asks you, "Why were you late yesterday?" you have five ready answers. ("I wasn't late, and besides, it was raining.")

Hidden agendas and the buried issues that lie beneath them can fatally poison a relationship. You might think you're not causing that much harm. You're just postponing the issue for a while, you say to yourself. You wonder how disastrous it really can be that instead of talking about your frustration that you don't have as much sex as you want, you talk about how nothing ever gets picked up around the house. Or that instead of discussing your anxieties that your partner seems too close to someone of the opposite sex at work, you talk to your partner about how he or she works too much.

That's where you're wrong. Perhaps the most devastating result of partners who operate on hidden agendas is that the real issues eventually burst forth in a torrid way. Do you remember how in the last chapter I talked about "cumulative reactions"? Each time a frustration is experienced yet suppressed, the associated emotional energy does not go away. It just gets stored up. And like a balloon that gets too much air, that frustration will explode. If you operate on a hidden agenda, you'll find yourself exploding in response to some seemingly trivial event. The magnitude of that response will leave your partner bewildered, angered, and certainly cautious about any future disagreement. The level of trust in your relationship will plummet. The hidden agenda may seem to protect you from having to deal with a dangerous truth, but in fact it does nothing but compound it. If you hide inside a hidden agenda, you still have an appointment with pain—pain that grows in intensity each time it is suppressed.

Characteristic #7: You Will Not Forgive

I barely need to elaborate on this characteristic, do I? At this very moment many of you are able to recall an incident from your past with your partner that was so hurtful to you, so devastating, that you can feel the tears stinging your eyes. You want to rage against the person who hurt you deeply. You think your anger might act as a kind of mystical curse on your partner. You hope it will make your partner suffer.

When you choose to bear anger at your partner, you build a wall around yourself. You become trapped in an emotional complex of such pain and agony that negative energy begins to dominate your entire life. Your resentment can literally become so pervasive as to crowd every other feeling out of your heart. What's more, your emotions do not remain specific to your partner. Bitterness and anger are such powerful forces that once they enter your heart, they change everything about you. They redefine who you are. If your heart has turned cold from your feelings of bitterness, for example, then that is the heart from which all your emotions spring. That is the heart that you will show to your children, to your parents, to your fellow human beings—and yes, to your partner. In effect, you make it almost impossible for yourself to love, and to be loved. It's as if you get up every morning and put on your clothes, and then you put on your pain and hurt, and off to work you go.

In many ways, your inability to forgive your partner—and yes, to forgive yourself for the destructive things you have done—is what gives rise to so much discord. Now, I recognize this is a very thorny issue. If you have been betrayed by your partner, the last thing you want to show is love. You don't want to look like a weakling who's basically asking your partner to steamroll right over you again. You want to bring down consequences on your partner, to make him or her pay.

And if a betrayal has taken place, there should be consequences—certain freedoms limited, certain penance paid. But what I'm saying is that if you wallow in your resentment, if you refuse to forgive and move on, then you're going to tear up your life. Forget your partner for the moment. I'm talking about you. At the beginning of this book I told you that the key to fulfillment in your life is to take back your power, to choose how you feel, to create your own experience. If you choose to carry on your resentments, then you guarantee yourself a life of misery.

Here are other ways this particular spirit infiltrates your life:

• You are consumed with such anger at your partner that you'll explode over the smallest disagreements or difficulty.

• You feel so bitter that you take a pessimistic view of life in general.

• Your body feels so physically unbalanced—the condition is called heterostasis—that you often experience sleep disturbance, nightmares, poor concentration, and fatigue. You develop severe headaches, back spasms, even heart attacks—all because your body's chemical balance is dramatically disrupted because of your stress.

• You cannot read a book or watch a television show

or movie without finding something in it that reminds you of your resentment.

• You keep in your memory bank all the imperfections in your partner, you remember all of the mistakes and failures he or she has made, and you bring them up constantly.

• You interpret many statements and actions of your partner in a negative fashion, based on the slimmest thread of evidence or often no evidence at all.

• You think you shouldn't yet forgive your partner because he or she is not acting sorry or apologetic enough.

• You think you shouldn't yet forgive your partner because he or she has not done enough things for you in order to pay penance.

• You try to control your partner through shame rather than seeking to inspire your partner.

You do have the power to forgive. You have the power to say to your partner, "You cannot hurt me and then control me. I am the one who makes the choices. I will not bond to you through hatred, anger, or resentment. I will not bond with you through fear. I will not be dragged into a darker world. By forgiving you, I am releasing me." This is one of the most important things you can learn in this book. By caring enough about yourself, you can break the bond of anger. You can break free from your prison of despair and rage.

But the only escape route is through forgiveness—to take the high moral ground and forgive the person who has hurt you. You forgive not for the other person. You forgive for yourself. Understand this: if you allow people who have transgressed against you to keep you locked in, then they

win. But if you become the emotional leader in your life—
and, in turn, the emotional leader for your partner—I
promise that you will get more of what you want and less of
what you don't want. Despite all the hurtful statements or
actions that have passed between the two of you, forgiveness is available. It is not too late unless you say it is too
late. Decide that you will stay the course, and you will realize that you can create your own experience.

Characteristic #8:
You Are the Bottomless Pit

Now it's time to turn to a different kind of bad spirit—the
spirit of insecurity. If you are afflicted with this one, then
you are too needy. You are so needy, in fact, that you consistently undermine your chances of success.

For you there is never enough of anything. You cannot
be satisfied. You can never be loved enough. You can never
be attended to enough. You can never be supported or appreciated enough. You can never look good enough, and
you can never perform well enough. You never relax, you
never enjoy, and you never accept anything at face value.

You feel, in some strange way, unworthy and undeserv-
ing of happiness and incapable of achieving your greatest
dreams. You'll say to yourself that you do not have what it
takes to be happy, to get results, to make progress. You'll
say you just don't have the time to get it all together. You'll
say you're just not smart enough. What's more, you are so
worried about your personal adequacy that you misinterpret
the meaning of your partner's statements about you—and
your misinterpretations always result in a negative conclusion about yourself. You say things to yourself like "My
partner got mad at me, so maybe I'm too unreasonable."

Or: "Maybe it would be better for me if I just keep quiet." Or, "Considering what my partner says about me, I must not have much of a personality, so I should just try to get along."

More than sabotaging yourself, you are sabotaging your partner. Because you act like a bottomless pit, your partner is frustrated by never seeming to be able to "fill you up." He or she never gets to know what it means to have a fully functioning and peaceful relationship. And even when you do get to a better place in your relationship, you'll say something like "This can't last." "It's too good." "This must be the calm before the storm." It's as if you are attached to the idea that you don't deserve to be happy and that you're even afraid to act happy because you might jinx something and the wheels will come off. The fatalistic observation "What I fear I create" is definitely true within a relationship.

It amazes me that a lot of insecure people I meet really believe they are being meek and accommodating in their relationships, that they are full of charity to their partners, that they are doing their best to fit in and not rock the boat. Wrong! That is a gigantic misconception. Because you have an insatiable appetite for reassurance and stroking, you can never give your partner any rest. You may also be consumed by a deadly jealousy over your partner because you think it is only a matter of time until your own true failures and shortcomings are discovered and your partner will abandon you. As a result, you'll entertain constant imagined threats from others that give you the opportunity to act jealous and demand of your partner that he or she renounce these other people in favor of you. You need to know, over and over, that your partner is really committed to you. Sometimes, you'll unconsciously try to drive your partner away just so you can get another dose of reassurance when one more time your partner proves his or her desire to hang in there. Manipulative and demanding, you keep your partner dancing forever, trying to find a way for you to be at peace.

We all want reassurance from our partners. That is perfectly healthy. But there is also a point at which it becomes toxic, where you constantly hunger for a fix of reassurance. There is something very wrong with your self-esteem if you incessantly fish for compliments and reassurance about your appearance, your worth, and your value. The classic case of the insecure spirit is the wife who constantly is asking about her cooking or what she's wearing. "Oh, that's too done, isn't it?" she'll ask her husband about her pot roast. She knows, of course, it's perfectly done. But she needs to be told. When she says, "I look fat in this dress, don't I?" what she is saying is, "Tell me I don't look fat."

Men do the same thing, in different ways. "Do you think my hair is getting thinner?" "Was it good for you?" The questions are different, but the message is the same: tell me I'm okay because I am unconvinced. With the insecure spirit, eighty percent of all questions are statements in disguise. What's more, those questions are demands in disguise. If you are dominated by the insecure spirit, you also conveniently give yourself permission not to take responsibility for holding up your end of the relationship. How could you be expected to be a fully functioning, contributing, and mature partner when you're not smart enough or good enough?

Here are some other signs that the insecure spirit has taken control:

- You talk yourself out of friendships and relationships because you think the person you like is out of your league.
- You fear rejection for voicing an opinion. You'd rather not say something than risk the disapproval of others, and when you do talk, you wonder if you're making the right impression.
- You find yourself saying "Thank you" or "I'm sorry" frequently and unnecessarily.
- You talk yourself out of trying something new with your partner, from horseback riding to counseling, because you don't want to look stupid.
- When you are complimented, you immediately downplay whatever you did that led to the compliment.
- When you buy presents for others, you worry if they are "right" or "good enough."
- You state your beliefs as questions, asking your partner what he or she feels about certain subjects that are important to you instead of declaring your position and taking a stand.
- Instead of expressing anger, you become tearful and play the victim.
- You are so sensitive and thin-skinned about any criticism that your partner cannot tease you or joke with you, and he or she sure as heck can't tell you the truth when you need to hear it.

- No matter what the question with regard to making plans, your answer is always the same: "I don't know, I don't care. Whatever you want to do."

If your partner ever grows weary of trying to fill the bottomless pit and raises the issue, you of course go into a self-pitying posture, and try to make your partner feel guilty by saying all you wanted to do was hear what he or she had to say because you respected his or her opinion so much. Your guilt act is not doing anything to contribute to the relationship. It's not true penance. You're acting chagrined in hopes that you can be restored quickly back to full status in the relationship. You fall on your sword. Once again you say you're sorry, and you put on a pretty good show. The more pained you become and the more guilty you look, the more you can manipulate your partner back into your fold. And pretty soon he or she does come back and says, "Oh, come on. Everything's okay." And bingo! You get your payoff.

If this spirit has its hooks in you, be honest with yourself and stop feeding the monster by constantly seeking the payoff of "one more fix" of reassurance. Right now take the first step to break from your old inhibiting mind-set and free yourself from the internalized sense of inadequacy and from the accusatory voices within you that tell you not to be too demanding or to want too much. Only then will you begin the journey of change and transformation. Indeed, as we move forward, I am confident that you will learn other ways to meet your needs of feeling self-worth and value.

Characteristic #9: You're Too Comfortable

This is antithetical to criticism, competitiveness, self-righteousness, and aggression, but it is a bad spirit all the same. Here, you become so passive that you get nestled in a "comfort zone" where the name of your game is to play it safe, not to reach, and maintain the status quo. The sameness of your relationship becomes like an old but not particularly good friend—one that's as comfortable as that baggy pair of sweat pants you wear when no one else is around. You don't challenge yourself, you don't strive for any kind of excellence. You become inert. And if you're not careful, you will find your days turning into weeks, weeks into months, months into years, and before you know it, you'll look up and it's all over.

All of us know someone who intended to get a college degree, but first laid out and worked for a year. That year turned into two years, and then three years, and eventually the person just never got around to getting back to college. So it is, if you're not careful, with your relationships. You get accustomed to where you are. You get used to a style of living, to a pattern with your partner that you decide is not really what you want, not very satisfying or challenging but is okay. You decide okay will do for now. It's not what you wanted, it's not what you dreamed about, but it becomes familiar and it is easy.

A comfort zone is not what you want out of a relationship. You know you are just skimming the surface in your relationship. You know you have a life of half-communication or non-sexuality with your partner. You know your days are dull and your minds are bored and restless. But you decide it's better for yourself if you don't reach for more. Instead of thinking, "Nothing ventured, nothing gained," you say, "Nothing ventured, nothing lost." You might try to look in command, with an array of material comforts and successes, perhaps even with fame and power, but on the inside you are cheating your partner and yourself.

I know that many of you are afflicted by this spirit. There have been surveys done with thousands upon thousands of everyday Americans, all of whom have a house, a job, 2.2 kids, and the barking dog, typical Americans from Anywhere, USA. And when they are asked if they are genuinely happy with their lives, they don't just say no—they say, "Hell, no." When they are then asked why they don't change, their answers are almost universally the same. In fact, the answers could be summed up in the words of one survey participant: "I'm doing what I'm doing today because it's what I was doing yesterday."

It's not that you have completely given up and gone into a fetal position—you'll learn about that bad spirit in just a few moments. The problem here is that there are no sure deals, and that means a bad four-letter word, risk. In the back of your mind there is the idea that you might not be able to change as much as you'd like. What if you admit that you want and need more, and then you are unable to get it? Now you have acknowledged that your life is not what you want and it is harder to just rock along. If you are really a creative comfort zone dweller, you may think far enough ahead even to think that if you do achieve a higher plane of existence, you will have the pressure of maintaining that higher level.

Trust me, I understand how, for so many of you, simply admitting that your relationship is not all that you want it to be is threatening. Saying that what you have is not enough is a genuine risk. It's definitely safer if you never admit that there is something else out there that you want.

Yes, your comfort zone might feel safe, but it is filled with compromise. If you're in a comfort zone, you are failing to meet your responsibilities in the relationship. You aren't contributing, you aren't stimulating, you're not energizing, you're simply not carrying your end of the deal. In all likelihood, your partner is trying to drag you along. Yet you remain lulled by complacency. You depend on the drab predictability of your life. You get in a daily rut of going to work, coming home, eating a fast dinner, and then heading to your remote control, or your book. Whatever it is for you, you have a more intimate relationship with that than with your partner. You certainly caress it more than you do your mate. If you're in your comfort zone, you can be certain that you've lost touch with your core of consciousness. You've stopped relying on your best instincts, values, talents, and wisdom.

Here are some other typical feelings and behaviors of the inert spirit:

- You never talk about such subjects as where your relationship is going, what your deepest desires are, what you dream about, what gives you passion.
- You're tired even after a good night's sleep, and you find it hard to keep your eyes open after dinner.
- You sit for extended periods of time watching television.
- You say to yourself you can't do things because you don't have the willpower.
- Your first reaction to almost any suggestion by your partner is "no." You don't have the desire

to go somewhere new or try something that is not part of the regular routine of your life.

- Anything involving risk to your current lifestyle is definitely avoided. As a result, your lifestyle offers no challenge and no stimulation.

- You feel emotional talk is bothersome and sort of silly. You always roll your eyes when you hear someone say, "Why don't you express your feelings?"

- You say "I don't know" to so many questions. "I don't know why that happened to me." "I wish I knew why I did that." What you're really saying is that you have closed your mind and decided it's not worth the work anymore of trying to understand what's happening to you.

I'm probably not the first to tell you that life isn't like the pizza man. It doesn't deliver. You've got to make the move. And if you don't make a move right now to correct a bogged-down, comfort zone life, it becomes easier and easier to just stagnate. To put it another way, if you keep believing what you've been believing, then you'll keep achieving what you've been achieving. Living in the comfort zone ensures that you will never be a real winner. The difference between winners and losers is that winners do things losers don't want to do. Winners are willing to take reasonable risk, and winners are willing to let themselves dream.

To break the inert spirit, you must break through denial, stop justifying your own passivity, and stop avoiding the challenge of change. It requires some courage and commitment—but as you'll soon see, it is not that difficult to step away once and for all from a life of dull complacency.

Characteristic #10: You've Given Up

The give-up spirit is what psychologists like to call "learned helplessness." That is the state of mind in which you believe that you are in an intractably permanent position. You believe the circumstances you find yourself in are so unchangeable that you can do nothing about it. It's what happens when so many of the bad spirits that I've already mentioned have crowded into your life that you cannot imagine there being any possible way out. You become so forlorn and lonely, so emotionally isolated and disconnected, so negative and cynical, so far from your core of consciousness, that you completely shut down that part of your brain that tells you there is any hope whatsoever. Here, you have basically decided you have no core of consciousness whatsoever.

Learned helplessness is a term coined back in the seventies by a brilliant researcher by the name of Martin E. P. Seligman and describes a different phenomenon than depression. Whereas depression is largely an emotional state, learned helplessness is a mental as well as emotional state. If you are afflicted with learned helplessness, you have come to believe so strongly that you are trapped that you lose both the willingness and the ability to learn.

Learned helplessness was best demonstrated in a series of animal experiments by Dr. Seligman and his colleagues. Don't skip over the next few paragraphs because you think an animal experiment has nothing to do with you. This has everything to do with how humans react to their relationships.

In the experiments, a dog was put into a twelve-by-twelve room in which one half of the floor was painted solid white and the other half painted with red and white stripes. At first the dog received painful but non-fatal electrical shocks whenever it moved to the striped portion of the floor. Predictably, the dog quickly learned that the white zone meant safety and that the striped portion meant danger. The dog would avoid the danger zone, even if tempted with food. Then, in phase two of the experiments, the conditions were reversed. The dog now received electrical shocks on the white side of the room, and the striped portion was the new safety zone. Once again, the dog demonstrated the ability to unlearn that which he had mastered and learn to stay in the striped zone.

In phase three of the experiments, there was no safety zone. The dog could go to the white side of the room and receive shocks or go to the striped portion of the room and receive shocks. For a while the dog made numerous and frantic attempts to find a remedy to its predicament, but soon the dog rightly perceived itself as helpless to escape punishment. He eventually gave up, rolled over on his back, and took the electrical shocks without fighting or attempting to escape.

Finally came phase four. The white zone was once again the safe area of the room, and the striped area was the new danger zone. The dog could once again control its own destiny. Sadly, the dog demonstrated an inability or unwillingness to relearn that there was again a safe zone. Even when dragging the dog physically into the safe zone, the dog could not or would not reprocess information and realize that there was now a safe place to go.

The dog had given up. It was in a state of learned helplessness. It was completely convinced that there was nothing it could do to extricate itself from the pain, so it closed the gates. It stopped processing new information even though it was readily available. It had given up and surrendered to fate. Its willingness to learn was completely and inextricably shut down.

This dog wasn't just going through a period of depression. It had completely stopped processing new information. It did not recognize that there was a behavioral alternative that would improve the quality of its existence.

That is precisely the condition which many of you are in when it comes to your relationship. You have shut down. At least when you were "inert" or "insecure," you thought about the relationship and knew there had to be a better way. But in this condition you have stopped entertaining the notion that improvements can be made to whatever has happened between you and your partner. You have stopped learning or gathering new information. Most significant, because you've shut down your information processor, you are unable to see even the most obvious opportunities to rejuvenate your relationship. You refuse to notice any change of spirit in your partner, and you refuse to notice any change of conditions or circumstances in your own life. You're like a caged bird that no longer sings, completely unable to realize that the cage door is once again open.

Here are some observable indications that you can use to determine whether or not learned helplessness has consumed you:

- You have consciously accepted a dull pain as a way of life.
- You feel a regular sense of malaise or lack of energy.
- You have surrendered to the reality of just "going through the motions" in a motionless relationship.

- You often think or say, "What's the use? It will never change."
- You no longer even bother to protest when attacked or abused by your partner.
- You think it's pointless to try to change because it will only make the other partner get angry.
- You feel lonely.
- You have begun to turn to other people or activities in search of fulfillment.
- You express disappointment in the relationship covertly, constantly becoming "ill," for instance, and having to spend days in bed, or even turning to prescription pills or alcohol or twice-a-week sessions with therapists.

This is a terribly epidemic problem. It is a pattern that is often seen in abusive relationships, where one partner believes there is nothing that can be done except continue taking the abuse handed down by the other partner. You might be reading this and thinking, "I'm not one of these people." But if you are consumed with defeatist attitudes— "I've already given too much and I'm too tired to change," "My partner will never change," "Nothing can change our relationship"—then you are already allowing your disappointment in your relationship to turn to pessimism and then to despair. You have decided that it is better to give up than to confront your despair. You are living in the emotional equivalent of a fetal position, accepting the pain in a relationship because you are convinced that you are not competent to change your plight in life.

I want you, right now, to listen to me: you're killing your spirit. People do change, and so can you and so can your partner. Unlike animals, who cannot be told that it is a new day and that they can control their fate, you can hear such a message, and you can reconsider your situation. In this book you are going to be given the tools to reconnect, to engage in productive measures, to rely on ideas that work—and to rebuild your best kind of spirit, that spirit that lets you believe in yourself and in your partner.

I have seen many, many relationships come back from the grave simply because one or both partners made the initial decision to change attitudes and feel hope. As I said in the introduction, all you have to do is want to want the relationship to work. Otherwise, the inert spirit and the learned helplessness that defines it will eventually devastate your life.

I recognize this has been a very tough chapter to read. It has focused almost entirely on the dark side of living and how we can rip apart our relationships. But the bigger danger comes when we don't acknowledge that dark side. Then we will never be alert to its arrival; we will not be ready to cast it out.

At this point you're ready to move forward, to proclaim, "No, I will not do this anymore. I will not let my competitiveness cause me to drive a wedge between me and my partner. I will not let my self-righteous attitude control me. I will not give in to my tendency to be dishonest and hide what I really think and feel. I will not become vicious and alienate my partner. I will not lose my self-esteem, and I will not be helpless."

The best part of your personality and your emotional life perhaps has atrophied somewhat, but it can be reconditioned. It's like working out with weights to build muscles. You do have the power to change. You may not always think of yourself as a leader, and you may not particularly feel like a leader in this relationship, but you are now. Because you now possess some powerful knowledge, and because you are in the process of gaining even more powerful knowledge, you have an opportunity to provide important direction in this relationship. Don't you dare cheat yourself out of the chance. You've come this far, now let's go do it.

FIVE

RECLAIMING YOUR CORE: THE PERSONAL RELATIONSHIP VALUES

Y ou will want to read this chapter with both eyes and stay focused. You can't afford to miss a thing. It is time to stop being a contaminator in your relationship, and start being a contributor. There is no middle ground. If you aren't constructively contributing to the relationship, then you are destructively contaminating it, and as your partner in this reconnection process, I want to activate the positives that I know are there—or at least can be there. The time has come to get your mind and your attitude right. Getting rid of the wrong thinking and bad spirits is not enough. You now have to reach into your heart and soul, and tap into your core because you, and you alone, can determine the quality of your life—you have the strength and depth of character to take your life and your relationship to a totally different level. But eliminating the negatives is not enough. It's time for "the cavalry" to arrive—the person you really are.

Don't think for a second that I'm talking about some

mystical state of inner being that will deliver you to the mountaintop. I'm not nearly so cosmic and avant-garde. I am simply referring to an ingrained set of attitudes based on a healthy core of who you are, a style of engagement that will become the backdrop for everything else that happens in your relationship. I'm talking about you tapping into that core of consciousness which will push your own life and your relationship to levels of intimacy and caring that you never dreamed possible. It can happen because you can and should believe in you.

I mean that literally and without exception. In relationships, just as in every other aspect of life, the spirit and attitude with which you do things is at least as important as your actual actions. I could go straight to a list of some cookbook-type, wonderfully creative, and clever romantic behaviors that you could plug into your relationship, but if you approached those activities with the wrong spirit, you would be doing yourself absolutely no good. To start the reconnection process with your partner, you must passionately adopt the proper spirit. The myths and the destructive mind-sets that we have talked so much about rip through your relationship with the same power and destructiveness as a hurricane rips through a city. But the alternative is also true. If you adopt a new way of thinking and feeling about yourself, you, your relationship, and your partner will reap amazing benefits. Nothing else, nothing less will do.

Now, I will be the first to admit that it would be nice if your partner were sitting beside you reading this book. Also, I know that the human tendency is to focus on our partners rather than ourselves. Don't worry, we will get to your partner, but remember what I told you in the first couple of pages of this book: I'm coming after you. This chapter is about reconnecting with your true and powerful persona. It's about saying, "I can get back to me, and that's where this must begin. I can bring out the best of who I am, my mind, and my heart—and I have the passion and power to use them."

The ten Personal Relationship Values that you are about to learn can be such a revolutionary pivotal point in your relational life that you'll be able to create positive change beginning immediately. Consciously reaching into your core of consciousness will cause you to start living with more integrity, honesty, compassion, and with genuine enthusiasm. In essence, the ten Personal Relationship Values will reprogram you for success. You're going to like yourself a whole lot better than you have in the past, and I'm betting that you'll notice that everyone else in your life, including your intimate partner, will as well.

What's more, these values are all things that are totally within your reach and control because they have always been a part of you. Your partner cannot give them to you, and your partner cannot take them away from you. A new and fresh wind will start blowing through your relationship solely as a result of your shifting positions. By breaking the stalemate of sitting around and waiting to see who's going to make a move first, by making the decision that you will no longer be the passive victim in your relationship, you will create energy, mystery, newness, and inspiration. Your constructive, healthy thinking will be infectious to everyone around you, especially your partner.

When you change, you change the entire balance of the relationship equation. At the very least, whatever happens, you will enjoy a peace that comes from knowing that you are doing everything that you can possibly do to breathe life into this relationship. Embrace and incorporate these powerful Personal Relationship Values. They are what winners and winning is all about. They are what you will be all about.

Personal Relationship Value #1:
Own Your Relationship

You are fully accountable for your relationship. This notion may be completely contrary to everything you usually think about your relationship, but it's true. How, you must be asking, can you be accountable for a relationship when your partner is being such a jerk? What kind of ridiculous idea is that?

I cannot say this too many times in too many different ways. Owning your relationship means that you accept responsibility for creating your own experience. You are the architect of your thoughts. You choose the attitudes that you bring into the relationship. You choose the emotions and feelings that will control your thoughts in the relationship. And you choose how you act and how you react to your partner in your relationship. You own your relationship. You are one hundred percent accountable for it.

That means you can never again believe you're a martyr suffering in your relationship because of an unworthy partner. Be honest: you may have gotten in the habit of whining and acting like the victim. But I am giving you a "whine warning" here. Say good-bye to that part of you and, good or bad, step up and own what is yours.

I know that it seems like I'm jumping up and down about this, but it's all because I want you to get real about how powerfully you can influence your relationship by the attitude with which you approach it. If you stop the gloom-and-doom mentality of a hapless victim and replace it with the positive, constructive thoughts of a mover and a shaker, you will immediately begin to see a change. You can create an internal dialogue that is healthy, constructive and joyful.

I don't mean that you should take some fatalistic position of being trapped. This is not about you saying, "Okay, I got into this relationship, and it's turned out bad, so I accept that I made a mistake." That's not ownership; that's whining. That's living in the past.

This is about you taking a new, right-now life position. It's about you creating a different lifestyle that will enhance your relationship. It's about you waking up in the morning with a refreshing realization that you are paddling and steering your own canoe. It's not about blaming yourself for where you've been; it's about directing yourself toward where you are going. Let me tell you as bluntly as I can: this Personal Relationship Value is the major building block to your new life. Only when you stop seeing yourself as a victim will you start to see yourself as a fully competent and potent force in your relationship. Your less than perfect relationship will no longer be a source of despair. It will be your opportunity to use your power. Problems truly are nothing more than opportunities to distinguish yourself. It is time to do just that.

Let me give you an example of how this value should manifest itself in your life. When there is something unfulfilling in your relationship, your very first step should not be to judge or criticize—there will be plenty of time to do that, if you must. Your first step should be to evaluate what you specifically are doing to cause that lack of fulfillment.

If you are living this Personal Relationship Value, you

don't just get mad if your mate is chronically late for appointments or dinner. You must instead candidly evaluate what you are doing to contribute to the occurrence of this action of your partner's. What payoff are you giving him or her? Are you being unassertive in a way that makes your partner feel you can be taken advantage of? What are you doing that keeps you and your partner from dealing with this issue? What are you doing to enable this behavior in your partner, and what can you do to make him or her genuinely change? By looking at yourself, instead of your partner, you're focusing on something you control instead of on something that you cannot.

When you own your relationship, you must hold up the mirror to look at yourself. You will finally realize that whatever it is your partner is doing, you are either eliciting, maintaining, or allowing that behavior. Your partner doesn't just act; he or she also reacts to you—to what you do or don't do. Your partner reacts to your tone and to your spirit. I'm not suggesting that you will always like what you see in that mirror. By being accountable and acknowledging that you have responsibility for where this relationship has ended up, you clearly will be coming face to face with some things that do not make you proud. You will have to be honest about the things you have done that have contaminated this relationship, and you will then have to resolve to stop and change those realities, decisions, and behaviors. Becoming accountable can at first be painful, but I promise that it will ultimately be very cleansing.

The time has come for you to take charge, to find a new level of personal power. When you do, you will have matured to a new level of functioning that will stand you head and shoulders above those who haven't heard the "whine warning" and continue to stumble through life being the victim. Let those unfortunate souls spend their lives complaining about what they do not control while you take hold and influence those things you can. That's what owning your relationship is all about. When you own your relationship, you don't hide behind anger and frustration with your partner. You decide how to start changing the stimuli that gets your partner to behave positively and constructively. You start changing the rewards and the consequences. You change the message and make it clear that you are not a victim but are instead a capable, competent, and self-directed individual who is willing to work and work hard on this intimate relationship.

When you are accountable, you are an agent of change. I am willing to bet that that is exactly what your relationship needs. As you're about to see in the remainder of the Personal Relationship Values, everything you're going to do from here on out will be designed to maximize your power in this relationship and to get yourself to start being honest.

When you do, you will start making permanent, healthy change—not only within your relationship, but within yourself.

Personal Relationship Value #2: Accept the Risk of Vulnerability

As I said in the previous chapter, being resistant to risk and changes that lead to risk is neither novel, nor is it illogical. Any time you are faced with adopting new thoughts and behaviors, particularly those that include opening yourself back up to a partner who has previously caused you pain, it's to be expected that some long-standing fears and anxieties will emerge. The tendency is natural, but it will not serve you here. You must take some risk and remember you are not alone; you have a partner, and we are going to do this together, step by step.

Even so, I'll bet that as you're reading this, you're starting to play the "What If" game. What if I get betrayed again? What if I get hurt? What if my newfound optimism is used against me to manipulate me?

There's nothing wrong with asking the questions. Any of you who have been hurt or disappointed naturally want to take steps to keep those feelings from ever coming back. Just as you stay away from a hot stove after you've burned your hand on it once, so you try to protect yourself from the chance to reexperience emotional pain. Just as you withdraw your hand from the hot stove, you withdraw your heart from a hurtful relationship.

But if you're going to play the "What If" game, you have to play it all the way to the end. That means if you are going to ask the "What If" questions, you have to answer the questions. What if your mate does in fact act badly and hurt your feelings? The realistic answer about what would happen is probably not nearly as bad or devastating as what you conjure up in your gloom-and-doom imagination. Monsters live in the dark. If you "turn on the light" by actually thinking through the answer, the monster that is your fear often becomes a mouse. By facing your fears, you will discover you are a whole lot tougher than you thought you were, and if things don't go just exactly right, you can still survive. You'll also discover that the pain you experience from anticipating some dreaded event is almost always worse than the pain associated with the dreaded event itself—that is, if it ever actually happens.

Face it, the true answer to the question is, "If my partner

does do something negative or hurtful when I open up and let myself care again, I won't like it, but I will survive. I will pick up my marbles and go on down the road, or scatter them out and play the game again, and again, and again until it works."

There is no question about it; getting back into a posture that involves emotion and caring and sharing makes you vulnerable. Letting yourself hope and dream again will make you vulnerable. Wanting and reaching out does make you vulnerable. But you and I both know that where you are now is hardly pain-free. At least by putting yourself on the line you have the chance of getting what you want as opposed to hurting with no chance of getting what you want. Not to venture is to lose yourself, and I won't let you do that.

I am not advocating that you lead with your chin. I am not advocating that you recklessly expose yourself to a hurtful partner who has not earned your trust. I know that, at one level, this may be very difficult. I know that you may have been hurt and disappointed and heartbroken, time and time again. But what I am asking you to do is resolve to trust yourself to be able to handle whatever your partner may do concerning this relationship. You must be willing to let yourself feel again, to believe that your relationship can be better. Just consider, for a moment, how well your protective devices are working. Residing behind a protective wall and living with loneliness and emptiness is certainly not without pain. You may feel that this kind of pain is safer because it has become familiar and because you seem to be in control, but it is pain nonetheless. The equation is simply this: you can remain behind the wall, with absolutely no hope of resolution or improvement in your relationship, or you can come out from behind the wall, possibly get hurt, but at least have a chance of creating what you want in your relationship.

Please do not let fear paralyze your life at this moment. If you feel too vulnerable, you might want to say to yourself right now that these new personal values and this reconnection program is merely an experiment that you're going to try for a couple of weeks. I am convinced that at the end of your "experiment," you will have such new insights and ideas that you will never want to be controlled again by your old fears. Think about it this way: your fear has been a huge catalyst in your past—perhaps the single most motivating force in your life. It has kept you from doing so many things. If you can be driven so far in one direction because of fear, imagine how far you can go in the other direction if fear is no longer there.

Personal Relationship Value #3:
Accept Your Partner

The number one need in all people, including you and your partner, is the need for acceptance. The number one fear among all people, including you and your partner, is that of rejection. The need for acceptance is so profound that I would venture to say that most, if not all, issues that cause conflict in a relationship ultimately come down to one or both partners feeling rejected—and, in turn, wanting to feel accepted.

So the message should be obvious. There should be no higher calling for you than to meet your partner's need for acceptance. If you want peace and tranquility, you must approach the task of managing your intimate relationship with a general spirit of acceptance. Sounds pretty simple, doesn't it?

But the problem is that when relationships get sideways, the spirit of acceptance is the first thing that goes out the window. You get upset over an event in your relationship, you get a chip on your shoulder, you get angry, you get frustrated—and as a result you soon find yourself behaving in a way that makes your partner feel unaccepted. And once you do that, once you send the message that you are rejecting rather than accepting, he or she begins to feel so unacceptable that withdrawal or retaliation takes place—and the war is on.

The spirit of acceptance is a core requirement for nourishing a reconnection. When you exhibit a spirit that indicates that you accept your partner, you're saying that even though you may not like everything that your partner is doing, things are still okay; we're going to get along right now, and most important, we are going to feel safe with each other. You're saying that despite our differences in personality and temperament, despite all the things I sometimes wish you were or weren't, the bottom line is that I accept you for you who are, and will always be there for you.

I hope you are beginning to understand why I say you have so much power to influence your relationship. You have the power to say, "I have to make my partner feel that I am not pushing him or her away just because we disagree about something. I can act out of a sense of goodwill so that even though we may vehemently disagree, I don't send a message of rejection. I can back off my old attitude of judgment and criticism and choose instead the accepting spirit."

Genuine change with your partner is never going to happen unless you first let your partner know that you are able to knock that chip off your shoulder, put aside your frustrations and anger and disappointment, put aside your critical perfectionism, and display a benevolent spirit. You need to make it known that you will be a safe, loving place for your partner to fall onto. If your partner experiences in you the spirit of acceptance, then it is most likely that he or she will find you approachable. By having two partners who are moving toward each other, rather than both trying to seek safety from pain, the chances of reconciliation are dramatically improved.

I often wonder how troubled relationships would turn out if couples spent as much time and emotional energy finding and focusing on things to admire in each other as opposed to spending that same energy focusing on and picking away at those things they don't like. What happens when you choose to approach your relationship with a spirit of acceptance is that you will automatically find yourself focusing on your partner's assets and qualities rather than on his or her shortcomings. You can and will choose to spend time thinking about that which you appreciate, rather than that which you wish was different.

Pain is the price that you pay for resisting the natural order of things—and nothing is more natural than supporting and accepting your intimate partner. The pain that you feel from resisting rather than accepting your partner is very likely much worse than the pain you experience during those times when your partner is doing something you don't like.

What I'm telling you here is to lighten up. Get off your partner's back. He or she is never going to be perfect, just as you will never be. Resolve in your heart to approach your partner with a benevolent spirit. I think you will be amazed at what you get back.

Personal Relationship Value #4:
Focus on the Friendship

Besides acceptance of your partner, another foundational value that quickly disappears in a distressed relationship is friendship. To put it simply, you forget to act like friends with your partner.

Perhaps it happened a long time ago, but you and your partner were once genuine friends. Very few of you leaped right into a slam-bang relationship. You were attracted to one another for some reason, you found each other appealing, and you thought there was potential—but at first you started out as friends.

You did the little daily things together that were nothing more than what any set of good friends would do.

As friends you supported each other and took an interest in what the other was doing. During conversations the two of you gave one another the benefit of the doubt. You didn't interpret his or her statements as some veiled message that he or she wasn't good enough. You laughed together. You kidded each other. You talked about things other than just problems. You did not approach each other with an attitude of "What can you do for me today?"

Then you moved from friendship into a serious relationship—from a fundamental camaraderie that contains little emotional baggage to an intimate situation that has many more complexities. In the complex world of your intimate relationship, even mundane conflicts take on exaggerated significance. The more you love and the more you have invested, the more it hurts when things go wrong. Sometimes, especially for those of you working difficult jobs and juggling lives with children, the concept of taking time to be with your partner as a friend was the last thing on your mind. You had too much to do. And as more time passed, you stopped hanging out together as you once did, calling each other during the day at work, finding the little delights in one another that you used to find when life was far simpler. In all likelihood, the very things that brought the two of you together as friends were ignored.

And I have no doubt the friendship was absolutely discarded if your relationship ran into problems and tensions emerged. You became overly sensitive to trying to meet much deeper needs, and all of a sudden you felt you were sitting at a poker table where the stakes had gotten way too high. Everything between you and your partner became loaded with meaning.

If you are in a problematic relationship today, you know what I mean. You probably treat total strangers, with whom you have nothing invested, with more care and energy than you do your life partner. The most simple dignities and kindnesses that are inherent in any friendship may no longer be found in your own relationship. Once you have had enough fights and conflicts with your partner, you tend to forget all the attributes you once admired and valued in that person and instead become all too aware of his or her negative qualities. You take the very things that used to make you admire that person during the friendship stage and turn them into negative traits during the relationship stage.

I suspect that if you look at what you and your partner spend the most time talking about and feeling, you will discover that the agenda of your relationship has become problem-driven. Even in strong relationships, too often people focus on the negatives in an effort to make the relationship all better. But by dwelling on what is wrong in your relationship—or to put it another way, by forgetting the friendship—it's easy to lose sight of what is right. I have often said that if all you deal with in your relationship are problems, then you will have a problem relationship. If you can simply begin to recapture the level of energy you originally invested in the friendship, you will not be plagued with the overwhelming stress that triggers so many of your own destructive attitudes.

Thus, in getting your mind right in this relationship, you have to take a step back from the depths of your problems and the pains of your intimate interactions—and you must focus on your friendship. You know your partner is not devoid of redeeming values, no matter how frustrating he or she may be to you at this point in time. You have to focus on those positive qualities, even if that means turning back the clock and remembering the early stages of your relationship—remembering again the characteristics about your intimate partner that attracted you and inspired admiration in you. Maybe it was something physical, or maybe it had to do with their personality or behavior. Whatever it was, there was something that caused you to reach out to this person or allow him or her to reach out to you. Be willing to turn back the clock and recall what it was that started the friendship that matured into this intimate relationship. If you have to, look through old picture albums and videos and reread some old love letters. Reach back into your history and find the commonalities and friendship that was the genesis of this relationship, and focus on that to the exclusion of all else.

If you need more help with how to reach back and get your hands around the friendship portion of your relationship, think about what you do with your friends now. Take stock of what kinds of conversations and activities you share with your friends, and see if you can recall similar activities that you once did with your mate. Did you and your partner used to talk about work, about favorite movies or television shows? Did you talk about other people and what was happening in their lives? Did you meet for lunch or walk in the mornings or evenings for exercise? What were the thoughts, feelings, conversations, and actions that defined your friendship?

The core elements of friendship are basically pretty simple. Friends treat each other in positive and rewarding ways that cause each other to say, "Hey, that felt pretty good. I think I'd like to do that again." Bottom line: if people feel better about themselves after having been around you, you will find that they value your company. Friends are also loyal and make sacrifices for each other. Friends are there for each other even when it would be easier not to. A really good friend is someone who's coming in the door when everyone else is running out. A good friend sticks with his friends in front of others, never criticizing him or her in public. A good friend approaches a relationship with a spirit of giving rather than the spirit of taking.

Can you remember what it was like when you and your partner didn't have so much of your self-worth tied up in each other? Can you remember the simpler times when the stakes were lower? Make no mistake: loving, intimate, committed relationships still maintain an underlying friendship. When built on a solid and deep friendship, a loving and intimate relationship becomes not only possible but inevitable. By focusing on the friendship, you are grooming the foundation upon which your more intimate relationship will be reformed.

Personal Relationship Value #5:
Promote Your Partner's Self-esteem

Okay, you're thinking, you've decided to own your relationship, take a risk, accept your partner for who he or she is, and then be your partner's friend. No sweat, right? You can pay those dues. You can make that contribution. "Now what, Dr. Phil, is that all I have to do?"

Hardly. There is yet another Personal Relationship Value you must adopt that requires you to significantly change the way you interact with your partner. It's great if you have these inner feelings about being accountable and being accepting and being a friend. But those spirits are only the first building blocks to getting you ready to be a contributor rather than a contaminator in your relationship. It's like my algebra teacher used to say, "These conditions are necessary but not sufficient."

Now you must resolve to interact with your partner in a way that protects or enhances their self-esteem. This is about bringing the spirit of acceptance into affirmative, interactive action. And that means you must actively work at promoting and protecting your partner's self-esteem.

The concept of self-esteem is easy to talk about and hard to really understand. It's particularly hard to focus on making your partner feel better about who he or she is if the two of you have been in a relationship that has been filled with bitterness, anger, frustration, and finger-pointing. As you have read the previous Personal Relationship Values, you might have been thinking, "Well, I can be accepting, and I can remember to be a friend." But can you really say to yourself that you can discipline yourself to resist making even justified criticisms and instead find some way to enhance your partner's self-esteem, no matter what he or she has said or done to hurt you?

What I'm talking about here goes beyond entering the relationship with a spirit of acceptance. To interact with your partner in a way that protects or enhances his or her self-esteem is easy in smooth waters when your partner is behaving admirably. What I'm talking about is finding the courage and creativity to do so at times when you feel compelled to be critical of your partner's conduct. To interact with your partner in this way means to affirmatively find some way to assert yourself and your right to be treated well, and yet do it in a way that leaves your partner's ego and sense of well-being intact. That means affirmatively putting a silver lining around every cloud.

This is a tall order, there is no doubt. But I'm telling you without equivocation: that is exactly what you must do. This value is going to be your relationship credo, and I mean this in its most literal sense. You must strive to help your mate maintain the feeling of worth and empowerment, the desire to operate at the highest level, to overcome self-defeating behavior, and to design a life full of happiness and fulfillment. No matter how you perceive your partner at this moment, require yourself to interact in a way that helps your partner believe he or she is a worthy and valuable person who also can take charge and become even more worthy and valuable.

Many of you out there are going to be saying, "Listen, McGraw, you have no idea of all the lousy things my partner has been doing." Oh, I bet I do. But from here on out, I don't want there ever to be a moment where your partner feels so belittled or even so despised that he or she feels there is no choice except to fight back, perhaps even to escalate the bad behavior just out of vengeance. This sounds old-fashioned, but you want your partner to feel "honored."

If you think I'm suggesting you ignore your partner's infirmities or take some codependent responsibility for your partner's bad behavior, then you're not coming close to hearing me. I never will ask you to excuse anything your partner does that brings you harm. I will never tell you to become blind to your partner's shortcomings, and I will never suggest that you are responsible for your partner's emotions. It is true, you cannot be responsible for how your partner feels. That is your partner's job. What I am talking about here is that you can help him or her do that job. You can make your partner's choices easier by reflecting back his or her virtues rather than shortcomings.

In great relationships, we are all held accountable for what we do. We must be confronted, sometimes given a good swift metaphorical kick in the pants, in order to change harmful behaviors. When you treat your partner in a way that protects or enhances his or her self-esteem, however, your partner will have a very different experience of any conflict between the two of you and any criticisms you may offer. Instead of trying to avoid you, or instead of trying to retaliate with greater intensity, your partner is likely to seek you out, to feel calm and confident instead of irritated, cooperative rather than combative. You don't want your partner to run from you when there is conflict because of the fear of browbeating. You want your partner to know that the two of you can work it out without either one of you having to be pounded down. Once your partner realizes this, the trust between the two of you accelerates.

Even if there is a situation where your partner is behaving outrageously—yelling or drinking or being irresponsible with money, letting down your children or breaking several commitments—you can deal with him or her in a way that clearly communicates that the behavior is unacceptable, yet in a way that ultimately promotes his or her self-esteem. You say to your partner, for instance, "I can't and won't tolerate your behavior, because I know you're a better man (or woman) than this. I cannot abide this because I know you're better than this. I know you can respond in a healthier, more positive way. And I won't let you be less than who you are. I'm going to require you to be that better person."

What I am asking you to do is hold yourself to a high standard. I am asking you to interact with your partner in a way that you can be proud of and in a way that no matter how negative the topic, you engage them in a way that does not communicate that they are a second-class citizen. By using the value of self-esteem, you create a much more nurturing atmosphere, one your partner will not want to abandon.

Personal Relationship Value #6: Aim Your Frustrations in the Right Direction

A wise and cynical man once said that the only sure things in life are death and taxes. I'm afraid his list was way too short. At a minimum, he should have also included frustrations with life. No matter how hard you work and no matter how well your life goes, you will encounter deep personal frustrations. Maybe you're picked on and unappreciated at work, and you store frustrations and negative feelings away. Or you stop by your mother's house on the way to church on Sunday morning, and she picks at you about one thing and then another. Or you step on the scales after you get out of the shower, and the news is not good.

You may go through your day or your week stockpiling frustrations, small and large, from any number of sources. The frustration builds and builds—and guess who comes cruising by? Your intimate partner. The problem, as far as your relationship is concerned, is that when you start looking for an outlet for venting your frustrations, your intimate partner is way too handy. A partner who didn't have one damn thing to do with any of the things that are bugging you.

I am not suggesting that you go after your partner consciously or purposely. But the fact that you don't mean to load up on your partner and blame them unfairly does not lessen the pain or unfairness that you visit upon him or her. You may attack just out of a general sense of irritability, without naming the source, or if you're really creative, you may manufacture some rationale so that you can get off your chest that frustration that comes from work, your mother, or the reading on your scales. Either way, you are dog-piling on your partner—and that means you are violating Personal Relationship Value #6.

Embracing this value has to be a very conscious decision. You have to work at sorting out the causes for your frustrations, and you must resist the impulsive temptation to pick at your partner because of your frustrations. Researchers have long agreed that the greatest stress that can be visited upon an individual is that which is associated with holding that person responsible for something he or she does not control. Think about how frustrating it would be if you all of a sudden were held responsible for the weather. It may change or it may not, but either way you can't influence it. Is it any less unfair of you to make your partner your scapegoat for life's irritations?

You and your partner, I am sure, have enough problems without you borrowing troubles from other parts of your life and grafting them onto your relationship. But as I have said many times, you can't change what you do not acknowledge—and one of the most powerful tools you have to make your relationship better is your simple acknowledgment that you are displacing much of your anger and frustration from other sources on to your mate. By aiming your frustrations at relevant rather than irrelevant targets, you ensure that you are not just spinning your wheels and deluding yourself into thinking that you are working on the problem. If you're upset about something at work, I'm betting you're going to find the solution at work. If you're frustrated with your mother, I'll bet you're going to resolve that either internally or in interactions with your mother, not your mate.

Moreover, be particularly cautious with regard to vague feelings of frustration with yourself. There's an old saying in psychology that goes, "There's something about that person that I just can't stand about me." When you are upset with yourself and lack the courage to get real about what it is that is so disappointing, it can be terribly tempting to criticize in your partner that which you find so distasteful in yourself. In effect, you are convicting an innocent person by unfairly focusing on your partner instead of yourself.

But once you start seeing that the negative things you are perceiving in your partner—incompetence, depression, etc.—are often things that are in yourself, you will literally alter the nature of your interactions with your partner. You will start eliminating so much of the noise that's on the line between you and your partner. You will not only be more efficient at problem-solving because you are dealing with real cause-and-effect associations, but just as importantly, you will not alienate one of your great support resources—your partner. All you have to do is stand back, take a look in the mirror, and make sure that the particular subject that makes you upset at the moment with your partner does not need to be fixed first in you. To do any less is a subtle but total denial of your responsibilities as a relationship partner.

Because you will now be acting out of an emotionally honest place in your life—because you will now be taking a long, hard look at yourself first—you will stop using your mate as a dumping ground. You will stop making your partner the "enemy" for invented reasons. You will stop denying the real source of your pain or frustration by disavowing the negative aspects of yourself.

I promise you, this shift of attitude will fundamentally change the spirit with which you approach your partner, as well as the efficiency with which you solve problems—because you are now focusing on the right target.

Personal Relationship Value #7:
Be Up-front and Forthright

Just as you will damage your relationship if you inappropriately dump anger and frustration on your partner that should be directed elsewhere, you will equally damage the relationship by keeping from your partner your most meaningful and honest feelings. In truth, when you do this, you are doing nothing more than outright lying to your partner.

By failing to communicate with emotional forthrightness, by resorting to the hidden agendas that we talked about in the last chapter, you are causing far more problems than you might imagine.

Nothing can be more frustrating than what is referred to as an incongruent communication, where an individual says one thing yet indicates something dramatically different with his or her nonverbal conduct. This issue was brought home to me many years ago. Shortly after I was married and still in graduate school, I came home to our apartment to find my wife, Robin, sitting in the corner, legs crossed, arms crossed, a scowl on her face and unwilling to look at or speak to me. Being young and not knowing any better, I charged the machine-gun nest and said, "Hey, what's wrong?" In a clipped, angry tone she spat out a one-word response, "Nothing!"

Now, I was only studying to be a psychologist at that point, but even in my neophyte status it was apparent to me that this was not a truthful response. In fact, my interpretation of her one-word response, "Nothing!" was, "There's plenty wrong, bucko, and you're it!" We went through about forty-five minutes of emotional denial that anything was wrong. A very, very long forty-five minutes, I might add, as I kept saying, "Tell me what's wrong," and she kept replying, "Nothing." We were in the same room, but we could have been miles apart. The point is that her response and persistence in saying that nothing was wrong when we both knew better was emotionally dishonest and unfulfilling for both of us.

You may be thinking about my incident with Robin, "Phil, she just didn't feel like talking about it at the time. You should have left her alone." That may well have been the circumstance, and may have been what I should have done. But I suggest that the better and more emotionally honest response from her would have been, "Phil, I don't feel like talking right now, okay? I am upset, and when I get my feelings sorted out I'll tell you, but what I feel right now is that I want you to back off and leave me alone." At that point it would be my duty to respect her wishes and give her the space that she needs. That would have been emotionally forthright, and we could perhaps have moved on to some type of a solution much sooner.

Each and every one of us is entitled to our particular feelings and emotions, and we must be responsible stewards of those feelings and emotions. We must strive to express them in mature and responsible ways. By the very nature of the fact that we are talking here about your primary intimate relationship in life, feelings and emotions are at the very core of the relationship. To own your relationship means to also own your feelings. By being appropriately honest about what you are feeling, you are giving your partner an important opportunity to deal with truth and reality.

Certainly, we have a choice as to when we decide to discuss an issue on our minds. However, it can reach the point of being maladaptive. There is a difference between a cooling-off period in which someone is allowed to sort out his or her thoughts, and a situation in which one of the partners is simply being evasive.

If you are upset, you cannot expect your partner to deal with what is going on if you are not honest about it. By being honest about your emotions, you base your relationship upon integrity rather than lies and deception.

I understand that this is a lot easier said than done. We all have the tendency to get nervous and defensive when we get close to dealing with meaningful emotional issues. Sometimes, we will switch our emotions to keep from expressing a real one. The best example I can point to is anger, the safest and most accessible emotion that we have. As I said, our number one fear is rejection. But instead of being forthright and telling our partner we fear rejection, we will act angry. What we are doing is essentially getting to our partners before they can get to us. We are rejecting them before they have the chance to be critical and reject us.

It is my strong belief that in the vast majority of cases, anger is a sham, a superficial covering for something else. It is expressed when we are afraid to express what we are really feeling, which almost always, in some combination, is hurt, fear, and frustration. When you are relating to your partner with anger—as good and as "emotional" as anger might feel—I suggest that you are hiding your true emotions and therefore violating this Personal Relationship Value. Only when you have the courage to look behind the anger and identify and express your true emotions are you dealing with honesty and integrity.

For your mind-set to be defined by emotional forthrightness, you will need to do a fair amount of introspection. You must be in touch with your feelings and why you are having them. If you are unwilling to investigate your true feelings in order to give them a voice, then you may be contaminating your relationship with emotional misdirection and misinformation. Have the courage to ask yourself the hard questions, and to give the answers an appropriate voice. Get real with yourself so you can be real with your partner. And don't be defensive when your partner has the insight and willingness to look behind your anger and challenge you to speak about what is really going on. Don't fail the test. Be willing to be introspective enough to identify and admit what is really going on with you.

Bottom line: give yourself permission to feel the way you feel, and require yourself to have the courage to give those feelings an appropriate voice. Require yourself to eliminate emotionally dishonest and non-forthright behaviors such as pouting, withdrawal, judgmentalism, and nitpicking. Just as you should not give your partner misdirection by being less than honest about your emotions, neither should you allow your partner to misdirect you, intentionally or otherwise, by dealing with the superficial at the expense of the meaningful.

Personal Relationship Value #8:
Make Yourself Happy Rather Than Right

Once again, this Personal Relationship Value calls upon you to refocus the point of view with which you approach life in general and relationships in particular. I want you to decide that you would rather be happy than right. Being right and being successful, particularly in the setting of relationships, are not even close to the same thing. The real measure that you should use in evaluating the quality of your behavior is not whether it is right, but whether it is working or not working.

You may have decided that some position that you are taking in your relationship is irrefutably correct. You might be 110 percent right, but you could still fail miserably. What I want you to do is to start evaluating the things you do in your relationship based on whether those thoughts, feelings, and actions are working or not working for you. Is your position getting you what you want or not? If it's not working, change it. Do what works, not what's right.

I had a father and son in therapy some years ago who taught me a lot about the flaws and fallacies of being right. J.B. was a chief master sergeant at our local air force base and was about as flexible as a bridge abutment. Darren, his sixteen-year-old son, was his absolute antithesis. Darren had long hair, baggy clothes, and a laid-back, go-with-the-flow attitude about life and everything in it.

J.B. wanted the boy to cut his hair, get some clothes that fit, and start "doing right." J.B.'s theory was that Darren should do what he was being told "because I'm his father, by God, and as long as he's living under my roof, eating my food, and spending my money, I've got the right to tell him what to do and how to do it." J.B. was right. According to the law and the patterns of our society, he did in fact have the "right" to tell that boy what to do. The problem is, his "rightness" wasn't working. He's wasn't being successful as a father, and therefore he wasn't happy and neither was Darren. What they were doing was destroying their relationship over a fight for control.

I would love to tell you that I did some marvelous therapy and that there was a happy ending to this story. But two and a half weeks after my initial session with J.B., Darren was playing in a high school basketball game, a sport at which he had excelled from an early age. It was the fourth quarter in a very close game, and Darren, the team's point guard, was bringing the ball down court with reckless abandon. At mid-court, he seemed to stumble and uncharacteristically fell facedown on the court. An autopsy revealed that he was dead before he ever hit the floor. The autopsy also revealed that Darren had a congenital heart defect that had been undiagnosed since birth. His father refused to let the funeral home cut his hair or put him in a suit in his casket. He was buried in long, flowing hair and baggy clothes.

J.B. does not melodramatically blame himself for his son's death, but I can tell you that he has spoken to me more than once about the time and happiness they wasted because of his obsessive need to be right. He could have been happy at least for a while, but instead he had to be right. I wonder if he would care who was right and who was wrong if he could have Darren back for one more day.

Think about all of the times, circumstances, and situations where you have gotten caught up in making yourself right rather than happy. Whether it is who said what to who, what's the best strategy for raising the children, how to spend your money, or how to deal with a difficult in-law, resolve to incorporate this Personal Relationship Value and do what works and generates good feelings rather than winning a "right fight." Failing to incorporate this principle can mean that you win a lot of battles, but you wind up losing the war. Seriously, whether you are a male or female reader, don't think that you are ever helping your relationship when you are grinding your partner into submission. Think about the times in your own past when you were the one who felt humiliated. Were you thinking, "Oh, I'm going to learn some good lessons here"? No, you were in all probability resentful and embittered—perhaps even worse. Don't think it's any different when you're on the "winning end" of that kind of exchange. The harder you fight to win, the bigger you lose.

I can hear some of you right now: "So what are you saying, Dr. Phil? Let my partner get away with some scumbag behavior—or let my partner lecture me even when both of us know I'm not the one who's wrong?"

Of course I am not suggesting that you turn into a little lamb, trudging meekly after your partner. I am not telling you to avoid arguments when they are necessary, to avoid stating what you believe and also to point out to your partner the behaviors that are hurting the relationship.

The point I am making, however, is that your goal should be to make you and your partner happy by doing what works rather than working so hard at showing your partner how you are right and how he or she is wrong. For example, you don't have to get mad every time you have the right to get mad. You don't have to lecture or scold every time your partner gives you the right to lecture or scold. You don't have to prove over and over that you know what you're talking about more than your partner does. You can choose a different emotion such as tolerance, understanding, compassion, or any other emotion that does not escalate the hostilities in your relationship.

Let's say that you know for an absolute fact that your partner creates problems in all of his or her relationships by being too controlling or too unreasonable. What if, instead of pointing out to him how right you are in your analysis of his behavior, you just decided to make a pivotal turn in your attitude? What if you decided to show your most loving and accepting side instead of trying to engage him or her one more time about their self-destructive behavior? What if you tried an empathetic approach, offering such enthusiasm and happiness about being with your partner that they might start reevaluating their own? That does not mean that you label yourself as wrong or have to endorse a behavior that you find offensive. It just means that maybe you change it by inspiration instead of confrontation.

I can assure you that when the struggle to be right takes on confrontational and domineering qualities, you have set your relationship up in a lose-lose scenario.

I remember once arguing with my wife, and I thought I was doing just great. I was making terrific points and resisting her points, and I knew I was about to win and emerge victorious. Hooray for me! Then all of a sudden she just stopped, the emotion drained from her voice, and with cold and scary eyes, she looked at me and said, "You're right. You're always right. How could I have been so foolish?"

Now, I'm not all dumb, so I recognized this was not a good development. So I quickly said, "No, I want to hear what you have to say; tell me what you think." To which she said, "No, it's okay, you're right, really. I don't know what I was thinking." As she walked out of the room, head held high, hair tossed back, I knew that I had won the battle, but I wasn't even close to happy. I wanted to jump up and say, "No, wait, I don't want to win anymore. I want to call Kings X and do this over. I don't want to be right, I want to be happy." In my mind I was thinking, "Boy, am I gonna pay for this one."

If you do not embrace this Personal Relationship Value, you may wind up living the tyranny of rightness. For you, being right serves the purpose of keeping you safe. It keeps you from having to risk making any changes in yourself. You are a one-trick pony who is so certain that what you are doing is right that you will ride your beliefs to the absolute bottom of the canyon, whereupon you crash and burn without ever having looked around to see if there were alternative ways of approaching the problem.

Some who live under this tyranny of rightness become

most insufferably self-righteous if his or her partner does not acknowledge the rightness in the proper manner. I'm talking about those times when you are in fact right. I'm talking about those times when your partner may have insensitively transgressed against you and is looking for some way to make amends.

So often one or the other partner will create a problem with some insensitive act and then be caught red-handed. If you are the partner that has been hurt, your preference may be for your guilty partner to come to you with great reverence, apologizing and asking your forgiveness. While that may be logical and justified, that may not be your partner's style. So often I have seen the guilty party make a joke or offer some type of self-effacing remark laced with humor, such as, "Well, I hope that doghouse is big enough for Fido and me both." In response to which I have heard many a partner say, "Oh, it's just all a big joke to you, isn't it? You don't care about my feelings; you just want to laugh it off." At which point the guilty party now feels rejected and rebuffed as well as imperfect. Just one time I would love to hear the guilty party look their partner in the eye and say, "No, I don't think it's funny. I'm just embarrassed at having done something so dumb, and I'm trying to lighten the mood a little bit so I can find some kind of face-saving way out of this mess. I just wanted us to get past the awkwardness of the pain and hurt that I have caused, and that's the only way I know how to do it. Sorry I'm not you."

As I said earlier, it's not so much what happens between partners that determines the outcome of a relationship as it is how they handle what happens. If you and your partner have a forgiving spirit and allow each other some measure of grace when one or the other of you seeks to reduce hostilities, your future will be bright. If instead you want your pound of flesh with full acknowledgment that you are the winner, your future will be dim.

By deciding to be happy rather than right, you will be receptive to your partner's attempts to de-escalate hostilities and return to civil interactions.

Personal Relationship Value #9: Allow Your Relationship to Transcend Turmoil

I know there are some therapists and authors out there who will tell you that a good relationship means a lack of conflict. Please. I do not believe that there has ever been a relationship that was free of turmoil, where one partner did not from time to time deeply hurt the other. There has never been a merging of two lives where significant problems of daily living did not occur.

When it comes to relationships, it's not a question of whether or not rough spots will occur. Fights and arguments are going to occur between you and your partner, and one way or the other, they are going to impact the relationship. The only question is how.

I'm talking about everyone here—not just people whose lives already are full of bitterness and contempt. Those of you who wake up every day wanting the best out of your relationship occasionally find yourselves losing control with your partners, feeling a little crazy as your temper rises, thinking dark and perhaps apocalyptic thoughts. It's a natural human impulse, and don't let any therapist tell you otherwise. Do you know how you often say to yourself in the privacy of your car when you get cut off by another driver on the highway, "I'd like to run that guy off the road"? Well, if you're honest with yourself, you do the same thing when your partner infuriates you. Somewhere in your psyche you say to yourself, "I'd like to run this person out of my life."

You have seen people who put the relationship on the line every time a problem arises. In those situations, ultimatums abound, and the relationship is at stake. Perhaps you've heard or even spoken some of the following:

"I hate it when you do this. I can't take this any
   more."

"You either stop this or I'm out of here."

"If you think I'm such a bad person, then why don't
   you just leave?"

"This isn't working. Why don't we just call the lawyers
   and get this over with?"

You are saying such things, of course, because you are afraid, you are insecure, and you are upset that you are not being heard. But that's not what comes out of your mouth. In those moments a desperation can overtake you with lightning-fast speed. You move into a mind-set that you are fighting for your life. Your sense of judgment and dignity disappears, and what comes out of your mouth are threats. You head to the front door and shout, "That's it! I'm leaving your ass!"

Let me tell you right now: this is dangerous saber rattling. You're hitting the panic button, and as a result you're knocking irreparable chinks into your relationship every time something goes wrong. If you are not careful—if you do not let the relationship transcend the problems, challenges, and turmoil of everyday life—you will bring that relationship to its knees.

True, you probably get back together the next day with

your partner and make apologies, and you think, "Well, that's over and done with." But it's not. You're leaving a residue. The next time a fight comes around, both you and your partner are going to be remembering the past thermonuclear reactions. Your partner might trigger a thermonuclear reaction of his or her own just to beat you to the punch.

Adopting this Personal Relationship Value means that you will vow that you will no longer use threats as a lever to manipulate and control your partner. Don't put your relationship in jeopardy whenever you have a dispute, no matter how meaningful. Give yourself permission to disagree, and give yourself permission to do so passionately—but do not make your relationship the stakes for which you are playing. Think about it as though your relationship sits on the limb of a tree overhanging a river. Yet the limb is so high that no matter how much splashing goes on in that river, it cannot splash high enough to reach the relationship. That does not mean that there's not a lot of sometimes violent thrashing and splashing going on in the river; the water just can't get high enough to reach the relationship.

There is a great feeling of liberation that comes with the commitment to treat your relationship as something sacred. It's not an extra burden. All you're doing, really, is getting rid of a false sense of urgency. You and your partner will find far less pressure in your lives once you know that neither of you are going to make threats every time something goes wrong in the relationship. If you realize your mate can be furious and it's not the end of the world, then you will start operating out of a calmer, more secure position.

I'm not telling you how to quarrel. I know that over the years each couple develops its own style of confrontation. I recognize that a lot of people like quarrels because it gives them a chance to let off steam or it whips up passion. Fine. I am telling you, however, that there must be a certain place where you stop. I don't care if you have to literally bite your tongue, you have to know how to break away from an argument before it turns into full-scale, relationship-threatening combat. You set a clear limit on the places a spirited discussion with your partner will not go. You resolve that your relationship will exist on a level above and independent of the turmoil, that there will be no more residue. Just by your putting this simple control on your life—that threats to the relationship are no longer an option—you will have made a gigantic step toward the process of reconnection.

Personal Relationship Value #10:
Put Motion into Your Emotion

As should be clear to you by now, I am hoping that as you instill these Personal Relationship Values into your life, you will begin to see and treat your relationship as a rare and valuable thing, one that must be diligently cared for and worked on. You must take the initiative and commit to always giving your partner the most positive stimulus possible. This Personal Relationship Value is about putting forth the best parts of who you are in hopes that it will raise the level upon which this entire relationship is played out.

By refusing to let yourself get bogged down or get sucked into ugly emotions and hateful interactions, you can and will create an environment in which anything less from your partner just doesn't seem to fit. By putting your best foot forward, you challenge and inspire your partner to do the same. You give him or her nothing but good things to react to by shoving aside mediocrity and demanding that your relationship be first-rate. You can no longer settle for living a second-class life with your partner. Ambivalence is no longer in your vocabulary. Passivity is no longer part of your behavioral repertoire, and hatefulness is no longer on your list of emotional choices. You must set the bar of excellence for yourself at an unprecedented high level, and then with tenacious determination strive to leap over it.

This value is about requiring more of yourself. Having good feelings is not enough. You must put motion into your emotion. Every day, at every step along the way in your relationship, you must ask of yourself, "Is what I'm doing and what I'm saying bringing us closer together, or pushing us further apart?" Every day, at every step along the way, you must ask of yourself, "Is what I'm doing helping us thrive in new ways as a couple, or am I keeping us stuck in our old patterns?"

As one who has worked with thousands of divorcees, I have observed an interesting phenomenon. I have seen that both men and women, six months to a year after a breakup, will start looking and sounding like completely new people. I have seen these relationship refugees suddenly have a new zest and energy for life.

You've probably seen it as many times as I have, and like me, you thought the reason for their new attitude was simply that they had gotten out of their crummy relationship. But over time I came to see it very differently. What I saw was that after losing at love, these relationship refugees had taken stock of themselves and decided they'd better clean up their act. They had become stagnant in their relationships and ceased to put their best foot forward. They had felt the sting of failure. They recognized that they needed to make some important changes. Realizing they had better get it in gear, these refugees lose twenty, thirty, or a hundred pounds, join a gym, develop new interests and activities that make them more interesting than stagnant. And here's what is sad to me: if those people had made those changes while still in their relationships, they would probably still be there. All they had to do was replace their stagnation with action, their apathy with interest. All they had to do was put some motion into their emotion.

That's what you have to do. You must turn the concept of love into a pro-active behavior. Instead of being like so many others who, consumed with negative messages about their relationships, don't have very high expectations—you must require yourself and therefore your relationship to be better.

I'm not talking here about being perfect. But I am talking about being proud, about taking great pride in your actions around your partner. The old saying "Familiarity breeds contempt" is sadly true. When we become too familiar with someone, we soon can become slovenly and undisciplined. Think about it: when you were first courting your intimate partner, you wanted to do everything you could to be impressive—and I don't mean impressive in some shallow way, but impressive as a human being. You not only groomed yourself and carefully selected your clothing, you put a smile on your face and presented yourself as positively as you could. You talked in a way that you hoped showed your best side.

Growing up with three sisters, I watched this mating

ritual for my entire young life. For example, my sisters wouldn't even consider eating in front of a date, even if they were starving. Why? Because it was unbecoming, in their view. My sisters, all married and obviously a whole lot less concerned with appearances, now will fight their husbands tooth and nail for the last chicken leg.

Contrast whatever your sensitivities were in the early stages of your relationship with how you ultimately have come to behave. I'll bet you now routinely say and do things you would never have considered doing in the early stages of your relationship. I'll bet you allow your partner to see you in ways that you would have died before permitting in the early going. It is, of course, human nature that we tend to relax once we become comfortable within a situation—and to a degree, that is healthy. You should not feel that you have to perform under a spotlight in your own home. As this relaxation takes over, however, there is a natural tendency to start requiring less and less of ourselves in a given situation. To put it another way, we are no longer on our best behavior because we are not trying to impress anyone. After all, a committed relationship has already been formed and the courtship is over.

You might be able to put on a happy face and interact with your partner in a warm and cordial fashion when the visitation committee from the church stops by, or when a neighbor visits. But the true attitude with which you approach your partner behind closed doors is a reflection of the quality and depth of your character. Granted, this relaxation of standards behind closed doors might initially seem harmless. But the result can turn ugly—for it's not just a behavioral shift of standards that's taking place, but a mental and emotional shift that is going on too. The sad fact is that as we get complacent, we often begin to permit ourselves indiscriminate volatility in our emotions. Instead of operating on our best behavior and with disciplined emotions, you may now say, "What the hell, I am mad and I don't care who knows it."

Here's the amazing irony. You probably hold yourself to a higher standard in your more meaningless, superficial relationships that don't much matter than you do in your intimate relationship that very much matters. You would never consider walking into your office and not greeting the people with whom you work, yet you will walk into your home and not so much as grunt in the direction of your partner. You wouldn't dream of going to a cocktail party or working lunch and snap at people, but you afford yourself that emotional outburst with your partner because you think you can. The person you supposedly love more than anyone else in the world is not afforded the common everyday courtesy of even your most casual acquaintances. You no longer say please and thank you. You no longer inquire as to your partner's state of being with a simple "How are you doing?" or "How are you feeling?" And when you get into a dispute, it is not very difficult for you to lose yourself in the heat of anger. You find yourself blurting out hostile put-downs.

Well, right now, resolve that this will all be coming to an end. I want you to resolve that never again will you be dragged down into the ugliness of a relationship fight that is so hard to undo. In short, even when behind closed doors, you must behave as though the world is watching, as though whatever you say or do will be played back on the evening news. If you keep that in your mind, then you will start holding yourself to a standard in which you invariably take the high road.

Your partner, of course, will benefit from your improved personal standards. You also will help elevate your relationship out of its emotional quagmire. Most important, you will be the greatest beneficiary of this new attitude. You will know that you have acted at all times with the deepest dignity, with the truest of giving spirits.

My great desire is for these Personal Relationship Values to rise to the level of what I call life decisions. I refer to life decisions as the most important things that define who you are. With life decisions, the debate is over. These are decisions that are not open for discussion and are not subject to being revisited. Life decisions occur in your heart, and carry a much deeper level of conviction than decisions that you might revisit on a day-to-day basis.

For example, some of your most obvious life decisions may include such things as "I will not cheat or lie to get ahead." "I will not steal what does not belong to me or what I have not earned." "I will not be unkind to my children or defenseless animals." "I will be respectful of the elderly."

Now these Personal Relationship Values must be added to your list of life decisions. They must become so inextricably ingrained into the fiber of your being that in time you will no longer consciously have to think about them.

When you add these Personal Relationship Values as part of your life decisions, I think you will find that you not only go through a vast change in the way you interact with all the people in your life, you go through a vast change in the way you interact with yourself.

Study each of the Personal Relationship Values, knowing that this is your new foundation from which you will think and feel. From this foundation your core of consciousness will become like a beacon in your life, guiding you in all that you do.

And get excited about what's happening. Up until now you probably have been living your life, and conducting your relationship, as if you've been trapped in one of those buildings where the windows were made of dark smoked glass. The tinted windows had seriously distorted your perception of the outside environment. Through that filter life always looked leaden with foreboding dark clouds. It's time now to step outside, to abandon your bad spirit once and for all and take up a new way of living.

Indeed, you are on the verge of creating a relationship that is going to be rich in emotional experience and one that will consistently become your soft place to fall. You also are on the verge of a brand-new life, one that honors the spirit of love that lives inside us all. Take the time to reread each of these Personal Relationship Values. Write them down. Stick them on the refrigerator door or on your bathroom mirror. Then write them on the tablet of your heart.

SIX

THE FORMULA FOR SUCCESS

I'm not the kind of guy who believes life can be summed up in a cute phrase. I don't think what you need to know to make your relationship work will fit on a bumper sticker or a refrigerator magnet. There are no quick fixes for relationships: that's just one more myth that has led so many people down the wrong road. Make no mistake. If you really want different results from your relationship, then you're going to have to devote meaningful and substantial time and effort to it.

However, there is a very clear, simple formula for rejuvenating a relationship, one that is unbelievably powerful in its effect. I'm not saying that it's easy to put the formula into action, but I am saying that it's easy to understand.

But before we talk about it, I want to be brutally honest. If you have skimmed over the preceding chapters, or have read them but not actually done the work assigned, then you're not ready for the success formula. I recognize that you may be extremely anxious to fix your relationship. But be assured that the quickest way from point A to point B is not always at the most hurried pace. If you haven't comprehended this book—if you haven't begun to feel this book's message in your bones—then I promise that you will screw up the formula. Have you honestly and carefully prepared yourself for what is to come? Test yourself. If any of the following statements are not true for you, then you are not ready:

- I realize that it's not too late.
- It is reasonable for me to want a rewarding and fulfilling relationship.
- I am entitled to, and deserve, a high-quality, caring relationship.
- I have identified the wrong thinking that has previously contaminated my relationship.
- I have identified the bad spirits that contaminated my relationship.
- I have embraced the Personal Relationship Values that will configure me for success.
- I have diagnosed and gotten real about the pain and problems in my relationship.
- I accept and acknowledge full ownership of my contribution to where this relationship is.
- I am committed to tapping into my core of consciousness.

If you can fully **endorse** each one of those statements with a resounding **True**, then you're ready for the formula for relationship success. Here it is:

The quality of a relationship is a function of the extent to which it is built on a solid underlying friendship and meets the needs of the two people involved.

Now you may be thinking, "That's it? That's the big formula I've been waiting for?" Yes, that's it, and believe me, it is elegant in its simplicity. Just remember, applying this formula will require your utmost commitment and integrity.

Let's start by establishing some definitions. Please note the formula's three key terms: friendship, needs, and quality. The friendship I am talking about is the one that began when your current intimate relationship sprang forth. It is the friendship that was there between you and your partner before the complications of love and romance muddied the waters. It is the friendship in which you regarded your now intimate partner with acceptance, approval, and desire. It is the fundamental relationship that was born out of shared meaning and experiences in which you put forth the effort to be a good friend to a good friend. It is that time in your relationship that you laughed, shared, and supported each other, not because you had to but because you wanted to.

The needs I'm talking about—your needs and your partner's needs—encompass a number of different categories. To say that you have a need in a particular area of your life is to acknowledge that you experience a void in that area. Soon enough we will examine your unique needs. But it is enough right now to understand that you do have needs in a number of different life categories, and that certain of these needs can be met only by other human beings. Just as important as understanding that you have complex needs is a realization that the word "need" is not a synonym for weakness. Rest assured that the fact you have needs, and that you must rely on another person to meet them, is a good and healthy thing.

The other key concept that must be defined is quality. If you experience your relationship as being rich with joy, excitement, and a sense of meaning, then you're likely to rate the relationship as one of high quality. If loneliness, fear, anger, and alienation characterize your experience, then you will of course rate the relationship as one of low quality.

Given these definitions of the two essential elements of the success formula, it should be apparent that two people in the same relationship can have two very different experiences of that relationship. You might rate the relationship as extremely high-quality because it fulfills all of your personal needs. On the other hand, your partner, reflecting on the very same interactions, will rate it much lower, because he or she is not getting certain basic needs met. One relationship, two people—each of them having very different experiences.

Please understand that this formula for relationship success doesn't work just some of the time—it works all of the time. If you are completely happy in your relationship, but your partner simply is not, then you can bet that your partner's needs are not being met. If your partner is happy and you are not, it's your needs that are unmet. It may well be that both of you perceive the relationship to be of poor quality because neither of you is having your needs met.

To make this formula work in your life, you've got two vitally important, complex, and dangerous jobs to complete.

Job One is to make your needs known. I'm not talking about some of your needs; I'm not distinguishing your "superficial" needs from the ones you think are more important. When I say that you've got to make your needs known, I mean all of your needs, including those at the deepest level.

Job Two is to work to discover the needs of your partner. This second job may not be an easy one, but it is just as important as the first. There's no point in judging whether your partner's needs are right, wrong, valid, or inappropriate. That is not your job right now. Your job is to *recognize* his or her needs.

You may be thinking, "Wait just a minute—I'm furious at my partner. What about the anger, the bitterness, the resentment, the conflict that we have between us right now? What about all that business?" Well, I intend to provide you with some step-by-step guidelines on how to work your way through those emotions. But for right now I am basically going to tell you to just get over it.

Remember the commitment that you have made: the goal is no longer to be right. The goal is no longer to win the fight. The only way to win, really win, is to reconnect with your partner in a loving and caring way. That's what I mean by telling you to get over it. Commit all of your focus and energy right now to getting this relationship back on solid, loving ground—and forget about the rest. We will talk later about getting your so-called pound of flesh. Just remember that you don't have to get mad every time you have the right to. Getting mad is not a requirement; it's just an option, an option you can choose to pass up.

Job #1: Make Your Needs Known

Making your needs known is much harder than you may think. I'm not talking about just blurting out whatever you think you need. Beware of the cheap, superficial answer. When I gave this same assignment to a woman patient some years ago, she immediately responded, "I can tell you right now what I need—I need him to shut up and quit bugging me." That wasn't exactly what I was thinking about, and it's not the kind of answer you want to give.

Most people can't really articulate their needs. They know they have them. They know how good it feels when those needs are met, and how bad it feels when they're not. But putting our needs into words can be very difficult.

What's more, some people who do know their needs will often go for years without ever telling them to their partners. Some of you are afraid that asking for what you want will cause conflict. You'll say, "I'll never get what I want anyway. My partner will think I'm being stupid or unrealistic, and we'll just end up getting more angry at each other. So what's the use?" Or you'll say, "My partner will feel like I'm criticizing him or her for not meeting my needs." Or you'll say, "I've asked before. It didn't do any good then. Why would it do some good now?" And there is the most well-worn excuse of all: "Why should I have to ask? My partner should know what I need without me having to say it."

If your partner is not meeting one of your needs, that is your responsibility. It is also very unfair to criticize your partner for not recognizing and meeting your needs when you don't know them yourself. Your partner can't read your mind; he or she can't guess what your needs are. The only chance your partner will ever have of connecting with you and responding to your needs depends upon your teaching your partner what really makes you tick. You must come to know yourself so well that you can teach your partner about yourself. If there are things about you that you have not yet discovered, now is the time to discover them.

Before we begin this process of identifying your needs, let me acknowledge the substantial risk that I'm asking you to take. It is the risk of intimacy. Once you accept the challenge of uncovering and identifying your deepest needs, and subsequently disclosing that information to your partner, you are admittedly putting yourself in a vulnerable position. You are providing your partner with especially sensitive information. To permit someone to have intimate knowledge of you means to take your guard down, to share with that person things you may previously have been afraid to acknowledge even to yourself. Intimacy means sharing what you dream about, strive for—and also sharing your weaknesses. You are giving your partner a lot of power with this knowledge

I won't try to minimize the step I'm asking you to take. Intimate self-disclosure is one of the scariest and most difficult things you'll ever do. The fact is that I am asking you to become intimately familiar with yourself, and then to share what you learn with another human being who could potentially use that information against you. It is my hope that you will decide it's a risk worth taking. I'm hoping you'll decide that you are strong enough to handle the risk, and that, should your partner prove to be a poor steward of this act of vulnerability and trust on your part, you can handle it.

Let me underscore that point by turning it around. If

and when you receive information of this gravity from your partner, you too take on a tremendous responsibility. Intimate self-disclosure by your partner means that you are being entrusted with the most fragile part of your partner's soul. You must treat it with reverence, dignity, and respect.

That doesn't mean, turn the television down. It means you turn it off or throw it out in the backyard if your partner comes to you and says, "It is time for me to tell you the intimate truth about me." It means you refuse to answer the phone, and you don't get distracted by the children. It means you find a time and a place that will allow you to have this exchange when there are no time limits, no deadlines, and no other demands on your attention. You must treat this information from your partner as if it were the finest china, so fragile and brittle that nothing short of the most delicate handling would be appropriate.

And then, you must never, ever permit yourself to use any of this intimate self-disclosure in a confrontation. It is not leverage, it is not a weapon of manipulation or one-upmanship. It is not to be joked about, made light of, or satirized. Receiving this information is a tremendous responsibility, and you risk doing huge damage if you mismanage it. Make no mistake: sharing this information is a risk; receiving it is a burden.

Resist the temptation to judge your partner's disclosures, or to explain them away. If your partner is describing to you a particular fear or area of self-doubt, it can be very tempting to say, "Oh, that's silly. You shouldn't feel that way," mistakenly assuming that you are easing your partner's mind. It's not silly to your partner, and your labeling it as such is not going to defuse the fear or self-doubt; doing so will only make your partner self-conscious. Tiptoe ever so lightly through your partner's intimate world. This is no time for the proverbial bull in the china shop. Be worthy of the trust.

The reverence with which I'm asking you to treat this information was once described by a participant in a relationship seminar. We had spent some time discussing this duty of stewardship, and many of the couples had taken their first, tentative steps into intimate self-disclosure. At our next meeting Bob, typically a man of few words, asked for a few minutes to tell us about his spot in the southern Rocky Mountains. It is a place he visits every year, without fail, although it's a challenging three-hour hike from the nearest navigable road. Twelve thousand feet above sea level, tucked between two jagged ridges, is a forest clearing that nobody knows about but Bob. He described it for us as a "pocket of peace," not more than two hundred feet in diameter, surrounded by white-trunked aspen trees. The handful of boulders that are sprinkled about are covered in moss, and the grass, though plentiful, gets such limited sunlight that it grows only a quarter of an inch every year. He told us that the turf is so delicate that he has found his boot prints there years after he made them. In telling us of this idyllic place, Bob spoke with a passion that charmed the entire assembly; it was as if we had each taken a seat on one of those green boulders and were trying not to disrupt the calm. Clearly, Bob's "spot" afforded him a sense of tranquility and utter contentment. All of us understood how fragile and beautiful a place it must be.

Bob then announced that he recognized there was another such place in his world, one just as fragile and precious. The second, he said, was the intimate and private world of the woman he loved. He said it had dawned on him, as she disclosed certain details about herself to him, that he needed to treat her private world with the same gentleness and respect with which he entered his private retreat every year. He said he was determined to afford her world as much reverence as he gave his Rocky Mountain paradise. At the time of his participation in the seminar, Bob was married to his fifth wife. I can assure you that this shift in sensitivity forever changed his perspective on that relationship. He has now been married to the same woman for twelve years, and they are happier than they've ever been. I wonder why.

It's important to point out that Bob was a self-made millionaire who had worked hard for everything he had achieved. At six-foot-six, physically chiseled, with a dominant personality, he had found it hard to admit that he needed anyone or anything. But in the course of that seminar Bob discovered some important personal realities of his own, which he then communicated to his wife. He was finally able to acknowledge to her that he really needed her endorsement and approval. He needed to know that she was proud of him. Bob told us that both of his parents had been killed when he was still very young, and that he had never felt there was anybody in the world who really believed in him and would be there for him. Admitting that he needed his wife's approval meant a great deal to Bob, and was an admission he might never have made until he learned that people were capable of honoring their innermost selves. This man who had been so fearful of his own vulnerability took a huge risk.

For her part, Bob's wife had never entertained the possibility that he needed anything at all from her, let alone her acceptance and approval. She saw him as he portrayed himself: the proverbial rock. When he trusted her enough to tell her how much he needed her, and was vulnerable enough to say he wanted and valued her support—in fact, that he hurt when he didn't get it—that moment changed their lives forever. For her to hear that he needed her made her feel, suddenly, extremely valuable. She was tremendously uplifted. Between this needful man and his loving wife, a trust and a sharing were born.

BUILDING YOUR PERSONAL PROFILE

Approach this exercise of self-discovery with an open spirit. Allow yourself to feel that it is natural, it is okay, to have needs in general, and to have your specific needs in particular. Don't think you have to justify or explain the why behind any of your needs. If you feel the need, that is enough. Your needs are not right or wrong, good or bad—they just are.

To give structure to your self-discovery, let me identify and define five categories of needs. These are: Emotional, Physical, Spiritual, Social, and Security. You may come up with other categories that make sense to you. That's fine: add as many as you want, or break these five into as many subcategories as you think are right for you. In any event, keep in mind as we go through these five that you cannot share with or teach your partner what you don't know yourself. Get real with yourself to give the formula for relationship success a chance.

For each of the five categories I have listed some of the most common, general needs that have been identified by the relationship partners with whom I've worked, both male and female. These lists are intended to stimulate your thoughts about the particular needs that are specific to you. Please remember that, because they are general, the listed needs should be considered as simply a place to start. You should be very specific about your own needs, to the point of including such details as time, place, frequency, and means of expression, as appropriate. As you come to an item that you think reflects a need within you, circle that item.

A note about emotional needs: this is a broad category that deals with how you need to feel. How you need to feel is up to you, not your partner. Your partner cannot make you feel the way you feel, but your partner can help you achieve your desired feelings by becoming aware of what they are and sensitive to the fact that they are important to you. At this point, don't worry about how you expect your partner to respond to these needs. Just identify them so that you can communicate them.

EMOTIONAL NEEDS

1. The need to feel, and be told, that you are loved
2. The need to feel, and be told, that you are a valued, vital part of your partner's life
3. The need to feel a sense of belonging to and with your partner
4. The need to feel respected as an individual
5. The need to feel needed for other than the tasks you perform (providing money, cooking, etc. . . .)
6. The need to feel that you are a priority in your partner's life
7. The need to feel special, above everyone else in your partner's life

8. The need to feel that your partner is proud to call you his or her own
9. The need to feel that you are trusted as a responsible partner
10. The need to feel that your partner would choose you again
11. The need to feel that you have and can be forgiven for transgressions and flaws
12. The need to feel accepted, flaws, fallacies, and all
13. The need to feel that you and your partner are, above all else, close and trusted friends
14. The need to feel desired
15. The need to feel appreciated for who and what you are and do
16. The need to feel passion between you and your relationship partner

PHYSICAL NEEDS

1. The need to be touched and caressed
2. The need to be kissed, even if casually
3. The need to be hugged or held
4. The need to feel that you are welcome in your partner's personal space
5. The need to be physically welcomed when encountering your partner
6. The need to feel that you are part of a couple when interacting with the world
7. The need to feel encouraged and welcomed by nonverbal communications
8. The need for tenderness
9. The need for a satisfying and rewarding sexual life

SPIRITUAL NEEDS

1. The need to feel that your personal spiritual values are supported without judgment
2. The need to feel that your partner respects your spiritual needs
3. The need to share a spiritual life, even if that spiritual life is experienced differently by you and your partner
4. The need to know and feel that your individual beliefs and differences are respected, if not shared

SOCIAL NEEDS

1. The need to be remembered with calls and acknowledgments when apart
2. The need to feel that your partner will plan and structure his or her activities to include you
3. The need to feel that social activities are shared rather than experienced individually
4. The need for appropriate tenderness and support when in public
5. The need to be encouraged and supported physically and emotionally when in public
6. The need to hear sweet things in a social environment
7. The need to be encouraged and supported in social situations
8. The need to be treated with politeness and regard in social situations
9. The need to share fun and joy in social situations
10. The need to share a connection expressed through awareness and sensitivity from your partner
11. The need to share joy and laughter

12. The need to feel that you are the most important person in your partner's life and awareness when in a crowded, busy social environment

SECURITY NEEDS

1. The need to know that your partner will stand by you in times of distress or conflict
2. The need to feel that your partner will rally to your aid if needed
3. The need to feel input and control with regard to the emotional aspects of the relationship
4. The need to be supported by your partner
5. The need to know that your partner is loyal and committed
6. The need to know that your relationship will not be put at risk and hang in the balance because of any disagreements and confrontations
7. The need to know that your partner is committed permanently
8. The need to know that your partner is there for you in times of third-party conflicts and problems
9. The need to know that your partner is your soft place to fall

Again, the items listed under each category are offered to stimulate your thinking, and are admittedly very general. It is a starting place to help you get in touch with yourself and your heartfelt needs as specifically and thoroughly as possibly. I encourage you again to give yourself permission to feel your needs and claim your needs without consideration for whether they are reasonable, rational, or even sensible. You will have time to review your work later,

Right now, err in the direction of overinclusiveness rather than risk leaving something out that might prove to be critical to the quality of your experience of this relationship.

ASSIGNMENT: Open your journal to a clean page, and write down the first category that you've just reviewed. Under this heading, as fully and completely as you can, describe your needs in that category. If Emotional Needs was your first category, write that down, then list under that heading those things that you feel you need in order to be fulfilled in your relationship to your partner. Now describe each need you've listed with language "from the heart": you can't share or teach what you don't know, so be as honest and descriptive as possible.

I do not intend for anyone ever to read what you are writing. This material is for your eyes only, and will serve as a guide for what you ultimately share with your partner, either orally or in writing. Take whatever steps you need to write in such a way that you avoid self-consciousness, and can write without fear of judgment or ridicule.

What needs are you discovering that have been thwarted or stifled for too long? Maybe you've identified needs you've pushed so far down that you had forgotten they were part of your dreams. Search out those needs that you've forgotten were ever included in your vision for your intimate life and relationship. To help you here, you may want to look back at the work you did in Chapter 2, when, as part of diagnosing your relationship, I asked you to write about your early dreams of what your special, romantic relationship would be like.

Remember, it is okay to want, and it is okay to expect.

This is not the time to play safe. Don't be conservative in expressing your needs. Lay them out. They have been buried, blunted, and frustrated long enough.

And don't let your fears control you during this exercise. So often we live silently under the burden of our fears rather than feeling silly admitting our vulnerabilities. But if you're truly giving yourself permission to reach inside your heart and claim your experience in this relationship in particular, and in this life in general, then identify your fears. They are a part of who you are. To stimulate your thinking, here are some examples:

- The broad and sweeping fear of rejection
- The fear of inadequacy, physical, mental, emotional, sexual, social, or in any other category where you fear that you may not measure up
- The fear of abandonment
- The fear of disappointing or letting down your partner

Again, these are very general categories of fears that I have often heard expressed by partners in a relationship. As before, they are offered for stimulus purposes only. I deal with this category of relationship experience here because it is reasonable for you to need your partner to help you deal with, manage, or overcome these fears. Once again, don't be self-conscious. Don't censor yourself based on your fear of how silly or irrational your fears might be.

ASSIGNMENT: In your journal, create a category of fears. With as much detail and descriptiveness as possible, list any fears that were not included in the descriptions you wrote for the five categories of needs above. Really dig to identify what you are afraid of. These may be overt fears or sensitivities you have, whether rational or irrational. If they are part of you, that is okay. Be honest enough to identify them.

The process you've just completed, of identifying your needs and fears, should affect you in more than one way. If you have really articulated all of those things that you need, and all of the fears that you need help dealing with, you should feel much closer to yourself than you did before. You should feel that you have gotten back in touch with who you are and what you value. That should be a very positive feeling for you. You may also be experiencing a certain degree of sadness or anger and frustration. By acknowledging the very important needs that you have, you cannot help but highlight in your mind and heart how much that you hold near and dear has gotten pushed to the side and ignored. Is it any wonder that your experience of this relationship has been so poor?

Whether your primary emotion is joy, sadness, anger, or excitement, deal with it just a little bit longer, because we are headed in the direction of changing your experience. In the meantime, we need to move on to Job Number Two.

Job #2:
Work to Discover the Needs of Your Partner

Properly done, this exercise will be fun, exciting, and—to say the least—challenging.

It is vitally important that you approach your building of this partner profile without a hint of a judgmental attitude. Take on the task of profiling your partner with the spirit and passion of an investigative reporter or biographer who is researching and writing about a mysterious, complex figure. You may not view your partner as mysterious and complex, but I can assure you that that is exactly what he or she is.

RED ALERT: The challenge of discovering your partner can be fraught with danger and difficulty. It may be that your partner is participating in this process and has therefore done the same personal profiling that you have. If that is the case, your job becomes much easier. If, however, your partner is not actively participating, then you are going to have to complete this discovery process "from the outside in" and without your partner's cooperation. That is okay—it makes things a little harder, but it's okay.

Your biggest area of danger lies in your fixed beliefs. It should be clear to you that your view of your partner has developed as a result of the experiences and interactions you've had thus far in your relationship. Some of these beliefs may be entirely accurate, while some of them may be the product of the distortion that comes with emotionality, conflict, and pain. If you allow fixed beliefs to distort your view of your partner and his or her needs, you are allowing history—accurate or otherwise—to control your present perceptions. It is extremely important that you resist this natural tendency. Tell yourself that you will view your partner through "current eyes" as opposed to old and potentially outdated fixed beliefs.

The second serious danger lies in making too many assumptions about what your partner thinks, feels, and intends in this relationship in particular and life in general. If in fact your partner is not participating in this process, then of course you can't avoid making certain assumptions. Nevertheless, you should make every effort to avoid blind assumptions. Use your investigative skills, and make sure you've got the data to support your conclusions about what your partner's wants, needs, fears, and points of pride are.

If you are alert to these two dangers, you can hold yourself to a higher standard of objective inquiry than might normally be the case.

Finally, before we begin the partner profiling process, let me recommend that you put this important challenge on what I call "project status." Project status means that you are making this challenge a high priority. It means that you are not going to simply "be aware of" wanting to learn and know more about your partner: you're going to make consistent, action-oriented efforts to get the job done. Putting this work on project status means that you will spend significant time and effort, on a regular basis, to achieve your goals. It means you'll approach the challenge with a sense of urgency and a timetable for completing it.

By the way, even if your partner isn't participating in this process, it is not important that you be subtle or discreet. On the contrary, it's quite possible that your partner will be flattered by the attention and effort that you're investing in getting to know him or her. Let's begin.

BUILDING THE PARTNER PROFILE

Professional salespeople know that "learning the customer" is an essential first step toward closing the sale. Admittedly, the clerk at the local discount store may not need to do a lot of research on you in order to sell you a toothbrush or a pair of shoelaces. But the more complex and more important the transaction is, the more likely it is that the salesperson involved is going to do some serious digging. That's because they know the more thoroughly they research the customer, the better the connection they'll make with that customer, and the more likely that interaction will result in a sale.

Take a real estate agent, for example. Before she even walks you through that first house or apartment, she's going to get as much history from you as she can. She'll find out how many kids you have, where you work, and how long you've been in the market for a home. If you've just got to have an extra bedroom for Fido, she'll want to know that. Before you've spent two hours with her, that agent will know plenty about what matters to you: what your priorities are, what bothers you about your current home, how you like to spend your free time.

All transactions involve the development of relationships, and all relationships involve transactions. The best relationships involve a thorough understanding of the other person so that the transactions can be meaningful. In business the currency is money. In intimate relationships the currency is defined by feelings and experiences. In the commerce and flow of relationships, you reward your partner not with money but with feelings of love, acceptance, belonging, and security. You are rewarded in the same way. You cannot give your partner what they need if you don't understand what they need. Your partner cannot give you what you need if they do not understand what it is. If you're the person hunting for the house or apartment in the scenario I just described, I submit to you that you're going to appreciate the extra effort that agent takes to get to know you. You'll recognize that she's trying to identify your unique needs so that she can meet them by steering you toward what will come closest to fulfilling those needs. In the long run, the profile that she creates of you, her customer, serves your interests and hers.

Suppose that you had to come up with a similar profile, this one involving not your business partner but instead your relationship partner. Since you cannot deal or react to what you don't know, it is going to be important to find and fill these informational voids. How well do you know him or her? You may feel as though you know your partner quite well—maybe all too well. But I suspect that you were surprised by some of the discoveries you made about yourself earlier in this chapter. Maybe there were needs you identified that you didn't know you had, or had never put into words.

In the same way, I think you're going to be very surprised by some of the discoveries you're about to make about your partner. You'll probably be surprised at what you didn't know about him or her.

As a first assessment of your partner awareness, take the following true/false quiz. Let me caution you not to work through this quiz with your partner—that would be cheating. Instead, let it be an honest appraisal of how well you know your partner as of right now.

PARTNER AWARENESS QUIZ

Read each statement and circle either True or False.

1. I can name my partner's three   **TRUE   FALSE**
   best friends.
2. I know what accomplishments   **TRUE   FALSE**
   my partner is most proud of.
3. I can identify the happiest time **TRUE   FALSE**
   in my partner's life.

4. I know what my partner considers   TRUE   FALSE
   to be his or her greatest losses
   in life.

5. I can describe what my partner   TRUE   FALSE
   considers to be his or her
   greatest area of difficulty in
   interacting with each of his
   parents.

6. I know what will probably be   TRUE   FALSE
   playing on the radio when my
   partner is driving somewhere.

7. I can name the relatives   TRUE   FALSE
   that my partner would most
   likely try to avoid at a family
   reunion.

8. I can describe the most traumatic   TRUE   FALSE
   event that occurred in my
   partner's childhood.

9. My partner has clearly identified   TRUE   FALSE
   for me what he or she wants in life.

10. I can identify the obstacles that   TRUE   FALSE
    my partner believes are preventing
    his getting what he wants.

11. I know which of my partner's   TRUE   FALSE
    physical features he or she is least
    happy about.

12. I can recall the very first   TRUE   FALSE
    impressions I had of my partner.

13. I know what section of the   TRUE   FALSE
    Sunday newspaper my partner is
    likely to turn to first.

14. I can describe, in some detail,   **TRUE**   **FALSE**
    the home environment in which
    my partner was raised.

15. I know what makes my partner   **TRUE**   **FALSE**
    laugh.

16. I know what my partner's parents   **TRUE**   **FALSE**
    would probably say is the thing
    about my partner that they are
    most proud of.

17. I can describe two or three   **TRUE**   **FALSE**
    decisions my partner made before
    we met that my partner now
    regrets—and my partner can do
    the same about me.

18. I know which part of a restaurant   **TRUE**   **FALSE**
    menu my partner is likely to look
    at first.

19. I can quote three things my   **TRUE**   **FALSE**
    partner says to me that he or she
    says to no one else in this world.

20. I am thoroughly familiar with   **TRUE**   **FALSE**
    my partner's religious beliefs.

SCORING: Give yourself one point for each true answer. If you scored higher than 10, it's fair to say that you've developed a pretty accurate profile of your partner. But it's not time to break out the champagne yet—not by a long shot. There's a great deal of exploration and discovery still to come. Likewise, a score of 10 or less suggests that the opportunity to create an in-depth profile of your partner may be coming at a critical time in your relationship. Whatever the case, I would suggest to you that there can be no more special feeling any of us has than to be focused on by our relationship partner. Knowing that our partner understands and appreciates, at a "heart level," our unique needs brings an energy and strength to the relationship that can be obtained in no other way.

The Partner Profile that you're about to construct is based on these fundamental truths about relationships:

- You cannot meet your partner's needs if you don't know what they are.
- You cannot know what your partner's needs are if you don't know your partner.

Consider this: Your relationship partner has a history, just as you do. There was a time when he or she lay in their mother's arms, a time when he or she was just learning to play, and still glowed with excitement at the new discoveries life offered. Like you, your partner has been scared, hurt, disappointed, and, at times, victorious. You may be thinking, "I already know all that." But how long has it been since you took the time to really reflect on all those various aspects of your partner's life? When was the last time you regarded your mate as a thinking, feeling human being, with a history and hopes and dreams? A real person with needs and pride and interests, a person trying to get through this world just like you, the best way they can. The time to deal with your partner in that way is now. To reconnect with your partner or to strengthen your connection with your partner, you must really know them from the inside out. The partner profile that we are about to build will walk you through a process of discovery or rediscovery that I believe will benefit you both in immeasurable ways.

Once you've begun the Partner Profile, you may think

that some of the material seems elementary, because you already know it so well. That's okay. One of the primary goals of the profile is to help you determine which things you genuinely know about your partner, as opposed to those things that are fixed beliefs: hardened assumptions you've formed about your partner over the course of the relationship that are wrong or outdated. Let the profile serve as a first step back from your fixed beliefs, and an opportunity to refocus on what makes your partner a unique individual.

Changing the way you consider another person can result in profound changes in your behavior and reactions toward him or her. When you challenge your own fixed beliefs about your partner, and replace them with new and fresh knowledge, you can close the distance between you. I liken it to the differences in perspective between bomber pilots and foot soldiers. The foot soldier must at times look his enemy in the eye and squeeze the trigger, fully aware that he is taking that other person's life. By contrast, the pilot who soars over a target at twenty-five thousand feet and seven hundred miles an hour has virtually no contact with the people whose lives he seeks to extinguish. For the pilot there is no blood; there is no cry of terror; he doesn't see the life flickering out in the other person's eyes. He's just bombing a target, a coordinate on a map.

I suggest that warfare from a distance, warfare from behind walls of coldness and impersonality, prolongs and dehumanizes conflict. Consider what would happen if combatants, on the eve of war, were forced to live among their enemies for a period of time beforehand. Suppose they had to watch their enemies getting their children ready for bed, reading them stories, rubbing their backs, and kissing them good night. Would they still so ferociously seek to destroy them?

Fixed beliefs and outdated stereotypic beliefs are like distorting lenses. They artificially lengthen the distance between you and your partner, making it virtually impossible for you to view each other up close and personal as unique human individuals. Of course, if colder and more prolonged conflict with your partner is your goal, then by all means hang on to the same fixed beliefs that have depersonalized your partner. Maintain those assumptions that have turned your partner into a "target" rather than a human being.

But I'm going to conclude instead that you're ready for a "revision" of your relationship. Think of the following Partner Profile as a chance to take a fresh look at your partner. Make it your objective, right now, to understand more about your relationship partner than you've ever known. If you'll agree with me that it makes sense to do your homework when the goal is to sell a piece of real estate, how much more important is it for you to understand the needs of the person with whom you're sharing your life? How much effort and insight does the "sale" of a lifelong, fulfilling relationship deserve?

I've designed the profile to stimulate some detective work on your part. Using your journal, answer the following questions about your partner as thoroughly as you can. Treat any unanswered questions as goals for your investigation and inquiry (this includes any false answers you gave to the Partner Awareness Quiz on page 194). In the first part, indicate whether or not you believe this was a relationship of high quality or low quality. Explain why you believe it was of high or low quality by referencing whether or not you believe the relationship met the needs of each partner in the five categories that we have identified:

- Emotional
- Physical
- Spiritual
- Social
- Security

In other words, in the questions regarding your partner's maternal relationship. if you believe the relationship was of low quality for your partner's mother, which of the above category of needs were not met?

Don't enlist your partner's help in answering these questions. For right now, do the best you can on your own.

As you work through the Partner Profile, you'll see that some questions can be answered with a simple yes or no. Others call for a sentence or two, while still others need a short paragraph in order to be answered properly. In deciding how much detail to give a particular answer, please keep the following in mind. The relationship strategies that I'm going to help you develop in later chapters will depend upon your ability to clearly articulate both your own needs and the needs of your partner.

You want to create strategies built on informed decisions, custom-built for your particular situation—not thrown together on half-truths and assumptions. So have the courage to be both thorough and honest in your answers. Treat this profile as an opportunity to reexamine what you think you know about your partner. Use the profile to root out and discard whatever fixed assumptions you have about your partner, and replace them with genuine insights. Again, the more thorough this Partner Profile is, the more effective you're going to be in finding new connections with your partner.

A final note before we get started: Some questions have to do with people who, while extremely important in the life of your partner, may have passed away. Please do the best you can to respond to all such questions accurately and thoroughly, treating them as if they were asking about a living person. As with the rest of the profile, avoid turning to your partner to fill in the gaps in your knowledge.

I. FAMILY HISTORY

Short Answer Section: Each of the following should be answered with a sentence or two in your journal.

A. PARTNER'S FULL NAME

1. How did your partner get his or her name?
2. Is your partner named after someone? Whom? What is the significance of that person in your partner's life, or in the lives of your partner's parents?
3. Is there any other special significance to your partner's name? Explain.
4. Does your partner like their name or not? Why?

B. AGE

1. Does your partner consider his or her age an issue? In what way?
2. Do they feel too old? Too young?
3. Does your partner desire to be a different age? Explain.
4. Are your ages the same or different? Is that a problem?

C. MATERNAL RELATIONSHIP

Circle Yes or No.

1. Is your partner's mother living?   YES   NO

2. If she is deceased, do you see any   YES   NO
   issue or problem there?

3. Does your partner consider this   YES   NO
   relationship an asset rather than
   a liability?

4. Do you consider your partner's   YES   NO
   relationship with his or her mother
   to be a healthy one?

5. Does your partner feel that his   YES   NO
   or her mother is proud of him
   or her?

6. Does your partner consistently treat   YES   NO
   this family member with dignity and
   respect?

7. By contrast, would you say that   YES   NO
   your partner tends to take advantage
   of or exploit this family member?

8. Is this relationship openly   YES   NO
   affectionate and warm?

9. Is guilt a major part of the   YES   NO
   relationship?

D. WRITTEN EXERCISE It's time now to address the mechanics of your partner's relationship with his or her mother. Use your journal to record your responses to the following stimulus questions. (Please keep in mind that these questions are designed to prompt your thinking about this important relationship. You should feel free to record other information that may occur to you.) If your partner's mother has passed away, you should of course treat these questions as being in the past tense.

1. How do the mother and child (your partner) handle problems? How do the two of them deal with frustrations? Do they freely express their separate views, or does your partner simply humor her? Can you describe the strategies that each of them uses when there is conflict between them? What behavior does each of them demonstrate?

2. What would you say is the best feature of this relationship? By contrast, what is the biggest problem you see in this relationship?

3. Are there times when your partner has felt that his or her mother has trespassed on private psychological territory? If so, how has your partner reacted to that violation of boundaries? Did your partner clearly communicate that an unacceptable trespass had occurred, or did he or she respond in some other fashion?

4. Would you say that your partner's relationship with his or her mother is generally positive or negative? Identify some things about the relationship that support that conclusion.

E. PATERNAL RELATIONSHIP
Circle Yes or No.

1. Is your partner's father living?   YES   NO

2. If he is deceased, do you see any   YES   NO
   issue or problem there?

3. Does your partner consider this   YES   NO
   relationship an asset rather than a
   liability?

4. Do you consider your partner's   YES   NO
   relationship with his or her father to
   be a healthy one?

5. Does your partner feel that his or her   **YES   NO**
   father is proud of him or her?
6. Does your partner consistently treat   **YES   NO**
   this family member with dignity and
   respect?
7. By contrast, would you say that your   **YES   NO**
   partner tends to take advantage of or
   exploit this family member?
8. Is this relationship openly affectionate   **YES   NO**
   and warm?
9. Is guilt a major part of the relationship?   **YES   NO**

F. WRITTEN EXERCISE Just as you did in thinking about your partner's mother, it's time now to address the mechanics of your partner's relationship with his or her father. Again, use your journal to record your responses to the following stimulus questions, keeping in mind that you should record other information that may occur to you.

1. How do the father and child (your partner) handle problems? How do the two of them deal with frustrations? Do they freely express their separate views, or does your partner simply humor his or her father? Can you describe the strategies that each of them uses when there is conflict between them? What behavior does each of them demonstrate?

2. What would you say is the best feature of this relationship? By contrast, what is the biggest problem you see in this relationship?

3. Has your partner sometimes felt that his or her father has trespassed across personal boundaries? If so, how does your partner react to that perceived trespass? Does

your partner clearly communicate that an unacceptable trespass has occurred, or does he or she respond in some other way?

4. Would you say that your partner's relationship with his or father is generally positive, or negative? Identify some things about the relationship that support that conclusion.

G. SIBLING RELATIONSHIP(S)

Circle Yes or No. Answer for each sibling.

1. Is this sibling still living?   YES NO

2. If he or she is deceased, do you see any issue or problem there?   YES NO

3. Does your partner consider this relationship an asset rather than a liability?   YES NO

4. Do you consider your partner's relationship with this brother or sister to be a healthy one?   YES NO

5. Does your partner feel that this sibling is proud of him or her?   YES NO

6. Does your partner consistently treat this family member with dignity and respect?   YES NO

7. By contrast, would you say that your partner tends to take advantage of or exploit this family member?   YES NO

8. Is this relationship openly affectionate and warm?   YES NO

9. Is guilt a major part of the relationship?   YES NO

H. WRITTEN EXERCISE As with the previous exercises, use your journal to record your responses to the following stimulus questions about your partner and his or her siblings. Any additional information inspired by the questions should, of course, be written down.

1. How do this sibling and your partner handle problems? How do the two of them deal with frustrations? Do they freely express their separate views, or does your partner attempt to humor this sibling? What strategies or behaviors does each of them use in handling conflict between them?

2. What's the biggest strength in this relationship? The biggest weakness?

3. Do your partner and this sibling respect each other's boundaries? When one of them perceives that the other has "stepped across the line," how does he or she deal with that issue?

4. Would you say that your partner's relationship with this sibling is generally positive, or negative? Identify some things about the relationship that support your evaluation.

Time-out: Before moving on to the next section of the profile, let me suggest that you put your journal aside for a moment. Take some time to relax, get comfortable, and "clear the cobwebs" so that you'll be mentally sharp and a hundred percent attentive to the next exercise.

II. RELATIONSHIP SKETCH

You have just answered some very focused questions about each member of your partner's family, including his or her parents. I'm going to ask you now to create a kind of mini-profile or study of the relationship between your partner's parents. To do that, it will be helpful for you to summon up a mental picture of them, using a series of questions to flesh out that picture and make it as detailed as possible.

Again, if one or both members of the couple are now deceased, try to visualize their relationship as you recall it, or to the best of your knowledge. These questions are written in the present tense, but of course you may be recalling things from the distant past. If stepparents are involved, apply the questions to those parental figures you think have been most influential in your partner's life. Let's also agree that you'll do the best you can to respond to these questions on your own. Avoid turning to your partner to supply this information.

They say it's best to read a recipe from beginning to end before you get started on a cake. Use the same approach here. Study the following questions carefully, one by one, all the way through, before attempting to write anything.

1. Picture your partner's parents together: In your imagination, where are they? If you picture them indoors, what room are they in? What are they doing?

2. Is the relationship between them characterized by lots of affection, or is it more standoffish? How do they express affection for each other? Do they use particular physical gestures to communicate affection for each other? Do they have favorite expressions or pet phrases that they share with each other?

3. Now try to picture them caught up in a conflict. Do their disagreements frequently escalate into all-out war? Or do they treat any kind of conflict as embarrassing and

unacceptable, such that even minor disagreements are quickly suppressed? How would you characterize their style of conflict? What strategies does each of them use for resolving the dispute? Perhaps each takes a stand, freely communicating his or her position. Maybe one of them quickly abandons the room, refusing to negotiate.

4. Have your partner's parents been faithful to each other?

5. Do they make each other laugh? How?

6. Are they friends with each other? Does each consider the other his or her best friend? If not, what need is left unfilled, such that he or she must turn outside the relationship to have that need met? By contrast, does each of them have a close-knit group of friends they just enjoy spending time with?

7. What kind of home environment have they created? Is there tension in the air? When visitors come calling, do those visitors immediately feel comfortable and welcome in the home? Or do they sit stiffly on the edges of their chairs, eager to escape?

8. What behavioral shortcomings or maladaptive behaviors do you see in your partner's parents? Maybe there are certain kinds of stresses or crises that one or both parents just can't handle very well. Think about those situations, and how the given parent is likely to react.

Now it's time to turn back to your journal. Using the preceding questions as prompts or guides, create a written description of the relationship between your partner's mother and father. Write about what you know of them, not as individuals but about the connection between them.

III. YOUR PARTNER'S OTHER RELATIONSHIPS

Now that we've explored, in some depth, your partner's family relationships, it's time to consider his or her other relationships. Treat the following as "short answer" questions, each deserving a sentence or two in your journal, in response. Again, avoid relying on your partner for information.

1. Who are your partner's best friends? Why are they his or her best friends? What is it about them that makes him or her want to spend time with them? How does he or she treat them?

2. Generally speaking, what is your partner's attitude toward the opposite sex?

3. Did your partner have best friends during childhood? Who were they?

4. What kind of people does your partner not like?

5. How does your partner feel about and treat the elderly?

6. How does your partner feel about and treat animals?

7. Other than you, to whom does your partner turn for companionship and warmth?

8. Has your partner ever been betrayed? Has your partner ever had his or her heart broken? By whom? What were the circumstances? How did your partner respond?

9. What has been your partner's prior relationship history? What do you know about his or her relationships before the one in which you are now a part?

10. What kind of social life and pattern does your partner prefer? Do weekends and free evenings

need to be filled with activity and new faces, or
would your partner just as soon stay home?
What's an ideal social occasion for your partner?

11. Does your partner have friends at work? What
does he or she like about them?

12. Is your partner liked by his or her peers? Why or
why not?

13. Does your partner seem to care what other people
think about him or her?

14. Would you consider your partner to be a loyal
person?

15. Is your partner faithful?

16. How does your partner feel about your family:
your parents, siblings, and relatives?

17. Which people, or what kinds of people, intimidate
your partner?

18. How does your partner feel about his or her
station in life? Does he feel that he is way
down in the pecking order, or is he proud of
where he is?

19. How does your partner relate to authority?

IV. YOUR PARTNER'S "ATTITUDE OF APPROACH"

This is a useful expression for capturing the manner in which
people engage the world. For example, when they enter a
room filled with unfamiliar faces, some people charge toward
the most crowded spot—they can't be comfortable until
they've placed themselves right in the middle of the action.
Other people prefer to seep into the room, like an aroma.

They may feel perfectly at ease within a few minutes—it's just that their attitude of approach is different. Everyone, including your partner, has an attitude of approach or style of being in the world.

MULTIPLE CHOICE: Think about your partner's unique way of being in the world, then answer the following by circling either a or b:

1. When the two of us arrive at a cocktail party or similar event where strangers are present, my partner would rather
    a. *hover around the edges of the crowd, waiting for someone else to initiate a conversation*
    b. *head straight for the partygoers who seem to be having the most fun*
2. I would describe my partner as being
    a. *more participative*
    b. *more passive*
3. I would describe my partner as being
    a. *more of a leader*
    b. *more of a follower*
4. My partner
    a. *is a courageous person*
    b. *plays the game of life with sweaty palms*
5. Generally speaking, my partner can be described as
    a. *lazy*
    b. *industrious*
6. My partner is
    a. *mostly content and satisfied with his or her life*
    b. *restless and frustrated*

7. My partner
   a. *lives in a comfort zone, refusing to step out of familiar boundaries*
   b. *has an adventuresome spirit, and welcomes fresh challenges*
8. My partner tends to be
   a. *flexible*
   b. *rigid*

SHORT ANSWER: Now answer the following Attitude of Approach questions with a sentence or two, in your journal, for each:

1. What does your partner think is funny?
2. What does your partner find offensive?
3. Does your partner ever reminisce? If so, about what?
4. How does your partner feel about his or her childhood?
5. Would you say your partner finds it easy to express himself or herself emotionally?
6. How does your partner respond when the environment is emotionally charged?

V. YOUR PARTNER'S "FRUSTRATION SET"

Just as you did with the relationship between your partner's parents, it will be highly useful for you to create a word picture of your partner's frustration set. By that I mean the factors that create stress and difficulty for your partner, and your partner's responses to those stresses. Before attempting to write anything, take some time to reflect on the following series of questions. For each question, see if you can summon up a vivid image of the subject matter—visualize the scene.

What are your partner's greatest frustrations? In considering this question, try to identify two or three sources of frustration that may be present in different areas of your partner's life

1. on the job
2. at home
3. dealing with particular family members
4. handling particular issues
5. Are there patterns to your partner's frustrations—that is, are there particular times and circumstances in which your partner is likely to feel especially upset?
6. Can you predict how your partner is likely to express his or her frustration? What does your partner do when frustrated?
7. Does your partner maintain a generally positive outlook, even when things aren't going well?
8. What does your partner do when angry?
9. Name three or four of your partner's pet peeves.
10. How important to your partner are peace and harmony?
11. Would you say your partner is forgiving or vindictive?
12. How competitive is your partner?
13. How does your partner feel about confrontation?
14. Is your partner a good sport? Is he or she a gracious winner?
15. Is your partner a whiner and a blamer, or does he or she generally accept what's done and seek to move on?

16. Does your partner have insecurities? What are they?
17. What does your partner do when hurt?
18. Does your partner feel appreciated?

Now turn to your journal and describe your partner's frustration environment, remembering to include the likely responses your partner will demonstrate when facing those frustrations.

VI. SUCCESS, FAILURE, AND LOSS

SHORT ANSWER: Each of the following should be answered with a sentence or two in your journal.

1. How does your partner define success? For example, does money define success? Or does success mean an absence of conflict? Does your partner decide that he or she is successful when the family is interacting peacefully, or when the home is running smoothly? What does success consist of for your partner?
2. What have been your partner's greatest successes in life? What have been his or her outstanding victories?
3. What have been your partner's greatest failures? What have been his or her most challenging defeats?
4. What are your partner's limitations? Does he or she acknowledge them?
5. Have there been one or more major tragedies in your partner's life? What were they?
6. Can your partner apologize when wrong?

VII. OCCUPATIONAL AND FINANCIAL CONCERNS

SHORT ANSWER:

1. How satisfied with his or her work is your partner?
2. If your partner could choose a different job, what would it be? What satisfactions would that job provide that your partner does not currently get from his or her work?
3. How does your partner feel about his or her financial position in life?
4. Is your partner financially responsible?

VIII. MIND AND BODY ISSUES

SHORT ANSWER:

1. What is the parental legacy that your partner has inherited:
   Medically?
   Psychologically?
   Relationally (i.e., in terms of his or her ability to have effective relationships)?
2. How intelligent is your partner?
3. How intelligent does your partner think he or she is?
4. How does your partner feel about his or her own appearance?
5. What is your partner's favorite sport?
6. What is your partner's desired level of sexual activity?
7. What are your partner's favorite foods?
8. What kind of music does your partner like best?

9. What is your partner's favorite art?
10. What are your partner's interests?
11. What hobbies does your partner have?

IX. PRINCIPLES AND PRIORITIES

1. Does your partner have and commit to principles? What are they? What beliefs does your partner have that rise to the level of conscious commitments?
2. Is there an area of your partner's life where they excel?
3. Is your partner especially committed to excellence in a particular area of his or her life?
4. What are your partner's political leanings?
5. What are your partner's top five priorities at this point in his or her life? List them.
6. Is your partner optimistic about the future?
7. About what is your partner most passionate?
8. About what in his or her life is your partner most proud?
9. What are your partner's greatest fears?
10. What does your partner do when afraid?
11. What does your partner's spiritual life consist of?
12. What are your partner's spiritual or religious beliefs about life after death?

Time-out: The following questions deserve your utmost focus and effort, so I'll again suggest that you take a break, step back a moment from your work so far, and do whatever you need to do to get fully ready. As before, read each question thoroughly before attempting to answer it.

I hope that, by this point in developing the profile, you recognize the delicate nature of your task. You are the caretaker of some precious data, information as valuable and fragile as the forest clearing described earlier. Of no part of the profile is this more true than the following series of questions, which are directed at some of the most sensitive and important information to be revealed by your work. Accordingly, I implore you first to devote your undivided attention and energy to each of them, and second, to treat your answers as being "for your eyes only."

FIRST QUESTION

If your partner could be anywhere they wanted to be
With anyone they wanted to be with
Doing anything they wanted to be doing . . .
What would it be?

SECOND QUESTION

What was the happiest time in your partner's life?
If it was some time in the past, why did it end?
What happened to change the happiness your partner
   felt: Did he or she change, or did the world change?

THIRD QUESTION

What does your partner want?
Your answer to this question should put words around
   the things you think your partner wants most from
   life. Once you have articulated your partner's
   wants, answer the following as well:
What are the obstacles to their having what they
   want?

FOURTH QUESTION

> Why did your partner choose you for an intimate relationship? Knowing what you know of your partner's family history, relationship history, and overall makeup, what do you think were the major factors that attracted him or her to you, and caused your partner to bring you into that private world?

FIFTH QUESTION

> What are your partner's major faults?

PUTTING IT ALL TOGETHER

In creating your Partner Profile, I trust that you've devoted a great deal of attention to each of the preceding questions, and have been willing to express yourself as honestly and thoroughly as you can. You may have discovered a variety of holes in your knowledge of your partner. There may be questions you simply couldn't begin to answer. Again, that's okay—it's much more important, at this stage, to have clearly outlined your understanding of your partner than to be worrying about all the things you may not yet know.

One critical step in the profile remains. Read over your personal profile, and recall that you addressed, from your own perspective, five separate categories of needs: emotional, physical, spiritual, social, and security. Before your Partner Profile can be considered complete, you've got to create the same kind of list from your partner's point of view.

To do this properly, you'll want to review the answers that you've given to the series of questions on the preceding pages. As you read over what you've written, place yourself in the role of detective. Sift through your answers to determine, from the unique perspective of your partner as you now understand him or her, your partner's:

- Emotional needs
- Physical needs
- Spiritual needs
- Social needs
- Security needs

Take some time right now to write down what you perceive to be your partner's needs in each of the five categories. For example, having read through the Partner Profile, you may be saying to yourself, "You know, as I look back over his life, there's nobody who's ever told him that he's special. He's never been affirmed that way by anybody in his life." Under Emotional Needs, you would therefore write, "He needs to know that he is special."

Three or four other such emotional needs may jump out at you as you review what you've written about your partner. In any case, put the Partner Profile under a kind of mental microscope until you have identified needs your partner has in each of the five need categories. This list will be complete only when you are satisfied that, for each of the five, you have identified your partner's most immediate needs in that category.

Once you have developed a list of needs in all five categories, go back to the first category you wrote down. We'll assume that it is Emotional Needs. Examine the first need that you've listed under Emotional Needs, and ask yourself the following question:

What are three things I can do, right now and consistently in the future, to fill the need that my partner has in this area?

Don't just ponder the question—answer it. Make a list of three specific action steps that you can take that will immediately address a need your partner has. If the first Emotional Need you listed was "He really needs to know that someone in this world just thinks he's special," then you might respond with the following three action steps (these are, of course, just examples):

1. "I can tell him that. I can just let it slip how lucky our kids are to have him as their father."

2. "When we're watching TV, and an obviously messed-up couple is portrayed, I can tell him how lucky I am to be married to someone so stable and solid."

3. "When we meet for lunch, I can mention how much I would always love him no matter what sort of job he had."

Stay with this last, vital segment of the Partner Profile until you have come up with three such action steps for each of your partner's needs, in each of the five categories. Please note that I'm not asking you to put them into action yet—how to implement each one of them, and incorporate it into an effective relationship strategy, is the subject of the next chapter.

Your goal right now is insight and understanding. You should not move on before you can say, with clarity, "That is a need my partner has, and these are three things I can do to respond to that need."

Having completed this substantial undertaking, you have

completed a giant step toward reconnecting or strengthening your connection with your partner. Continue to "massage" this information. You are discovering or perhaps rediscovering that person with whom you have the closest relationship in this world. Be encouraged and empowered; you are on the right track.

RECONNECTING WITH YOUR PARTNER

So far everything you've done has been intrapersonal, or completely within you. But now it's time to go interactive. It's time to bring in your partner. And that means it's time for you to become a leader.

As I said earlier, knowledge is power. Whether or not you generally consider yourself to be a leader, I can assure you that because of the knowledge you now have, you are in the leadership role in your relationship. You are in the prime position to create a meaningful reconnection within your relationship. You have never been better configured, and unless your partner has matched you step by step as you have progressed through this book, you are in a far better position to guide this relationship in a positive direction than is your partner. You have acknowledged the truth, gotten yourself out of denial, developed the right thinking and the right spirit, identified the needs of yourself and your partner, and then come up with specific action steps that each of you can take to help meet the other's needs.

Let me be very clear about the objective of involving your partner. You are ready to take decisive action to get what you want and need, and to get your partner what he or she wants and needs. I don't want you to finish this book thinking, "Well, at least now I have some insight." Insight without action is worthless. You should settle for nothing less than changed lives and a changed relationship. You have been settling for less for too long, and you also have lived too long with all the things that you haven't wanted.

From here on out, the measure of success must be results—it will be determined purely by where your relationship is one month from now, six months from now, or five years from now. This is the only criterion that matters. If in that time period your relationship is the same or worse than it is right now, then you have not done your job, and I have not done mine.

Get clear in your mind what success means for you in this context. When we typically think about success, we think about money, beauty, achievement, or material things. That definition is no good here. When I speak of success in the context of relationships, I'm referring to peace and harmony, to a reality for you and your mate that gives you what you hoped and dreamed about when you were both young. As you remember, I told you at the very start of this book that it is not too late and not unreasonable to want the relationship you dreamed about. But let me remind you: it is all up to you. There is no middle ground, and there is no excuse. In the past, when you brought wrong thinking and wrong attitudes to your relationship, you were destined to contaminate it. That was a bad deal, but you didn't know any better. You don't have that excuse now because you do know better. You now have the power to control and inspire your relationship. All you have to do is step up, do it, and then claim the results.

And let me once again be clear about what claiming means. It doesn't mean you control this relationship just for your own ends. Your goal is to create a win/win situation. Remember that element of the formula that says "meets the needs of the two people involved." Obviously, all of us view life from the perspective of how it relates to and affects us personally. We want events to work out in our favor. But I'm telling you right now, in the relationship context you absolutely, unequivocally cannot win if your partner doesn't also win. If your objective is just to get what you want so that only you can be happy, you are going to fail. You will drown in selfishness and you will not be happy.

So it is time to reopen negotiations and redefine this relationship. It is time to begin again with better information and with better spirit than you ever have had before. You have started this relationship rescue just by picking up this book, and continued it by working on yourself first. When you go interactive, your partner now has his or her first chance to contribute to the process. Maybe they will step right up as a willing spirit, and maybe they won't. But either way, it is time to step up the intensity of your Project Status because you're now going to have to wake up every day asking yourself the question: "What can I do today to make my relationship better?"

I am not saying that answering that question will be easy, or that carrying out your plans will be easy. I also know that you may still retain some feelings of fear and ambivalence. But don't be led by those feelings. Don't sabotage yourself by giving in to doubts. You don't have to wonder if it is going to be hard, because I am telling you right now it is going to be hard. But I am also telling you that you have the tools and that your relationship is worth it. Refuse to live in your own private hell, stuck in bitterness and resentment, sitting with your partner in some den or living room with nothing more than a two-foot end table separating you. A table that practically becomes a canyon that neither one of you can or will reach across. Refuse to be part of the statistic in America that describes two people as ships passing in the night.

Claim the courage to be the one who reaches across that table and takes your partner's hand and says, "I want to talk about falling in love with you all over again." It doesn't matter if your partner deserves it; it doesn't matter if you think he or she ought to be doing that to you instead of vice versa. You are now the leader. You are the one that has amassed the knowledge, done the work, and prepared your spirit and soul. Use that energy to put the past behind you, reach out and break the stalemate that separates you and your partner. The goal of this book is not to get you to a point in your life where you find yourself sitting alone at home after a failed relationship saying, "It wasn't my fault." This book is designed to make you find happiness, even if a big part of you wants to walk away.

Before we begin the actual daily program, I want to give you a little help as you prepare to approach your partner and open a new dialogue. You will probably face one of three scenarios. First, and certainly most desirable, is that your partner is already involved; he or she has been reading the book with you and has participated in and completed all of the assignments. If that is your situation, you are truly blessed. The second scenario involves a partner who has not been progressing through this book elbow to elbow with you but nonetheless is a willing spirit. If this is your situation, your partner is about to get very excited and be very flattered at the hard work and energy that you have invested in your relationship and in profiling him or her. If this is your scenario, you too are blessed and stand on the threshold of change.

The third scenario, however, involves a partner who is not a willing spirit. In all honesty, many of you are going to have to deal with this scenario. Your partner, for any number of reasons, has not read the book, is not willing to work on the relationship, and might say to you, "Well, look what's happened. You've read a few pages of a book and now you're a big-time expert!" Or he or she may say, "What's some bald-headed shrink know about me and my life? He is just another jerk peddling some book."

He or she might tell you that all this talk about the "relationship" will only make the relationship worse. He or she might be genuinely afraid of hearing that you have deep needs because he or she doubts that they can be met. Or maybe your partner doesn't want to get into this program because of an unwillingness to dredge up painful memories or episodes from the past. It may be that your partner thinks that it's pointless to work on such issues because of a friend who came out of some marital therapy sessions completely shattered and angry. Last, but not least, he or she may think all the problems are because of you, and he or she will just get angrier and angrier at what you're trying to do. If your relationship has not been working and from your partner's point of view "the thrill is gone," he or she may be totally unmotivated. Your partner may be depressed, withdrawn, and defensive. That may not be what you want, but if that is the deal you have, then it is what it is.

Be patient and keep moving right along. You can still, acting alone, make a huge difference in the relationship. You can provide a healing influence on your partner's anger or frustration. Remember, you are about to express yourself in a way that your partner probably has never before experienced. In the past you've been unable to state your needs or fully hear what your partner's needs are. You've been unable to escape your bad spirit while trying to communicate with your partner. You've been unable to open up with the kinds of Personal Relationship Values that you now have learned. Instead of hammering away at your partner about your problems, or just ignoring your partner altogether and turning away, you will now be able to make the lines of communication much clearer and much more effective.

I won't try to pretend that the task will be easy if your partner won't get involved. But it isn't impossible. You know from your own life experiences that it is difficult for someone to go against the flow forever. If you absolutely refuse to give up, if you absolutely refuse to take no for an answer, and you continue to think, feel, and behave in a constructive way, it will have a positive effect. If you have to, come back and reread this page every single day. I know that it can be lonely, and I know that it can look like an unbelievably steep hill that you have to climb. But stay the course. Trust your ability to make a difference, and never forget that small and subtle changes can start the relationship moving in the right direction.

Even if you are working in isolation, the experience of the relationship should begin to improve—and with that improvement will come a more benevolent spirit of cooperation from your partner. I know that your partner will eventually begin to appreciate your efforts. You may have to prime the pump for a long period of time before you get your partner's attention. You may have to patiently allow your partner time to accept that he or she too is hurting, scared, lost, and completely frustrated with regard to what to do. But let your partner see that you are sincerely trying to understand and meet his or her needs. Just by taking some action with regard to your relationship, you are about to experience a liberating power.

No matter what your personal situation is with your partner, you can generally follow the same strategy for reconnecting that will lead to a win/win result—which is why I am going to give you a very specific step-by-step process for accomplishing a relationship reconnection. If you look at the accompanying flow chart, you will see the specific steps that I believe you and your partner should follow. I want you to look at the flow chart to get an overall picture; then I will give you a more detailed discussion of the key points to consider in each step of the flow chart. After you have studied the chart and read the ten sections on executing each step, I will offer a few do's and don'ts about how to interact with your partner in such a way as to minimize backlash or resistance.

Step 1: Open the Reconnection Dialogue

As you begin your new dialogue with your partner, I think that you ought to be a little manipulative. I do not believe that manipulation is in and of itself a bad thing. It's only negative if it is self-serving and destructive. But it's a healthy endeavor to use your knowledge and powers of

Reconnection Flow Chart

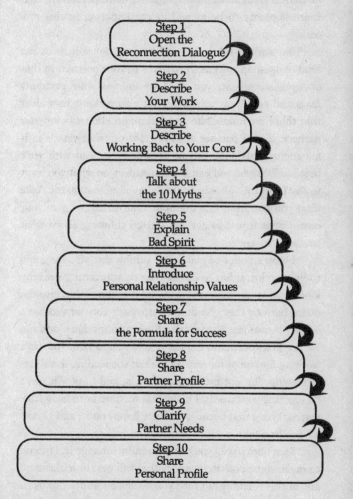

Step 1
Open the
Reconnection Dialogue

Step 2
Describe
Your Work

Step 3
Describe
Working Back to Your Core

Step 4
Talk about
the 10 Myths

Step 5
Explain
Bad Spirit

Step 6
Introduce
Personal Relationship Values

Step 7
Share
the Formula for Success

Step 8
Share
Partner Profile

Step 9
Clarify
Partner Needs

Step 10
Share
Personal Profile

persuasion to manipulate someone into a constructive position. In this situation I want your partner motivated right at the very beginning, to have no trouble perceiving that there is plenty to be gained by participating in this process.

That's why I think it would be good for you to have a kind of opening statement to make to your partner. In that opening statement, you need to address your partner's fears and points of resistance, but also make it very clear that there are immediate and meaningful benefits for your partner. If your partner can see right up front what's in it for them, resistance will be lessened. So lead with your best stuff. Maybe you can get some ideas on what you want to say from the following sample opening statement. Take what you like from this example, if anything, or plan your own. I offer it just to get you started thinking about what you want to say.

"I have an offer to make, and I think that you are going to like it a lot. It has to do with our relationship. Now, stop looking at your watch and deciding it is time to go give the dog a bath or that you have to run over to your mother's house. Please just sit down and listen to me for a minute. We are in a stalemate. You know it as well as I do. This isn't working for you or for me. We are not succeeding in this relationship. It's not meeting my needs, and I know it can't be meeting your needs. I know that we have both been frustrated. I hate that because we were happy once, and I know we can be again.

"I am here to tell you that I intend to change it. I intend to make some positive changes that will give us a chance. I got in this relationship with you because I wanted to be in this relationship with you. There were so many things about you that attracted me to you. I loved those things about you then, and I love them about you now. Our problem, my problem, is that we stopped focusing on those things that brought us together. I confess that I made the mistake of forgetting about those things that made me care about you so deeply and started focusing on things that I don't care about at all. I started focusing on negatives and problems and irritations. The truth of the matter is that I have not been a very good friend. I have not been a good friend to you, and I have not been a good friend to me, because I stopped being very much fun and we stopped having much fun. And the worst of all, we have stopped being there for each other.

"I have a commitment that I want to make to you. I commit to making this relationship better. I commit to focusing on my love for you rather than my criticisms of you. I commit to accepting you for who you are and supporting you for what you want. I am committed to making our decision right. I intend for you to have what you want and need in this relationship, and I intend for me to have what I want and need in this relationship.

"I want to start fresh. I forgive myself for the foolish things that I have done in this relationship, and I forgive you for the foolish things that you have done in this relationship. I just didn't get it before, but I do now. I'm convinced this relationship business is just not that hard. I just forgot about what was important. All of the things that I have criticized you for or been frustrated about, I am putting behind me. You're either going to do them or you're not, and I am telling you right now you are off the hook. I don't blame you for me being unhappy. I own my own situation, and I am no longer blaming you or anyone else for it.

"I am one hundred percent accountable for what I have created in this relationship. This is not a fifty-fifty deal. I am one hundred percent accountable for my life. I happen to believe that you are also one hundred percent accountable, but that is your deal and that's not what I'm here to talk about. I am telling you that I own my own feelings, and blaming you is an insult to me. It is an insult to me because blaming you means that I am incompetent and can't control my own destiny or create my own experience. That's not right because I can control my own destiny and I will control my own destiny.

"I ask of you only one thing, and that is that you be a willing spirit in helping me help you. You may not be the least bit excited about getting involved in working on our relationship. If that's where you are, that is fine. I can't tell you how to feel, but if you could at least want to want to, that is enough for me. Take it a step at a time if you have to, but try to be a willing spirit and participate in the things that I have been working very hard on, and I commit to you that we will emerge from the other side of this process in a way that both of us will value."

Okay, so there you have it. Now, with your opening statement completed—and please, don't think it has to be that long (I was giving you a variety of ideas)—allow your partner to respond. If he or she is suspicious, paranoid, or resistant, don't show any tension or impatience. It's perfectly natural that your partner might feel a little threatened. If he or she says, "So what are you now, Sigmund Freud," don't take the bait. Respond in as nonjudgmental way as you possibly can. You could say, for instance, "Not at all. I can't begin to tell you how much I don't know about relationships and human behavior, but what I do know is that I want us to be happy. I hope you'll give what I have been working on a try and work with me here, but if not, I understand. Maybe at some point in the future you'll change your mind." Whatever your words, stay the course, live what you've learned, and be patient.

Assuming that your partner is at least willing to sit still while you share some of the things you've been doing, then move on to Step 2. This may be in the same sitting, or you may feel like you need to give it a break and do Step 2 at a later time.

Step 2:
Describe the Work You Have Been Doing

It will be useful here to give your partner an overview of everything you have been doing to get the reconnection process in gear. But how do you do that without showing signs of arrogance? Trust me, at this stage in the game you do not want to come across as some condescending know-it-all. You want to interact with your partner in a way that protects their self-esteem. The key, then, is to be as un-threatening as you possibly can. You could start off by saying something as simple as "Listen, I've been reading a book written by this bald-headed Texan that I think you would like. And I have to tell you, it's a plain-talk, action-oriented book that makes a lot of sense. And this guy's not much into a bunch of pop-psychology, did-you-hate-your-mother kind of thinking."

Rather than provide you another script as I did in Step 1, I offer the following talking points for your consideration. These are points that, however interwoven, should be covered in some fashion during Step 2.

Tell your partner, without yet getting into much detail,

that you have been guided through an interesting diagnostic process in the book to determine what is working and what is not working in the relationship.

The author, "Dr. Phil," requires you to measure things based on results. He doesn't much care what you or I intend to happen; he really encourages us to look at outcomes.

Guilt, fault, blame, and shame are all about living in the past. This book tells you that you have to move forward and look ahead, not back. The message is pretty simple: "If what you're doing is not working, change it."

Talk to your partner about how you have identified some seriously wrong thinking on your own part and that you are now trying to adopt some constructive thinking Again, don't go into great detail. (You almost want to be a little tantalizing about what you've learned so that your partner will say, "Oh, yeah? Tell me more.")

Explain that you have been working to identify some really self-destructive attitudes that you have inadvertently brought into the relationship.

Explain that you have begun identifying what your needs and fears are, and those that you think are true for your partner.

Tell your partner that the author has given you a very commonsense formula for making a relationship succeed.

Again, reassure your partner that you don't believe that you are now some kind of relationship expert, but that you have learned and are continuing to learn what you believe are some pretty darn important things for getting along in a relationship.

If your partner asks for more explanation or some examples of this wrong thinking or wrong attitudes that you have been using, then give those examples. However, if he or she asks about these needs and fears that you have identified, do your best to delay until you get to that step. If you have the opportunity to share some of the key concepts you have learned before you get into relationship specific discussions, those discussions are likely to go much better.

Remember, meet your partner where he or she is. Don't force the process. Think back to how lost you were just a short time ago, and you might appreciate how your partner could feel overwhelmed if you push too hard. Be patient. When you sense your partner's ready, move on to Step 3.

Step 3:
Describe Your Efforts to Get Back to Your Core of Consciousness

Now it's time to get a little more specific about what you have learned. Share with your partner the concept of the core of consciousness and your drive to tap into it. Here is just an example of what you might want to say: "I've really worked hard and struggled to get back to what the book refers to as my core of consciousness. That's not nearly as fancy as it sounds. In fact, it's about as down to earth as you could possibly get. It's down to earth because it talks about that place where we find who we really are. It talks about that place where our self-worth, self-esteem, and dignity are located within us. I recognize that same place in you. I recognize that your self-worth, self-esteem, and dignity shine just as brightly as mine can. But you, just like me, have had it clouded by the world and all of the problems that we've encountered along the way. I've been getting back in touch with my core of consciousness, and I feel better about me and as a result, I feel better about you. I know that if you'll do the same thing, we can meet on a completely different plane that can do nothing but help our relationship."

If you're on a roll, keep going. If you need to take a break and come back tomorrow, then do so. Remember, get your partner as involved in the conversation as possible and encourage questions and answers. If he or she wants to discuss anything that you said, that is great. But remember to do so in keeping with everything that you have learned. Win-win, always win-win.

Step 4:
Talk about the Ten Relationship Myths

You don't have to elaborate on all the myths, but an explanation of one or more of them may help pique your partner's interest. You may want to explain what I mean when I said myth. Remember, your partner is probably as frustrated as you have been. Your partner has probably been feeling as inept and confused as you, due to an inability to make this relationship better. Let your partner know my views on the fact that nobody ever told either of you how to do this correctly and therefore you've been just casting about in the dark. Let him or her know that it's no wonder this relationship has gotten in trouble because you've been believing and applying wrong thinking. Here is again just an example of what you might consider saying:

"I was really surprised to hear that some of the things I believed in so strongly were simply not true. Some of them seemed so commonsensical I had just taken them at face value. Number four is a good example. I always believed that in order to have a good relationship, we had to resolve our conflicts and be good problem-solvers. Dr. Phil says very plainly that we will probably never resolve the major conflicts we have in our relationship. He says if we are married fifty years, we will probably still disagree on the core issues that we are at odds over today and that, believe it or not, that's okay. He says that most of those disagreements are just a product of men and women merging two lives into one. I needed to hear that because I was so frustrated that I couldn't move my position to your point of view or get you to move yours to my point of view. It was refreshing to hear that the only way that has anything to do with the future of our relationship is if we let it, instead of just accepting our differences and choosing to live peacefully."

These myths can be good stimuli for discussions. Go through them as much as your partner seems willing to. Again, don't be judgmental and, for God's sake, don't use your partner as a bad example. If it feels right, go to the next step.

Step 5: Explain the Bad Spirit

Let your partner know that you have taken a very self-critical look at the spirit with which you have approached and functioned within this relationship—and that by confronting your own bad spirit, you have started to transform your life. Again, don't be academic. It will be helpful to your partner if you personalize how a particular negative spirit has affected you. Let me give you a possible example:

"Among the bad spirits that Dr. Phil talks about is one he calls the 'hidden agenda.' That's where you kind of hide the ball by nit-picking over little stuff instead of discussing the really important issues. I don't know about you, but I confess that I have at times been a chicken in this relationship, when a little bit of courage would have made a huge difference. There have been times when I would focus on some trivial event between us because I did not have the courage or energy to talk about what was really bothering me. I realize now that I cheated you out of an opportunity to deal with me at a realistic level. To say the least, that little pearl of wisdom gave me a wake-up call."

Give a specific example of when you have allowed one of your bad spirits to dominate you. Choose something he or she will remember, and be as precise as to time, place, and person as you possibly can.

Again, discuss as many of the bad spirits in as much detail as your partner would like. Remember to focus on you and not on your partner. There will be plenty of time for partner focus whenever they are ready to take a harder look at their own behavior.

Step 6:
Introduce the Personal Relationship Values

I recommend that you spend some extra time here because it is these Personal Relationship Values that will move you and your partner into the more positive aspects of your relationship in the future. Discuss these as goals to strive for. Do not suggest that because you adopt or endorse these Personal Relationship Values that you think you are a shining example of any or all of them. Let me offer another example of what you might want to say about one of those values:

"I really liked it when Dr. McGraw talked about the Personal Relationship Value that he calls 'Focus on the Friendship.' It reminded me that you and I used to be such good friends. I used to really value talking to you and sharing my thoughts and feelings with you. But I want you to know that I allowed myself to be distracted from that.

"Dr. McGraw says that if we are ever going to be lovers and mates, it will be because we are first and foremost good friends. I found a lot of strength and hope in that because I know we were friends once, and I am convinced that we can be friends again—the kind of friends who cannot imagine life without each other."

Reminiscing here can be useful. Remind yourself and your partner of friendly activities you used to share, whether it was dating or watching each other play sports or walking through the neighborhood. If you can reconnect with memories of some of the times of good friendship, it can help create some positive momentum.

As you progress through the Personal Relationship Values, strive to find as many of these specific examples in your history as you possibly can. By specific examples I simply mean situations and circumstances in which you were living one or more of the Personal Relationship Values and it was working for you. By reminding your partner and yourself that at one time these Personal Relationship Values carried the day, both of you will draw confidence that can be built on going forward. If it feels right, move on to the next step. If it doesn't, it's okay to take a break. It may take several hours, several days, or several weeks to ultimately get through all of the steps.

Step 7:
Share the Formula for Success in a Relationship

At this point I hope you have that formula memorized, so that you can look right in your partner's eye and say it. ("The quality of the relationship is a function of the extent to which it is built on a solid underlying friendship and meets the needs of the two people involved.") Then offer an overview of the explanations that you have been given about the formula thus far. I suggest you get a dialogue going with your partner about the formula by saying something like this:

"In a very commonsense way, Dr. McGraw has convinced me that if I want to have a high-quality relationship, I've got to learn to meet your needs and teach you what mine are so that you have a chance to meet them. Frankly, I haven't held up to my end of the deal, which I now realize has made your job really hard. First, I didn't take the time to really figure out what my needs were. I couldn't tell you what I didn't know, so you had no chance to meet my needs. To be honest, I think I would have been too chicken to tell you what my needs were anyway, for fear that you would laugh at them or reject them. That wasn't fair to you. I guess I thought you could read my mind. Now, all this is probably no great revelation to you, but it was good information for me.

"And that's not all. The book made me realize that I hadn't worked to discover what your needs are, and then do the best I could to meet those needs. So that is my goal—to get our needs met. I know that if you and I just begin working together to understand and communicate our needs, then we will be moving back toward each other instead of down our separate roads. I must tell you, this formula gives me great hope."

Discuss this formula as much as your partner is willing. The commonsense nature of the formula makes it easy to get your minds around. Obviously, you want your partner to adopt and acknowledge the formula just as you have. Whether that happens in your first conversation or later, continue to refer to the friendship and refer to the needs of each of you when you are discussing your relationship.

Do not move on to the next step until you have a reasonable period of time, at least one to two hours. This is a time that you will need to do some serious reality testing to see if you are reading your partner right. If you have disagreements, be gentle but also trust your perceptions. You have probably worked harder and more objectively on your partner's profile than he or she ever has.

Step 8: Share Your Partner Profile

We are now at an extremely critical part of the reconnection process, and here you must be very careful and unthreatening as you share the Partner Profile that you have built. Your partner is going to be very curious about this part of your work. He or she will no doubt be flattered that you have put so much time, effort, and energy into profiling what you believe are his or her hopes, dreams, and needs. Let's face it, everyone likes to be the star. Everyone likes to be the focus of attention and energy.

But you must present your profile in a validating way. Otherwise, you risk isolating your partner, and losing a prime opportunity for the two of you to come together. While everybody likes to be the star, it is also easy for your partner to feel threatened by being put under a microscope. If your partner has painful memories and events in their history and you announce that you have been digging around, you might arouse some degree of anxiety in your partner. Again, be as unthreatening as you possibly can.

Here is a way to let your partner know what you have done:

"One of the things I've been doing for the last two weeks is building what Dr. McGraw calls a Partner Profile. It's a detailed process that is designed to remind me about what I know and value about you. It also is designed to point out to me what I do not but should know about the person I am spending my life with. I want to tell you what I have come up with, but I also want you to know that it has a lot of holes in it. There are things that I should have known about you that I just don't know, and I am hoping that you will help me fill in the blanks and then tell me the things that I may have gotten wrong about you. I had to start somewhere, but I am really excited to show you the profile that I built."

I recommend that you then walk your partner through the profile, item by item, so that he or she knows what conclusions you have made. What will invariably happen is that a dialogue between the two of you will begin. Your partner, for example, will look at something you've written on the profile and say, "Well, no, I really didn't hate my brother for doing that." Be prepared for your partner to say that you are wrong, and make sure you do not engage in a debate over your conclusions. If your partner feels backed into a corner, you're headed for trouble. But if he or she feels that you are flexible and open, then an environment will be created where both of you feel safe to share what you are thinking without fear of an argument.

Be gentle but open as you go through this profile. Make sure your partner understands that you are not necessarily interested in being right in what you have concluded. Make sure that your partner understands that you just want to know what the truth is so that it can help you to understand who they are and what they need. If you are wrong, you are wrong. But do try to find out what is right. Be sure to focus on your partner's accomplishments and those things that you know he or she is or should be proud of.

Your partner may be embarrassed when you talk about the needs, so be sensitive to that and move patiently and delicately.

Step 9: Clarify Your Partner's Needs

This is your chance not only to get heartfelt responses from your partner about how accurately you have identified his or her needs, but also to accurately determine how best you should respond to those needs.

I know I have said this before, but it is worth repeating: when talking about your partner's needs, characterize them in an uncritical way. For example, if you are a woman and you believe that your husband has an incessant need for reassurance and approval, you are going to offend him by stating that need in such a blunt fashion. It infers that his need makes him dysfunctional in some way. You'll risk losing him in this process of reconnecting. A better way to express that need is to ask yourself what it is that underlies this obsessive, insatiable behavior for reassurance and flattery. It certainly would be more beneficial for you to tell him that you believe one of his needs is a need for a higher degree of self-worth. You should look behind the expression or manifestation of his need and identify what most likely underlies it. I know this puts some pressure on you to be analytical, and you may feel like you are "playing psychologist." You do have to take some risk here. Be honest but be diplomatic in communicating what you think your partner's needs are.

What's more, as you share with your partner what you have discerned his or her needs to be in each of the five areas we have already talked about—emotional, physical, spiritual, social, and security—explain that your lists are to be considered merely as a place to start. These needs you have listed, and the three things that you propose to do under each need, should be considered at this point only as a stimulus for further discussion between the two of you. Again, allow your partner to disagree and replace your interpretation of a need with one of his or her own. Urge your partner to challenge what you have written. You might say, "Do you see where I wrote down these three things about how to meet this need of yours? Can you tell me if that is what you need from me, and will those three things do it for you?" This kind of interaction can be among the healthiest conversations that you have ever had in this relationship, because both of you will realize that you are talking about something important.

And please, stay patient during this discussion. Don't forget that because you have been doing most of the work, you are probably way ahead of your partner in the evolution of your thinking about your relationship. If he or she denies a need or a fear that you believe is absolutely real, give your partner time to come around. Stay patient yet persistent. You might wait a few days before going back to that particular need and readdressing it.

Step 10:
Sharing Your Own Personal Profile

This final step is all about you—and yes, it's going to be a little scary. As you perhaps remember what I wrote earlier about the risks of intimacy, you are now taking a giant risk by sharing your deepest, innermost needs and fears. You're jumping off the high dive.

Yet this step is critically important to you. Don't be shy, and don't be unassertive when you talk about it. In this life the most you will ever get is what you ask for. Have the courage to name it so you have the opportunity to claim it. Tell your partner what you need. Don't hold back about telling him or her what specific things can be done to meet those needs. I recommend introducing this step with a statement along the lines of the following:

"I will be honest in telling you that this is probably the scariest part of this whole process for me. For a long time I have been putting walls up around myself to protect me from you. I am not proud of what I did, but I did it. I thought I would feel safe behind those walls. But I wasn't. I was lonely. So now I'm going to come from behind those protective walls and be vulnerable to you. It's frightening, but it is a risk I am willing to take because I know this is the way for us to be close again. And I need that, I need it very badly.

"I only ask that you hear what I am saying with your heart as well as with your ears, and that you not judge me for what I am telling you. By telling you my needs and my fears, I am telling you how to hurt and control me. I am doing it because I want to trust you. I hope that you will respect the risk that I am taking.

"Just as I identified three things that I wanted to do to help meet your needs in this step, I was required in this book to identify three things that I would really love for you to do to help deal with my needs and fears. I don't want you to think I am demanding that you do certain things. I am just identifying what in a perfect world I think I would really value and appreciate. So here goes."

As you progress through your Personal Profile, don't hesitate to relate back to your Partner Profile and the parallels and similarities between your needs and fears. Remember, you are just two people trying to find some measure of happiness in a very fast-paced and often unforgiving world. Do not feel that it is weak to talk about needs. It is because of needs, after all, that the two of you came together in the first place.

You have completed the steps of the flow chart, and you have established a very important beginning. Through the communication between you and your partner, intimacy is seeping back into your life. It is taking root, and perhaps already starting to bloom.

To help you keep things moving in the right direction, here is a simple list of do's and don'ts for dealing with your partner during this important phase:

Do	Don't
Be patient	Push too hard
Be humble	Come across as a know-it-all
Be accountable	Be judgmental
Be strong	Take the bait if provoked
Be specific	Be mysterious
Be totally open	Hide anything
Use "I" statements	Use your partner as a bad example

You and your partner have just completed some vital work. The two of you have shared vital information about your minds and your hearts. You no doubt have inspired your partner to renew his or her own commitment to a better relational life. Even if your partner has shown only a flicker of willingness, don't be discouraged. A flicker can quickly lead to a burning flame.

But this is just a beginning. Always remember, relationships are managed, they are not cured. Whatever has happened through these discussions, you must keep in mind that this is an ongoing process. You must continue to seek clarity in your conversations with your partner. You must work hard to ensure that your perceptions of yourself and your partner are on the mark. And you must be patient with yourself as well as your partner. These are new skills that you are learning, and like any new skills you learn, you can master them only through practice. And I mean you have to practice them often.

That's where we are headed next in our reconnection process. We are going to engage in two very important elements to make you successful. Those elements are programming and action. You must be committed to let this process take as long as it takes, and you cannot let the setbacks discourage you.

FOURTEEN DAYS OF LOVING WITH HONESTY

I told you at the very start of this book that I wasn't going to be satisfied just having you peel back the layers of your relationship so that you could study it. I didn't want to produce one more book that would let you intellectually figure out what's happened between you and your partner. You can sit around and talk about this until the world looks flat, and you still won't change anything.

My goal, plain and simple, has been to focus on how to fix what's broke rather than to focus on why it is broken. And if there is one thing I know after twenty years of working with couples, you don't fix things just by thinking more about them. In fact, analysis is paralysis. You don't get better just by getting smarter. You have to take decisive and effective action and follow a specific program.

I would cheat you terribly if I was not crystal clear here. You will never permanently reconnect with your partner through a few isolated changes or by relying on simple willpower. *You have to have a program.* True, at this moment you might feel so inspired to make your relationship better that you're willing to run through a wall.

The problem is that such willpower has been the cause of more failed attempts in people's lives than I could ever begin to describe. Willpower is a myth. The problem with trying to use willpower to achieve and sustain a behavioral change is that it is fueled by emotion. And as we all know, our emotions are, at best, fickle. They come and they go. When your emotions start running down—and they will— even your best-laid plans will fall flat.

Think about how many diets or New Year's resolutions you have undertaken when you were so excited and convinced that you could make changes in your life. Inevitably, a few days or few weeks later, those emotions that made you so pumped up started to fade and you began to get tired or distracted. You succumbed again to the safety of food or the warmth of your couch and the drone of your television. As a result, you've probably gone through cycles— losing the same twenty pounds twenty times or rejoining the same gym year after year—believing this time it will all be different.

You have probably done the same in your relationships. You may have resolved not to fight and yell anymore—or perhaps resolved never again to feel insecure with your partner—only to have your willpower falter and your conviction and commitment decline within a few days. At that point you most likely reverted to the same behaviors and emotions that had plagued you before you thought you had it all figured out.

Your relationship can indeed be different—and I mean different for the long term—but only if you adopt a program that does not depend merely on willpower. Programming, with appropriate goals, time management, scheduling, and accountability, will carry you when willpower and emotion have long since faded.

How can a "program" fix the results of the emotional roller coaster of a relationship? The answer is in the structure. A good program is structured enough so that it props you up and propels you forward during those times that you don't feel like performing. If you program yourself, your environment, and those around you in such a way as to support your goals, then you have programmed your world in a way to help you sustain your commitment.

I admit, it's easy to make quick, temporary changes when you are excited and your emotional energy is high. The key is to have a program that pulls for your performance when the emotions are gone and you are tired or confused or discouraged. Changing a chronic problem that has proven itself to be resistant to change is done one day, one step at a time.

And speaking of steps: as significant as it is that you have made the first major steps toward reconnecting, never forget that you have made only the first steps. You have to practice at tapping into your core of consciousness over and over until it becomes second nature. Actions, not intentions, are what will rescue your relationship and reconnect you with your partner. And it is only action that will keep you going. Just as a downhill skier starts off slowly at the top of the hill but quickly becomes unstoppable as he or she progresses down the slope, your relationship will pick up the same momentum—as long as you have a specific plan for getting down the mountain to the finish line.

What I'm going to do in this chapter is give you a

fourteen-day program that will build this magnificent momentum in your relationship. The daily activities you're about to do are very straightforward and, most important, are designed to make you take action. Each day requires important new behavior. Consistent with putting your relationship on what I call Project Status, you are going to be required to do certain things within yourself and certain things interactively with your partner.

I'll be honest with you: what you're about to do in this chapter might at times feel uncomfortable. It has been designed to stretch you and to require you to be vulnerable. It has not been designed to be comfortable and easy. If something is easy, then that means you already know how to do it. The challenge is to move on to new behaviors that yield new rewards and that kill off that old negative voice inside you that is telling you it's much easier to go back to your former life and simply avoid dealing with the issues between you and your partner.

All I ask is that you follow what I ask you to do. You don't have to like it, you don't even have to understand it, you just have to do it day in and day out, trusting that the results will come. Remember, the misunderstanding that caused your relationship to go into distress was an active process on the part of you and your partner—and now you must take equally strong action to head the relationship back the right way. Even those of you who are in good relationships will find these techniques meaningful, for they will reinforce those building blocks that make a relationship strong.

I recommend that you schedule specific times for each of the assigned tasks. Then I want you to protect that time just as you do your other important activities of daily living. For example, you would not even consider getting up in the morning and going to work without putting on clothes or brushing your hair. You would never say, "Well, I am running a little behind, I will just wear my pajamas to work." That is exactly what is required here if you expect to succeed. You make the time, and then you use the time.

Furthermore, both you and your partner should do the assignments exactly as outlined. This is a real chance to help and support each other in your efforts. Some of the instructions and requirements may seem extremely specific. They are, and what's more, they are not specific by accident. I have not chosen these assignments or the specific words within each assignment in some random fashion. Do it exactly, precisely as outlined. If, for example, the instruction requires you to sit silently, then sit silently. Don't sit kind of silently with just a little bit of small talk. Follow the instructions. Old habits between two people die hard, which means you must consciously commit yourself to avoid letting these scheduled interactions deteriorate into combativeness. The precision of the language will keep you out of trouble.

One other thing: Get along during these exercises. Guard against coming across to your partner as the know-it-all expert. You have been the leader to this point and you still are, but you are also a co-equal member of this relationship team who must participate on a level playing field. Guard against setting yourself up as an authority figure, or you will elicit rebellion. What you want here is cooperation.

Each day you will be given a morning assignment and an evening activity. If you have a willing partner, you may, of course, do as many other activities as you wish to improve the relationship. But at the least, do these minimum pre-scribed activities. If your partner is not yet willing to do the evening activity with you, don't stop the program by any means; do it alone. Keep up with your morning assignments and press on with your optimistic new spirit, and I cannot imagine your partner not eventually coming around.

Day 1

MORNING ASSIGNMENT

Your morning assignment is in part to select something that you can actively, affirmatively do sometime during the day that will accomplish one or more of the following three things:

1. Accomplish one of the specific acts that you previously identified in your Partner Profile that will meet one of the needs of your partner

2. Relieve tension

3. Introduce something positive into your relationship. Whatever you choose, it must be something that is observable and discernible by your partner. It could be as simple as a phone call during the day, a hug and kiss in the morning or evening, or an affectionate note tucked into a pocket that addresses one of your partner's needs.

Does this seem too simple, or seem like it is not enough to do? Trust me, action, not intention, is the key to success. Little things add up. That is why the consistency of programming is so important. Your relationship does not need some dramatic concentrated event as much as it needs a consistent infusion of positive energy and action. Don't be impatient; just put one foot in front of the other, day after day, with simple acts of kindness and attention.

As a second part of your morning assignment each day you are to carry out a simple "concept review" of the principles that you have been working so hard to master. As part of a little extra work that I want you to do this first morning, get a card and list the following:

1. Your Core of Consciousness
2. The Ten Myths about Relationships
3. The Ten Characteristics of Bad Spirit
4. The Ten Personal Relationship Values

Keep this card close by for the next fourteen days. Today, read over each of the lists and select one item to reread in the book before getting your day under way. For instance, you could select Value 4 from the Personal Relationship Values: "Focus on the Friendship." Turn back to page 143 and read that section again about the importance that friendship has as a foundation to your relationship.

EVENING ACTIVITY

Your evening activities, because they are directly interactive, are extremely important. To program yourself for the highest probability of success, choose a time when competing or interfering activities are at a minimum. Specifically, that means when dinner is over, the television is turned off, the kids are in bed, and the phone is off the hook. You will need about thirty uninterrupted minutes.

Get two chairs and arrange them so that they are facing each other in close proximity. The chairs should be arranged in such a way that a clock is visible from the chairs or, even better, use a simple timer with a bell. Timing in this activity is going to be important. You and your partner now sit in the chairs, with one of you having your knees slightly apart and touching the front edge of your partner's chair. The other partner should have his or her knees together so that they can fit between the first partner's knees. Both of you put your hands in your lap as opposed to folded across your chest. From the moment you sit down, make and maintain eye contact. This is what is referred to as a dyad. That is simply a term that describes a two-person unit wherein the partners are face to face and are involved in active eye contact.

We will use the dyad arrangement every night. You and your partner will be assigned topics or given questions about which you will interact in a very structured fashion while sitting in this dyad. It is very important that you strictly adhere to all of the instructions for each assignment and that you remain in the dyad position. Do not vary or depart from the instructions in any way, and do not break your dyad arrangement until completion of all assignments.

I know this sounds rigid, but let's face it, when this deal has been left up to you two in the past, you have demonstrated an impressive ability to run it off in the ditch. So, let's try it my way at least for these fourteen days. I caution you about being judgmental and labeling this as just too weird. There is nothing weird about sitting across from your partner and looking him or her in the eye in an undistracted way. The fact that it is so structured and has all of these rules is just to keep you from screwing up and deteriorating into some kind of argument or otherwise destructive interaction.

Here's your first assignment in the dyad—and don't laugh.

Sitting silently, make eye contact with your partner for two uninterrupted minutes. The emphasis here is on silence. Do not make small talk. Do not chatter. Look your partner in the eye. This might seem like an eternity, but, trust me, you must do it if you are ever going to start acknowledging your partner as a thinking, feeling, caring human being. Rarely do couples, especially those in distress, take the time to just look at each other as human beings—to look at one another without any judgments or questions or concerns. All I want you to do is look at each other and consider what you are seeing. No talking.

Next, it is time to talk to one another—but only in a very structured fashion. Each night I'm going to give you three topics to discuss. With each topic I am going to start a sentence, and it is up to you to finish it in as many different ways and with as much embellishment and honest disclosure as you possibly can. There is a specific pattern in the way you must talk to each other. The partner who is to speak first (it can be either one of you) shares his or her thoughts and feelings about the assigned subject matter for three uninterrupted minutes while maintaining eye contact with the second partner, who is to keep time and signal when the three minutes is up. You must stop talking when your time is up. If you sit there stuttering and stammering for two minutes and forty-five seconds and then finally really get going, I don't care. When three minutes is up, so is your turn. Don't waste it.

At the conclusion of the first partner's remarks, the second partner can make only one response: "Thank you for caring enough to share, and I promise to weigh it carefully." No other statement may be made. The second partner or listener cannot argue, disagree, agree, or ask questions. Commit the response to memory and give it precisely and dutifully each time your partner completes his or her sharing.

Then it's the second partner's turn. He or she will take three minutes and respond to the same subject matter as the first partner while being timed by the first partner. Again, eye contact is to be maintained throughout the entire response, and the first partner's only response can be: "Thank you for caring enough to share, and I promise to weigh it carefully."

For your first evening there are three topics. To make sure there is no misunderstanding, I will take you through the routine of exactly what should happen. Tonight and each successive night, keep your book handy so you can read the assignments exactly and follow the pattern precisely.

Here is your agenda for evening number 1. You need the book and timer. Arrange your dyad and maintain eye contact silently for two minutes.

Topic 1

PARTNER A: "I chose you as the person with whom
I would form an intimate relationship
because . . ."

Three minutes

PARTNER B: "Thank you for caring enough to share,
and I promise to weigh it carefully."

PARTNER B: "I chose you as the person with whom I
would form an intimate relationship
because . . ."

Three minutes

PARTNER A: "Thank you for caring enough to share, and I promise to weigh it carefully."

Topic 2

PARTNER A: "My greatest fear in opening up to you has been . . ."

Three minutes

Hint: Use "I" statements, not "you" statements. Avoid saying, "My greatest fear in opening up to you has been that you would not handle it well." Instead, offer statements such as "My greatest fear in opening up to you has been that I didn't trust myself enough because . . ."

PARTNER B: "Thank you for caring enough to share, and I promise to weigh it carefully."

PARTNER B: "My greatest fear in opening up to you has been . . ."

Three minutes

PARTNER A: "Thank you for caring enough to share, and I promise to weigh it carefully."

Topic 3

PARTNER A: "What I hope to gain by opening up to you is . . ."

Three minutes

PARTNER B: "Thank you for caring enough to share, and I promise to weigh it carefully."

PARTNER B: "What I hope to gain by opening up to you
is . . ."

Three minutes

PARTNER B: "Thank you for caring enough to share, and
I promise to weigh it carefully."

Thirty-second hug.

That's right. You read that correctly. Thirty seconds of
hugging. The hug is an unspeakably effective tool for healing. It is also one of the best ways I know of that you and your
partner can let each other know that this evening's exercise
is not just some little game you two are playing, but an honest, sincere attempt to make a difference. With this hug you
two are saying that both of you are hanging in there.

Day 2

MORNING ACTIVITY:

For a detailed explanation of morning activities, see Day 1
on page 253.

EVENING ACTIVITY:

Set up the dyad, having your book and a clock or timer
handy. Remember to choose a time that is free of distraction.

STEP 1: Silently make and maintain eye contact. Two
minutes

STEP 2: Topics for intimate disclosure:

PARTNER A: "I feel that my greatest contributions to this
relationship are . . ."

Three minutes

PARTNER B: "Thank you for caring enough to share, and
I promise to weigh it carefully."

PARTNER B: "I feel that my greatest contributions to this
relationship are . . ."

Three minutes

PARTNER A: "Thank you for caring enough to share, and
I promise to weigh it carefully."

PARTNER A: "I feel I have contaminated this relationship
by . . ."

Three minutes

PARTNER B: "Thank you for caring enough to share, and
I promise to weigh it carefully."

PARTNER B: "I feel I have contaminated this relationship
by . . ."

Three minutes

PARTNER A: "Thank you for caring enough to share, and
I promise to weigh it carefully."

PARTNER A: "I am most excited about our future
because . . ."

Three minutes

PARTNER B: "Thank you for caring enough to share, and
I promise to weigh it carefully."

PARTNER B: "I am most excited about our future
because . . ."

Three minutes

PARTNER A: "Thank you for caring enough to share, and
I promise to weigh it carefully."

STEP 3: Standing hug for thirty seconds.

STEP 4: Start a journal for yourself—for your eyes only. Get
a notebook and record your thoughts and feelings
about what's happened so far in your new program.
It can be important for you to be able to return to
your journal and review these thoughts and feelings in the weeks and months to come. Spend five
minutes minimum writing in your journal.

Day 3

MORNING ACTIVITY:

For a detailed explanation of morning activities, see Day 1
on page 253.

EVENING ASSIGNMENT:

Set up the dyad, having your book and a clock or timer
handy. Remember to choose a time that is free of distraction.

STEP 1: Silently make and maintain eye contact for two
minutes.

STEP 2: Topics for intimate disclosure:

PARTNER A: "The negatives that I took away from my
mother and father's relationship are . . ."

Three minutes

PARTNER B: "Thank you for caring enough to share, and
I promise to weigh it carefully."

PARTNER B: "The negatives that I took away from my
mother and father's relationship are . . ."

Three minutes

PARTNER A: "Thank you for caring enough to share, and
I promise to weigh it carefully."

PARTNER A: "The most positive things I took away from my
mother and father's relationship were . . ."

Three minutes

PARTNER B: "Thank you for caring enough to share, and
I promise to weigh it carefully."

PARTNER B: "The most positive things I took away
from my mother and father's relationship
were . . ."

Three minutes

PARTNER A: "Thank you for caring enough to share, and
I promise to weigh it carefully."

PARTNER A: "Our relationship has such a better chance
because . . ."

Three minutes

PARTNER B: "Thank you for caring enough to share, and
I promise to weigh it carefully."

PARTNER B: "Our relationship has such a better chance
because . . ."

Three minutes

PARTNER A: "Thank you for caring enough to share, and I promise to weigh it carefully."

STEP 3: Standing hug for thirty seconds.

STEP 4: Please record your thoughts and feelings in your personal, "for your eyes only" journal. It can be important for you to be able to return to your journal and review these thoughts and feelings in the weeks and months to come. Spend five minutes minimum.

Day 4

MORNING ACTIVITY:

For a detailed explanation of morning activities, see Day 1 on page 253.

EVENING ASSIGNMENT:

Set up the dyad, having your book and a clock or timer handy. Remember to choose a time that is free of distraction.

STEP 1: Silently make and maintain eye contact for two minutes.

STEP 2: Topics for intimate disclosure:

PARTNER A: "You should love and cherish me because . . ."

Three minutes

PARTNER B: "Thank you for caring enough to share, and I promise to weigh it carefully."

PARTNER B: "You should love and cherish me be- cause . . ."

Three minutes

PARTNER A: "Thank you for caring enough to share, and I promise to weigh it carefully."

PARTNER A: "If I lost you, it would hurt me because . . ."
                                              Three minutes

PARTNER B: "Thank you for caring enough to share, and I promise to weigh it carefully."

PARTNER B: "If I lost you, it would hurt me because . . ."
                                              Three minutes

PARTNER A: "Thank you for caring enough to share, and I promise to weigh it carefully."

PARTNER A: "My sincere dreams for our relationship are . . ."
                                              Three minutes

PARTNER B: "Thank you for caring enough to share, and I promise to weigh it carefully."

PARTNER B: "My sincere dreams for our relationship are . . ."
                                              Three minutes

PARTNER A: "Thank you for caring enough to share, and I promise to weigh it carefully."

STEP 3: Standing hug for thirty seconds.
STEP 4: Please record your thoughts and feelings in your personal journal for five minutes minimum.

Day 5

MORNING ACTIVITY:
For a detailed explanation of morning activities, see Day 1 on page 253.

EVENING ASSIGNMENT:
Set up the dyad, having your book and a clock or timer handy. Remember to choose a time that is free of distraction.

STEP 1: Silently make and maintain eye contact for two minutes.

STEP 2: Topics for intimate disclosure:

PARTNER A: "Agreements that I have made with you and then broken or failed to live up to are . . ."

Three minutes

PARTNER B: "Thank you for caring enough to share, and I promise to weigh it carefully."

PARTNER B: "Agreements that I have made with you and then broken or failed to live up to are . . ."

Three minutes

PARTNER A: "Thank you for caring enough to share, and I promise to weigh it carefully."

PARTNER A: "It hurts me when you break agreements because . . ."

Three minutes

PARTNER B: "Thank you for caring enough to share, and I promise to weigh it carefully."

PARTNER B: "It hurts me when you break agreements because . . ."

Three minutes

PARTNER A: "Thank you for caring enough to share, and I promise to weigh it carefully."

PARTNER A: "I feel better about myself when I treat you with dignity and respect because . . ."

Three minutes

PARTNER B: "Thank you for caring enough to share, and I promise to weigh it carefully."

PARTNER B: "I feel better about myself when I treat you with dignity and respect because . . ."

Three minutes

PARTNER A: "Thank you for caring enough to share, and I promise to weigh it carefully."

STEP 3: Standing hug for thirty seconds.
STEP 4: Please record your thoughts and feelings in your personal journal for five minutes minimum.

Footnote for Day 5: Because none of us are perfect, we all make agreements that we fail to keep. Maybe it is something as simple as taking out the trash or calling if we are going to be late, or as complex as agreeing to love and respect our partner. Even small broken agreements can put bumps in the road for our relationships. Such behavior can and does send a message to your partner that he or she was not important enough to you to win out in the competition for your time and energy. I am sure that you always have an excuse, sometimes even one that sounds pretty good. But that does not change the result.

Examine this issue honestly and from the heart. Be specific in detailing the agreements that you have broken. Force yourself to identify the specific instances. For example, "I broke an agreement with you when I said I would pick up the dry cleaning a week ago Tuesday. I broke an agreement when I said I would not let your brother irritate me. I broke an agreement with you when I said I would really try to make our relationship work, and then I started pouting and did not do it." Do not explain or justify them to your partner, just acknowledge them by listing them. Your three minutes may be filled up by agreements you have broken in the recent past, or you may include those that are from years gone by.

Day 6

MORNING ACTIVITY:
For a detailed explanation of morning activities, see Day 1 on page 253.

EVENING ASSIGNMENT:
Set up the dyad, having your book and a clock or timer handy. Remember to choose a time that is free of distraction.

STEP 1: Silently make and maintain eye contact for two minutes.

STEP 2: Topics for intimate disclosure:

PARTNER A: "When I have forgiveness and acceptance instead of judgment in my heart for you, that helps me because . . ."

Three minutes

PARTNER B: "Thank you for caring enough to share, and I promise to weigh it carefully."

PARTNER B: "When I have forgiveness and acceptance instead of judgment in my heart for you, that helps me because . . ."

Three minutes

PARTNER A: "Thank you for caring enough to share, and I promise to weigh it carefully."

PARTNER A: "When I have forgiveness and acceptance instead of judgment in my heart for me, that helps me because . . ."

Three minutes

PARTNER B: "Thank you for caring enough to share, and I promise to weigh it carefully."

PARTNER B: "When I have forgiveness and acceptance instead of judgment in my heart for me, that helps me because . . ."

Three minutes

PARTNER A: "Thank you for caring enough to share, and I promise to weigh it carefully."

PARTNER A: "I want and need your forgiveness because . . ."

Three minutes

PARTNER B: "Thank you for caring enough to share, and I promise to weigh it carefully."

PARTNER B: "I want and need your forgiveness because . . ."

Three minutes

PARTNER A: "Thank you for caring enough to share, and I promise to weigh it carefully."

STEP 3: Standing hug for thirty seconds.
STEP 4: Please record your thoughts and feelings in your personal journal for five minutes minimum.

Day 7

MORNING ACTIVITY:
For a detailed explanation of morning activities, see Day 1 on page 253.

EVENING ASSIGNMENT:
Set up the dyad, having your book and a clock or timer handy. Remember to choose a time that is free of distraction.

STEP 1: Silently make and maintain eye contact for two minutes.

STEP 2: Topics for intimate disclosure:

PARTNER A: "The things that are going well for me in my life are . . ."

Three minutes

PARTNER B: "Thank you for caring enough to share, and I promise to weigh it carefully."

PARTNER B: "The things that are going well for me in my life are . . ."

Three minutes

PARTNER A: "Thank you for caring enough to share, and I promise to weigh it carefully."

PARTNER A: "The things that are not going well for me in my life are . . ."

Three minutes

PARTNER B: "Thank you for caring enough to share, and I promise to weigh it carefully."

PARTNER B: "The things that are not going well for me in my life are . . ."

Three minutes

PARTNER A: "Thank you for caring enough to share, and I promise to weigh it carefully."

PARTNER A: "The excuses I would typically make if our
relationship does not turn out well are . . ."

Three minutes

PARTNER B: "Thank you for caring enough to share, and
I promise to weigh it carefully."

PARTNER B: "The excuses I would typically make if our
relationship does not turn out well are . . ."

Three minutes

PARTNER A: "Thank you for caring enough to share, and
I promise to weigh it carefully."

STEP 3: Standing hug for thirty seconds.

STEP 4: Please record your thoughts and feelings
in your personal journal for five minutes
minimum.

Day 8

MORNING ACTIVITY:

For a detailed explanation of morning activities, see Day 1
on page 253.

EVENING ASSIGNMENT:

Set up the dyad, having your book and a clock or timer
handy. Remember to choose a time that is free of distraction.

STEP 1: Silently make and maintain eye contact for two
minutes.

STEP 2: Topics for intimate disclosure:

PARTNER A: "Our greatest barriers to a successful relationship have been . . ."

Three minutes

PARTNER B: "Thank you for caring enough to share, and
I promise to weigh it carefully."

PARTNER B: "Our greatest barriers to a successful relationship have been . . ."

Three minutes

PARTNER A: "Thank you for caring enough to share, and
I promise to weigh it carefully."

PARTNER A: "Our greatest assets in having a successful
relationship are . . ."

Three minutes

PARTNER B: "Thank you for caring enough to share, and
I promise to weigh it carefully."

PARTNER B: "Our greatest assets in having a successful
relationship are . . ."

Three minutes

PARTNER A: "Thank you for caring enough to share, and
I promise to weigh it carefully."

PARTNER A: "Our relationship is worth all of our hard
work because . . ."

Three minutes

PARTNER B: "Thank you for caring enough to share, and I promise to weigh it carefully."

PARTNER B: "Our relationship is worth all of our hard work because . . ."

Three minutes

PARTNER A: "Thank you for caring enough to share, and I promise to weigh it carefully."

STEP 3: Standing hug for thirty seconds.

STEP 4: Please record your thoughts and feelings in your personal journal for five minutes minimum.

Day 9

MORNING ACTIVITY:

For a detailed explanation of morning activities, see Day 1 on page 253.

EVENING ASSIGNMENT:

Set up the dyad, having your book and a clock or timer handy. Remember to choose a time that is free of distraction.

STEP 1: Silently make and maintain eye contact for two minutes.

STEP 2: Topics for intimate disclosure:

PARTNER A: "My 'tapes' or fixed beliefs about men are . . ."

Three minutes

PARTNER B: "Thank you for caring enough to share, and I promise to weigh it carefully."

PARTNER B: "My 'tapes' or fixed beliefs about men
are . . ."

Three minutes

PARTNER A: "Thank you for caring enough to share, and
I promise to weigh it carefully."

PARTNER A: "My 'tapes' or fixed beliefs about women
are . . ."

Three minutes

PARTNER B: "Thank you for caring enough to share, and
I promise to weigh it carefully."

PARTNER B: "My 'tapes' or fixed beliefs about women
are . . ."

Three minutes

PARTNER A: "Thank you for caring enough to share, and
I promise to weigh it carefully."

PARTNER A: "My 'tapes' or fixed beliefs about relationships
are . . ."

Three minutes

PARTNER B: "Thank you for caring enough to share, and
I promise to weigh it carefully."

PARTNER B: "My 'tapes' or fixed beliefs about relationships are . . ."

Three minutes

PARTNER A: "Thank you for caring enough to share, and
I promise to weigh it carefully."

STEP 3: Standing hug for thirty seconds.
STEP 4: Please record your thoughts and feelings in your personal journal for five minutes minimum.

Footnote to Day 9: "Tapes" are those seemingly mindless but recurrent thoughts and beliefs that we have about certain things in our lives. These tapes are fixed beliefs that have run through your mind so many times that they are almost if not completely automatic, and can only be eliminated or compensated for when consciously acknowledged. Examples: Men are driven by sex. Men are insensitive. Women are flighty. Women are manipulative.

Day 10

MORNING ACTIVITY:
For a detailed explanation of morning activities, see Day 1 on page 253.

EVENING ASSIGNMENT:
Set up the dyad, having your book and a clock or timer handy. Remember to choose a time that is free of distraction.

STEP 1: Silently make and maintain eye contact for two minutes.
STEP 2: Topics for intimate disclosure:

PARTNER A: "What I like least about me is . . ."

Three minutes

PARTNER B: "Thank you for caring enough to share, and I promise to weigh it carefully."

PARTNER B: "What I like least about me is . . ."

Three minutes

PARTNER A: "Thank you for caring enough to share, and I promise to weigh it carefully."

PARTNER A: "What I like most about me is . . ."

Three minutes

PARTNER B: "Thank you for caring enough to share, and I promise to weigh it carefully."

PARTNER B: "What I like most about me is . . ."

Three minutes

PARTNER A: "Thank you for caring enough to share, and I promise to weigh it carefully."

PARTNER A: "What I like least about you is . . ."

Three minutes

PARTNER B: "Thank you for caring enough to share, and I promise to weigh it carefully."

PARTNER B: "What I like least about you is . . ."

Three minutes

PARTNER A: "Thank you for caring enough to share, and I promise to weigh it carefully."

PARTNER A: "What I like best about you is . . ."

Three minutes

PARTNER B: "Thank you for caring enough to share, and
I promise to weigh it carefully."

PARTNER B: "What I like best about you is . . ."

Three minutes

PARTNER A: "Thank you for caring enough to share, and
I promise to weigh it carefully."

STEP 3: Standing hug for thirty seconds.
STEP 4: Please record your thoughts and feelings in your
personal journal for five minutes minimum.

Day 11

MORNING ACTIVITY:
For a detailed explanation of morning activities, see Day 1
on page 253.

EVENING ASSIGNMENT:
Set up the dyad, having your book and a clock or timer
handy. Remember to choose a time that is free of distraction. (See chart of categories on page 280.)

STEP 1: Silently make and maintain eye contact for two
minutes.
STEP 2: Topics for intimate disclosure:

PARTNER A: "Of the five categories available, I feel
that I best fit the _____ category
because . . ."

Three minutes

PARTNER B: "Thank you for caring enough to share, and
I promise to weigh it carefully."

PARTNER B: "Of the five categories available, I feel that
I best fit the _____ category because . . ."

                                           Three minutes

PARTNER A: "Thank you for caring enough to share, and
I promise to weigh it carefully."

PARTNER A: "Of the five categories available, I think
you best fit the _____ category
because . . ."

                                           Three minutes

PARTNER B: "Thank you for caring enough to share, and
I promise to weigh it carefully."

PARTNER B: "Of the five categories available, I think you
best fit the _____ category because . . ."

                                           Three minutes

PARTNER A: "Thank you for caring enough to share, and
I promise to weigh it carefully."

PARTNER A: "I can best use my category to contribute to
our relationship by . . ."

                                           Three minutes

PARTNER B: "Thank you for caring enough to share, and
I promise to weigh it carefully."

PARTNER B: "I can best use my category to contribute to our relationship by . . ."

> Three minutes

PARTNER A: "Thank you for caring enough to share, and I promise to weigh it carefully."

PARTNER A: "I could possibly contaminate our relationship if I allowed my defining characteristics to . . ."

> Three minutes

PARTNER B: "Thank you for caring enough to share, and I promise to weigh it carefully."

PARTNER B: "I could possibly contaminate our relationship if I allowed my defining characteristics to . . ."

> Three minutes

PARTNER A: "Thank you for caring enough to share, and I promise to weigh it carefully."

STEP 3: Standing hug for thirty seconds.
STEP 4: Please record your thoughts and feelings in your personal journal for five minutes minimum.

Day 11 footnote: In order to complete this evening's assignment, look at the chart on the following page. This chart depicts five different personality types. For the sake of imagery, I have assigned an animal to each personality type that typifies how those personality types would probably be seen. Have some fun with this, but also give it careful consideration as you answer the dyad questions.

PERSONALITY TYPES
CONTRIBUTIONS/CONTAMINATIONS

Wolf	Lion	Dog	Owl	Beaver
Promoter	Controller	Supporter	Analyzer	Workaholic
Smooth	Runs things	Anything goes	Take it apart	Earn way
Persuasive	Willful	Easy way	Figure out	Never rest
Own rules	Leader	Laid-back	Suspicious	Perfection
Always sells	My way	Gullible	Judgmental	Sweet virtue
		Testing		

Day 12

MORNING ACTIVITY:
For a detailed explanation of morning activities, see Day 1 on page 253.

EVENING ASSIGNMENT:
Set up the dyad, having your book and a clock or timer handy. Remember to choose a time that is free of distraction.

STEP 1: Silently make and maintain eye contact for two minutes.

STEP 2: Topics for intimate disclosure:

PARTNER A: "The greatest pain I have experienced in my life was when . . ."

Three minutes

PARTNER B: "Thank you for caring enough to share, and I promise to weigh it carefully."

PARTNER B: "The greatest pain I have experienced in my life was when . . ."

Three minutes

PARTNER A: "Thank you for caring enough to share, and I promise to weigh it carefully."

PARTNER A: "The worst loneliness I have ever experienced in my life was when . . ."

Three minutes

PARTNER B: "Thank you for caring enough to share, and I promise to weigh it carefully."

PARTNER B: "The worst loneliness I have ever experienced in my life was when . . ."

Three minutes

PARTNER A: "Thank you for caring enough to share, and I promise to weigh it carefully."

PARTNER A: "I have never felt more loved and valued than when . . ."

Three minutes

PARTNER B: "Thank you for caring enough to share, and I promise to weigh it carefully."

PARTNER B: "I have never felt more loved and valued than when . . ."

Three minutes

PARTNER A: "Thank you for caring enough to share, and I promise to weigh it carefully."

STEP 3: Standing hug for thirty seconds.
STEP 4: Please record your thoughts and feelings in your personal journal, five minutes minimum.

Day 13

MORNING ACTIVITY:

For a detailed explanation of morning activities, see Day 1 on page 253.

EVENING ASSIGNMENT:

Set up the dyad, having your book and a clock or timer handy. Remember to choose a time that is free of distraction.

STEP 1: Silently make and maintain eye contact for two minutes.
STEP 2: Topics for intimate disclosure:

PARTNER A: "If I had the power to change your experiences of life in any way, I would . . ."

Three minutes

PARTNER B: "Thank you for caring enough to share, and I promise to weigh it carefully."

PARTNER B: "If I had the power to change your experiences of life in any way, I would . . ."

> Three minutes

PARTNER A: "Thank you for caring enough to share, and I promise to weigh it carefully."

PARTNER A: "I am most proud of you when . . ."

> Three minutes

PARTNER B: "Thank you for caring enough to share, and I promise to weigh it carefully."

PARTNER B: "I am most proud of you when . . ."

> Three minutes

PARTNER A: "Thank you for caring enough to share, and I promise to weigh it carefully."

PARTNER A: "I want you to feel really special because . . ."

> Three minutes

PARTNER B: "Thank you for caring enough to share, and I promise to weigh it carefully."

PARTNER B: "I want you to feel really special because . . ."

> Three minutes

PARTNER A: "Thank you for caring enough to share, and I promise to weigh it carefully."

STEP 3: Standing hug for thirty seconds.

STEP 4: Please record your thoughts and feelings in your personal journal for five minutes minimum.

Day 14

MORNING ACTIVITY:

For a detailed explanation of morning activities, see Day 1 on page 253.

EVENING ASSIGNMENT:

Set up the dyad, having your book and a clock or timer handy. Remember to choose a time that is free of distraction.

STEP 1: Silently make and maintain eye contact for two minutes.

STEP 2: Topics for intimate disclosure:

PARTNER A: "I think you are the most sexy and sensual when you . . ."

> Three minutes

PARTNER B: "Thank you for caring enough to share, and I promise to weigh it carefully."

PARTNER B: "I think you are the most sexy and sensual when you . . ."

> Three minutes

PARTNER A: "Thank you for caring enough to share, and I promise to weigh it carefully."

PARTNER A: "You make me feel sexy and sensual when you . . ."

> Three minutes

PARTNER B: "Thank you for caring enough to share, and I promise to weigh it carefully."

PARTNER B: "You make me feel sexy and sensual when you . . ."

Three minutes

PARTNER A: "Thank you for caring enough to share, and I promise to weigh it carefully."

PARTNER A: "The gifts I see in you are . . ."

Three minutes

PARTNER B: "Thank you for caring enough to share, and I promise to weigh it carefully."

PARTNER B: "The gifts I see in you are . . ."

Three minutes

PARTNER A: "Thank you for caring enough to share, and I promise to weigh it carefully."

STEP 3: Standing hug for thirty seconds.
STEP 4: Please record your thoughts and feelings in your personal journal for five minutes minimum.

Day 14 footnote: All of us have unique talents, skills, and characteristics. They are God-given gifts that are unique to each one of us. Acknowledging and articulating the gifts that we observe in our partners can be very affirming. Think carefully about the gifts that you see and experience in your partner, and describe them fully and with passion.

Clearly, this is not a complete program. Almost every day from here on out will test your ability to reconnect. You'll still have to confront the negative thinking and bad spirit that has hampered your relationship in the past. You'll strive constantly to revise your distorted thinking about your partner, and you'll continue to need to work on building the right spirit. You'll have to practice, practice, practice. But after these fourteen days I know you'll be on the right track. I know that if you regularly apply the concepts that you've been reading about in this book, you're going to find the kind of connection you once only dreamed about. You're going to continue to make powerful changes in your life. And I think it's important that you and your partner make that very statement to yourselves.

In fact, I want you to make a life decision about your relationship in the form of a jointly drafted mission statement for your relationship. This mission statement will be all about defining your relationship in terms of your hopes, dreams, and commitments. It can become like the North Star that has been used to guide mariners and navigators for centuries. If seamen from the earliest times became lost or confused, they had only to find their North Star, focus on it, and everything else fell into its rightful place. That is exactly what I want to create in your relationship. By jointly drafting a mission statement, you create a reference point upon which you can constantly focus to keep your relationship on track.

This affirmation should be a product of your combined thinking. Here is an example that was shared with me by a couple some years ago:

"We, Jeff and Diane, resolve to live the relationship credo and treat each other with dignity and respect. We commit to the friendship upon which our love is based and to live with acceptance rather than criticism of each other. We resolve to never again fight in front of our children and to never again put our relationship on the line because of some argument. We will be imperfect, but with God's help and a committed love, we will prevail. Signed, Jeff and Diane."

In the space offered below, I want you to create your own North Star for your relationship. It should be unique to you and your partner. It may also be dynamic in that it can change as your relationship changes. But the core of it should always be your defining philosophy about what you want, need, and expect. Make sure your mission statement is displayed prominently in your home so that you can be constantly reminded of its contents.

Your Mission Statement:

_____

_____

_____

_____

_____

_____

_____

_____

_____

NINE

RED ALERT: RELATIONSHIPS ARE MANAGED, NOT CURED

After all you've gone through—busting myths about a relationship, aiming the harsh spotlight at your darker side, embracing a new set of Personal Relationship Values, and then engaging in a detailed reconnection program—you are probably feeling pretty good about yourself right now. And you should. But we both know that if you are thinking that you're going to be sailing forevermore through smooth relationship waters, then you need to go back to page one of this book and start all over, because you didn't get the message of this book—and you didn't get it in a big way.

As I have said many times in the preceding chapters, you have spent your whole life working real hard at doing the wrong things and creating a lifestyle that supports maintaining a really bad relationship. You have set up that lifestyle, based upon those self-defeating parts of your personality that cause you enormous distress and frustration—and believe me, the simple fact that you now recognize that you have a lifestyle that works to the detriment of your relationship does not fix the problem.

I will say this over and over: no degree of good intentions will get you what you want. The reason that eighty-five percent of those who quit drinking start back within a year, and that almost ninety percent of those who lose weight gain it back within a year is because they never gave up the lifestyle that supported their self-destructive behavior.

Alcoholics set up their world so that they can keep drinking even though they consciously confess they want to stop. Heavy people set up their world to keep them overweight. They make sure that their lives revolve around food. They may have insight and they may try for short periods of time to exercise willpower in the midst of a weight-sustaining environment, but they never really change their lifestyle. And yes, you have set up your world and chosen your lifestyle in a way that supports the existence of a bad relationship.

So don't even begin to think that a new formula for relational happiness is some magic pill, or that fourteen days of new conditioning will transform you. You have to abandon your old lifestyle and consciously embrace your core of consciousness. Nothing short of deconstructing your world and putting it back together—with a new lifestyle that is consistent with whatever it takes to support a positive rather than a negative relationship—will give you long-lasting change. Think about it this way: if you have lived lifestyle A and it generated a bad relationship, and then through your hard work and this book you shifted to lifestyle B and that generated a rewarding relationship, what makes you think that if you drift back to lifestyle A, you won't return to the same relationship problems you originally had? *If you want different, you have to do different.*

You've got another inherent problem in keeping your relationship on track. You and your partner are programmed for conflict. The fact that you are involved with a member of the opposite sex—and I emphasize the word "opposite"—means that you are trying to mesh your life with someone who is physically, mentally, emotionally, and socially different than you. You and your partner are as naturally compatible as cats and dogs, and take my word for it: there is no book, no speaker, and no therapist who can erase that natural difference.

There are going to be points in the future—maybe tomorrow, maybe next week, maybe next year—when those differences will cause the two of you to draw lines in the sand and dare each other to step over. When that happens, if you are not managing those differences with a great degree of awareness, then you are going to go spiraling right back down to the bottom.

I hope I'm not knocking a dent in your enthusiasm. Believe me, because of what you have learned in this book, you are now part of a very small group of people who know what it takes to make a relationship work. But there's a big difference between knowing and doing, between being capable of change and living a commitment to change. What you're about to go through is no different from someone drifting downriver in a canoe and then turning to head back upstream—only to find that it requires furious paddling just to hold one's place against the inexorable force of the current. You've made a U-turn back to a positive direction, but never forget that you still must paddle upstream against the current for the rest of your life. All of your history, all of your role models, all of your expectations, continue to flow in a negative direction against you. It will not be easy, but it is doable.

I want you to be part of that small group who has the courage to keep paddling and eventually to beat the river. And that means you need to have a program in place to keep your relationship healthy. I hope it's been exciting for you to have been operating under the intense and specific relationship programming that I have given you, completing your series of exercises and questionnaires and daily assignments. But that connect-the-dot phase of the process is now over. You are now heading into a major danger zone, where you and your relationship are unbelievably vulnerable.

For me to state it any less emphatically would be to cheat you. That's why, as we come to the end of the book, I'm not about to start caressing you and giving you lots of pats on the back, telling you that all that's left for you to do is write a love letter to your partner and bask in the serenity of a healed relationship. I want to make sure you've got a strategy in place so that you hang on to what you have worked so hard to gain.

If you do not have a real strategy with which to handle the future, then you'll fall on your butt. And I mean quickly. There is a natural tendency to relax immediately after you achieve something you have been working for. You have made real progress, but this is not a time to relax. This is the time to really make some positive progress because things are flowing your way. Never fall into the trap of just working on your relationship when it is in trouble. Relationships are much like every other element of your existence. If, for example, the only time you ever worked on your health was when you were sick, you would never have a durable, healthy lifestyle. You must work on your health particularly when you are well, and the same goes for your relational health. If you fail to create and execute a good management strategy, then this book will end up being just something you happened to read once before returning to your old lifestyle. Once again, let me remind you: relationships are never cured, they are managed. You need a strategy for reconnecting in the long term, one that takes into account the powerful negative pull of your long-term history and the real-world challenges you will face in trying to keep your relationship flourishing.

Think ahead, way ahead. I am as concerned with what you and your partner are doing next summer or next Christmas as I am with what you are doing next week. Your short-term management is critical to creating momentum and a new positive history—and the long term is important because it is your life. I want you to come up with careful, thoughtful, mature, and realistic planning about the way you conduct your lifestyle. New Year's–type resolutions, made of hollow promises, won't cut it. The plan must be specific, and it must be broken down to the daily level.

I know you don't want to be told about having to do more hard work, but if you really and truly want this relationship to stay on the right track, then you must do this right. Think about it this way: even though it was unintentional, you've been "working" very hard for many years at making your relationship wrong. You already have been programming your relationship for a very long time, only you've been inadvertently programming it to fail. All I'm asking you to do is take the same amount of time and energy that you spent in support of a painful and unrewarding relationship and invest it to reprogram your relationship so that it becomes something better. Yes, it's work, but this time around, the work will truly be a labor of love with both short- and long term rewards.

PRIORITY MANAGEMENT

The first trick to managing your new relationship is to pay close attention to your priorities. Priority management is simple and effective if and only if you are clear on what those priorities are. Do you remember that I spoke in an earlier chapter about the concept of life decisions? These are the decisions that we make at a very deep level of heart-felt conviction, as opposed to the decisions we make out of simple intellectual deduction. Your rescue of your relationship must be that kind of life decision, a priority so important it becomes the standard against which you evaluate every thought, feeling, and behavior that you have. You have only to ask yourself the simple question "Does this thought, feeling, or behavior support my priority of maintaining this relationship?" If the answer is no, if you are doing something that does not support your priority, then you're in trouble. My rule is this: if you catch yourself at any time doing something that is not in support of your top priority, or is in fact antagonistic to your top priority, stop what you are doing and change to something that is consistent with your priority.

Your overall attitude about your relationship is like a piston in your engine. This is where the change begins. And by attitude, I don't mean willpower that helps you build up a short-term burst of energy that will lead to some change. Willpower is what gets you to lose weight in two weeks so you'll look good for a wedding. If you have a major project that must be completed by a certain tight deadline—or else you lose your job—willpower is what helps you get it done. But willpower is never going to be enough. I don't care how committed, pumped up, and excited you currently feel about your relationship, that energy is absolutely going to fade. Careers, children, family, the flu, and a million other "damn dailies" will disrupt your momentum and drain the emotional energy away.

What I hope you can do is to get past needing to feel motivated and take control of your motives, to change your inner psychology so that you routinely will want to get up every morning and make a positive difference in your relationship. Trust me, this is not dreamy self-help double talk that sounds good but means nothing. The fact is that there is a fundamental difference between those who live ordinary lives and those who rise above their circumstances to create something far more significant and rewarding for themselves. The difference in these people is their belief system. They never say that they should or ought to find a better life. They say they must find a better life, and they identify and execute the actions to get it. They demand excellence. They never look for shortcuts that make their lives easier but fail to generate the desired results. There is a hunger at the very forefront of their lives which drives them to do much more than just get by or even do well. They are driven to be outstanding.

These people decide what they want and they go after it. They take action rather than getting bogged down in analysis and intention.

You must be driven in just such a way to make your relationship outstanding. That is your priority. You must take pride in and be challenged by the fact that you have a higher calling now. You cannot mealy-mouth around about your decision to improve your relationship, and you can't run hot and cold from one day to the next. You can't allow yourself to stick your toe in the water to see how it goes. Apathy, tentativeness, and playing it safe never accomplish anything. Your new priorities allow for no second-guessing. If you play mind games and constantly revisit your priorities, your commitment will be halfhearted and inconsistent. If you try to play the relationship game from behind a wall of protection, you will fail. Nothing worth having comes without risk—and a wonderful and rewarding relationship is no exception.

A tried and true formula fits the need here: Be—Do—Have. Be committed, do what it takes, and you will have what you want. Don't decide to work on this for some preset period of time. You have to commit to work on this "until." You work on this until you have what you want.

Your new priorities might seem so powerful right now that you cannot imagine ever forgetting them. But don't forget these are new priorities, and you need to keep familiarizing yourself with them. You've done some hard work to get this far; stay with what you have learned and incorporated. Toward that end, I strongly recommend that you "dance with who brung ya." Go back into the book and read about the danger of the myths and bad spirits seeping back into your life. Continue to raise your game by studying the Personal Relationship Values so that you may better embrace them. Reread these passages and honestly evaluate how consistently you are living those values. Clarity of vision has really helped deliver you to this threshold. Don't give yourself the chance to get fuzzy ever again.

BEHAVIOR MANAGEMENT

The second task in managing your relationship is behaving your way to happiness. Don't confuse this with the less genuine technique of "fake it till you make it." You aren't faking your relationship in any way. You genuinely do want a healthy, happy, and productive partnership. If you begin to behave in ways that define and reflect your priorities, then you will begin to enjoy the consequences of that kind of behavior. You can move toward happiness simply by behaving in ways that define what happy means to you in the relationship context.

It has long been my theory that bored people are boring, and depressed people are depressing. If bored people would do more interesting things—i.e., not "act" so boring—they would have a very different experience of life. If depressed people, even those who are biochemically deficient, would "act" more enthusiastic about life, then they'd be happier. The old saying that "you can't get a hit without swinging" is definitely true. You can't get happier if you do not get into the game. By getting into the game, by acting the way that you want your life to be, you give yourself the chance of experiencing the rewards that come from those kinds of behaviors. For example, if you like the way it feels when your partner looks at you and laughs or smiles, then do something that gives your partner the chance to look at you and laugh or smile. Create what you want by doing what you can.

I know what I'm about to say is a cliché, but to be great, you must act great. Even if it doesn't yet feel great to be with your partner, you can move in that direction if you choose to conduct yourself with passion, even if it is a conscious rather than spontaneous choice. Even if you feel you haven't completely tapped into your core of consciousness, you can get there soon if you act as if you have. Even during those times in your reconnection process when you feel ambivalent and when you wonder just how much progress is being made, you must continue to behave like a winner. One of the ways to help nurture your desire is to behave the way you know you will feel when you fully have it. You know it is true that moping around never got anybody anything. Jack it up and get excited about what is going on in your life, even if it means giving yourself and your relationship an optimistic benefit of the doubt. Before you know it, positive action and interaction will become the rule rather than the exception. As any psychologist will tell you, new feelings follow new behavior.

Indeed, an action-oriented spirit, where you put everything that you have learned into motion, is critical to keeping your momentum alive. Notice that the word "reconnect" is a verb. If you are reconnecting, you aren't just thinking and feeling, you are doing—and don't confine your new behaviors to just those that are interactive with your partner. Remember that the relationship lives or dies in the lifestyle and environment in which it occurs. Creating a new, relationship-friendly lifestyle means making substantial, observable changes. As a good barometer, I can tell you that if people who know you do not find it glaringly obvious that you have changed the way you live, then you have not made dramatic enough changes. You do not make a difference just by wanting different; you make a difference when you do different.

Your partner will know it too. Your partner will sense in you a revitalization of the heart and a revitalization of your interest, which means he or she cannot help but get caught up in your passion too. To be loved, admired, and adored by someone is of no consequence if that person remains a secret admirer. If your partner has to read your mind to know how you feel, you are not being seductively mysterious, and you are not being the least bit intriguing. You are just lazy and unwilling to take the risk of reaching out.

I will confess that men are the most typical offenders in this area. For years and years I have encountered and counseled men who, when pushed, reveal that they often think sweet and adoring thoughts or contemplate caring and supportive actions, yet most typically they say nothing, do nothing, and therefore risk nothing. Tragically, I have often heard these confessions from men as they are exiting a failed relationship, abandoned by a partner who feels unwanted and unappreciated.

Now, this does not mean that you must act like a high school cheerleader and put on an over-the-top, rah-rah attitude about your relationship. But showing your commitment, behaving with commitment, is a way of letting your partner know that you are not going to give up the first time something bad happens between the two of you. Your behavior says that your commitment is unconditional. You are saying that you are fully and totally involved, that you are not holding back because you aren't sure. You are behaving with an openness and enthusiasm that is saying to him or her that you want to be on this journey with no one else. You are saying that you are looking out for the best interests of you and your partner, that you are not going to intentionally cause hurt, and that you are going to be available when he or she needs you. Love as a behavior creates an enormous amount of good feelings between you and the object of your behavior: your partner. Believe and behave as though a better relationship will happen, and I guarantee you, your partner will begin to believe and behave as though it can happen, too. Winners invariably tell you that they can see their victory and success and experience it in their mind and heart as a way of keeping themselves moving toward that which they so very much want.

And remember one other thing that I have been harping on in this book: the best predictor of future behavior is relevant past behavior. In addition to the fact that a new lifestyle will change what is happening in your relationship on a day-to-day basis, it will also have the important effect of beginning to build a new and positive history for you, one day at a time. As I have said many times, days turn into weeks, weeks turn into months, and soon your relevant past behavior is positive and productive—and thus the most accurate prediction for the future becomes more of the same.

GOALS MANAGEMENT

As part of the reprogramming of your life in general and your relationship in particular, you must have a particular plan to deal with what you know will be the weakest spots in your relationship. Your particular weakness could be fighting, or it could be withdrawal. You might have a specific tendency to get vicious in certain situations, or you may be stuck in your comfort zone, or maybe you react to trouble spots in your relationship by flirting a little too much with someone of the opposite sex at work.

Whatever your trouble spot is—and I'm sure you already know it—you need to have a "goals" plan in place to overcome these prominent weaknesses in your relationship. If, for example, you believe that the quality and/or frequency of sexual interaction is a weakness in your relationship, then you must have a specific, conscious plan to change it. Your goals could be as simple and direct as committing to initiate sexual interaction a set number of times per week. Or it can be as indirect as getting more exercise to increase your energy level, dressing or grooming better to be more appealing, or creating more times alone in which sexual interactions can occur.

By the same token, you need a similar goals plan to build on the greatest strengths of your relationship. For example, if you believe your time together on weekends or vacations is one of the most valuable parts of your life, then come up with goals to make sure you enhance those times together and increase the opportunity for them to happen again. If the two of you really enjoy and relate well in social situations, then make sure that you engage in them frequently.

This goal setting is a critical part of your management program, and it is not something you can let slide just because your relationship is improving and things are "some better." Being some better can be seductive. It can cause you to lose your sense of urgency and drive, because the pain of the relationship is lessened. I promise you, it is a short drop back into the pain from whence you came. It's very easy to ignore the problems which need work because you want to let sleeping dogs lie, and it's similarly easy to take the good things in your relationship for granted and let them stagnate. Be an active goal setter and pursuer, and keep up the momentum.

Your long-term management philosophy should be one

that is based on perpetual ascendancy. I am not suggesting that you should not appreciate and enjoy where you are, but the reality is that you can end up in just another comfort zone and become stagnant once again. Because relationships are managed and not cured, your task is an ongoing one. You must always have some relationship goal in your window of focus with specifically defined behaviors for achieving it. Remember, a good manager is never reactive. A good manager doesn't wake up every day and simply react to what happens. You must be proactive by setting goals and making plans for their attainment. By remaining cognizant of your strengths and weaknesses—and setting goals and making action-oriented plans for their attainment—you are meeting the requirements of being an active relationship manager.

Here are some simple yet critical criteria and characteristics of well-defined and therefore attainable goals. Be extremely specific in defining what you want. Break your goal down into the specific behaviors or observable elements that define it. For example, if you want more harmony in your relationship, you must be specific about what you mean by harmony. Does it mean an absence of fighting and arguing, a daily hour of quiet time with your partner, a walk through your neighborhood or park with a strict rule against discussing problems during the walk? Whatever events define your goal, specify them.

Write your goals down. Formulating objectives in your mind does not require the crystallization and objectivity that writing them down in a coherent manner provides. Be specific and thorough in writing out your goals.

Be specific as to time. A goal without a schedule is nothing more than a dream or fantasy with which you entertain yourself. Once you say when you want to achieve a carefully defined goal, it takes on a completely different air.

Break down the steps. Clearly, some goals take time and have a lot of different parts and pieces. Make a realistic assessment of the time required, and divide that time into interval steps. Make the intervals short enough that not much time elapses before you take a measurement of your progress.

Create accountability. Establish a checkpoint person in your life to whom you require yourself to report on your progress. It can be a family member, friend, or even your partner. At least once a week, if not in shorter intervals, you must look someone in the eye whom you respect and report on your compliance to your program.

Have clear outcome criteria. Objectively define what will define success. Again, be specific so you know when you have arrived.

DIFFERENCE MANAGEMENT

I will confess that I personally spent years secretly and sometimes not so secretly believing that my wife, Robin, was nuts. I could not have been more convinced that I was right, and like a complete idiot I frequently told her so. The logic of my reasoning seemed so clear. I would listen to her talk and say to myself, "That's just not possible [because it didn't agree with my logical thinking]. How could someone so brilliant and capable be so screwed up in her thinking?"

I was, at the time, fully crippled by a strong belief in Myth #1. I believed a great relationship existed only when both partners fully understood each other. As a result, I was sometimes overwhelmed with frustration by what was happening between Robin and myself. I was trying to understand Robin through the use of my male logic, and she was trying to understand me from her point of view. Talk about trying to put square pegs in round holes.

The inconsistencies in the way she would reason or do things would sometimes just leave me standing there with my mouth open. For example, I had watched her deliver our firstborn, and could obviously see that she had a tolerance for pain that would shame any man. Then one day she slammed two fingers in the car door in the middle of the afternoon, and when I didn't cancel a half dozen patients to come home and put ice on it, she was deeply offended that I was not there in her time of need, and concluded that I didn't love her any more. What happened to being tough?

Or I can be at home on a two-foot ladder, changing a lightbulb, and she'll say, "Oh, be careful, don't fall. Be careful." Ten minutes later, we can be in the car pulling up to an intersection, and an entire herd of Hell's Angels circle the car. She'll say, "Phil, that man is staring at me. Tell him to mind his own damn business." "What? Robin, there's twelve of them. They will kill us and eat our young. Three minutes ago you were afraid I'm going to fall off a two-foot ladder, and now you want me to get out and throttle a flock of Hell's Angels." It was clear I didn't even almost get it.

We seem so different, it's unbelievable. If Robin and I need to be somewhere at nine o'clock in the morning, I will get up at eight-thirty, so I'll have some extra time. I mean, it's not like I have to do my hair. I shower, shake like a wet dog, and I'm ready. Robin, on the other hand, slithers out of bed about four-thirty, and it starts. At first it's the lights.

Strange lights glow from under the bathroom door, and then these gaseous clouds of powdery stuff appear. It looks like the Twilight Zone in there. And then you start to hear the noises. One of them is this bizarre steamy sound. Now, I've been in there in the middle of the afternoon when Robin's not at home, and I swear I can't find anything that makes those noises.

So anyway, I lie there until I'm finally about to wet the bed and I am forced to get up and go through "the Zone." I don't want to, I wish I didn't have to, but I have no choice. I get in okay and I am sleepily stumbling my way back out, almost making a clean getaway, when she says, "Umm, wait a minute," and then she asks one of those questions to which there is no right answer. I want to run for the hills, but I look up and sure enough, everything she owns is hanging around the dressing room. She takes a dress down, holds it up in front of her, and asks, "Is this slenderizing?" Oh, no! No way! If I say yes, it's "So I need something slenderizing?" If I say no, I'm really toast because that was my best shot. I mean, there is no right answer. You might as well just chew your foot off to get out of the trap and hop away.

Obviously, I am just having some fun with you here to make a point. Just like Robin and me, you and your mate have enormous differences, and no amount of work can bridge that gap. As a result, you have to learn to manage your relationship despite the differences. What's more, you need to embrace those differences, find value in them. Resisting the differences by being judgmental about them will cause you nothing but pain. Your reconnection program will collapse in a pile of smoldering accusations and angry stares. Your life will be filled with total frustration, your head shaking constantly in disbelief.

I am embarrassed to confess to you how many years I spent being frustrated with my wife, judging and resisting her for doing exactly what God designed her to do. God didn't design us to be the same; he designed us to be different. He made us different because we have different jobs in this world, and yet we criticize each other for being who we are. Men criticize women because they are emotional, sensitive, and intuitive rather than one-dimensionally logical. Women are supposed to be that way, and those characteristics don't preclude intelligent, insightful, and decisive thinking. They just do it differently.

Women have more of those characteristics than do most men because God contemplated that women would fill a role in the cycle and plan of life for which those characteristics would be ideally suited. God gave men less of those qualities and more of certain other qualities such as logic and physical strength, because he determined that those characteristics would lend themselves well to certain jobs that he contemplated for the males in society. It's not a matter of hierarchy. It's not that emotionality, sensitivity, and intuitiveness are second-class—just as it's not true that classic male characteristics are second-class. There's nothing wrong with the differences between a man and woman, unless you decide it's wrong.

I've told you the price you pay for resisting the natural order of things. I've paid that price. But today I am so thankful that Robin is the way she is. I now realize I would have ruined everything if I could have changed her years ago. Robin, I think, feels the same way about me. Years ago she was grouching about how I can be occasionally rude and crude, and I said, "If you could change how I acted, how I talked, how I thought, and how I expressed my feelings, what would you change?" She got all starry-eyed and described this caring, sensitive, emotional, tearful man who liked to get a blanket and go out in the woods and talk about our feelings. I said, "What you're telling me is you want a middle linebacker who fought for everything I ever got to become some kind of a ballet dancer who writes poetry. But I guarantee you that's not what you want. You weren't attracted to me because of my sensitivities. You were attracted to me because, among other things, I made you feel safe and secure, I protected you and protected our cave." She later confessed that if she had changed me to what she said she wanted, I wouldn't have still been the person she chose to spend the rest of her life with.

We now have both made the commitment to see our different views of a situation and our different ways of expressing thoughts as complementary attributes. I don't need to be as sensitive and emotional as she is, and because of my presence, she does not have to be as linear and logical in her thinking as I am. But together our very different styles work out just great. She will never see situations as I do, and may well forever think that I am cold and callous in my handling of certain things. Similarly, I will never understand how or why she can be so undone over certain situations, but I recognize that it is those characteristics and traits that create a warmth in our home and family that is so urgently needed. I want to be married to somebody who has the qualities and characteristics that are not primary within me so that that person can bring things to the table that help complete me. What's more, I promise you my wife does not want to be married to someone exactly like her.

We could talk forever about the differences between

men and women. What men define as solving the problem and what women define as solving the problem are two different things, for instance. Men are interested in the solution, while women are also interested in the journey to the solution. Men like to get to the point; women like to nourish details. The key here is that if your differences are not managed, they become destructive. Management does not mean one partner seeing a situation through the eyes of the other partner. It doesn't mean always understanding the other partner. It just means that being different is okay and should not be a source of frustration.

One good thing about a troubled relationship history is that you are no longer naive about how difficult or ugly it can get. You are a seasoned veteran with a powerful education. The tuition of pain that you paid was extremely high, so don't waste it. Research has shown that it is actually not what happens or doesn't happen that causes most people to get upset; it is whether or not what happened violated their expectancies.

When conflict arises, as you know it will, you won't panic. You will simply say to yourself, "This is the very thing we talked about. We knew it would happen and we know how to deal with it. We won't panic, and we won't put our relationship on the line just because we are encountering some of the normal challenges of two merged lives."

ADMIRATION MANAGEMENT

This might seem like an odd topic to you. What is managing your admiration? How do you do something like that? The reality is that just as you can forget to build on the strengths of your relationship, so too can you forget to work at rediscovering, finding, and focusing on the qualities in your partner which you can and should admire. Remember, couples who deal only with their problems have a problem relationship. Even in strong relationships people too often focus on the negatives, hoping to resolve them in an effort to make the relationship better. But if you dwell on what is wrong, it's easy to lose sight of what is right. If you dwell on the flaws and fallacies, it's easy to forget the admiration. Indeed, if you concentrate on the negative messages about your relationship, your expectations for your relationship and your partner will not be very high. You need instead a plan to remind yourself of all your partner's admirable qualities, and to remind you that the negative side of your partner doesn't cancel out everything else.

This is a different part of your programming from simply accepting your differences. You need to go beyond just accepting your partner, and actively work to create value in the way in which your partner is different. By doing so, you make a conscious commitment to develop and nurture your admiration of your partner. Focus on the admirable qualities so you can build on them. By becoming your partner's greatest fan, you will routinely choose to focus on those things about him or her that are unique and inspiring. You didn't choose this person because they were a hapless loser; you chose them because you saw things in them that moved you in a positive direction. Fan the flames of respect, honor, and admiration on a conscious level and work to be proud of your partner.

Remember, you don't need to understand or agree with your partner's style or nuances to appreciate them. I don't understand electricity very well at all, but I sure do use it and I sure do appreciate it. Perhaps your partner's manner of being in this world is very much the same.

Once I started to focus on my wife's best qualities rather than being critical of her differences, I began to reap benefits I didn't expect. Instead of resisting her, I came to rely on her. I didn't just stop at recognizing her differences as strengths. I began to value all of her in a more mature, complete manner.

TEN

THE DOCTOR IS "IN"

A s I have progressed through the process of writing and designing this book, I have frequently tried to put myself in the position of you, the reader, to try to get a feel for what you would want and need to hear about at different stages along the way. It occurs to me at this point that if I were you and had been working so long and hard through the many strategic steps that we have covered, I would probably be wishing that I could have a face-to-face sit-down to fine-tune my own personal relationship and ask a few specific questions. I can almost hear the thinking: "Hey, Doc, we get it, we really do, but we could sure use a session or two to get some specific thinking and clarity on a few key issues." I wish we could do that, but we can't.

Since we can't sit down together, I wanted to do the next best thing, and that is anticipate the questions I think you would ask if we were sitting face-to-face. While I know that every individual situation is different, I also know that there are many core elements that apply to certain subject matters, regardless of the specific circumstances.

So while I do not have the benefit of hearing your personal situation before I respond, I know that there are certain points I would make in every situation. I believe that by giving you some straightforward talk about these common denominators, I can give you a running start on handling some meaningful challenges in your particular relationship. I offer these thoughts and suggestions now so you can build on them.

To make sure I chose the right topics to talk about, I reviewed case histories of literally thousands and thousands of couples that I have encountered individually and in seminars to identify the most oft-asked questions. I hope that I cover at least some of your questions in the following sections.

Some of the topics merely make couples uncomfortable, while others are so explosive that the couples are likely to end their relationship if they cannot find some way to manage the problem.

I am not talking about Hollywood romance and drama. I am talking about the day-to-day issues that real couples face in the real world. For example, I suspect that if you are married with children, you are rolling out of bed early during the school year and scrambling to get your kids, yourself, and your partner all up and out the door in some sort of reasonable repair, that you're exhausted by the end of the day, that you face money and budgetary challenges, time challenges, physical and emotional tiredness. Not very entertaining challenges, but real nonetheless. I can tell you, at my house the morning light is usually unwelcome, but we yield and are soon shoveling Cheerios, packing lunches, and telling the dog to shut up and quit jumping on the door. If I put a rose on her pillow at night or she on mine, we would be picking thorns out of our cheeks because half of the time we lie down and are asleep before our heads hit the pillow.

So let's talk about a short list of very hot topics: sex, money, children, and even those moments when you look across the kitchen table at your partner and murmur, "What the hell have I gotten into? I'm hooked up with a crazy person."

So find your question on the list and trust that if you sat before me on the therapist's couch, this is, at a minimum, what I would tell you.

QUESTION: Sex in our relationship is on a serious decline. Should we be concerned, and what should we do?

As I said earlier, it is nothing short of mythical denial to think that sex becomes unimportant at any stage of an intimate relationship. For healthy couples, sex is a natural extension of a good relationship. This is one of those lifestyle patterns that we have talked about throughout the book. Low priorities get little if any time and energy. If you want a good sexual relationship, it needs to be embedded in a good overall relationship.

Make sure you understood what I just said. Sex is not the foundation of a healthy relationship; it is a natural extension of a relationship in which giving and receiving mutual support and comfort are common.

In other words, you and your partner cannot expect to have a lifestyle in which you spend an entire day or several days full of insensitivity, hostilities, inattention, and combativeness—and then hope to throw a switch and give and receive with each other through sexual intimacy. To have a fully functioning and healthy sexual relationship, relationship partners must have a substantial degree of mental, emotional, and physical trust. Sex involves vulnerability: it is an act that can flow freely only against this backdrop of trust. (As I use the term, sex is a spectrum of physical intimacies that runs from simple and superficial touching and caressing through the act of intercourse and its aftermath.)

So when people say to me they are having sexual frustrations, my first thought is that the frustration may have little, if anything, to do with sexuality itself. I suggest the couple examine its relationship at large to determine whether or not the two of them are creating a foundation or backdrop with which normal and healthy sexual intimacy is consistent.

If you expect to ignore your partner in the morning, bark at them two or three times during the day, argue with them in the evening, and then fall into their arms for a fanciful sexual adventure at night, it is no wonder you are having frustration. If, on the other hand, you and your partner are interacting in a healthful and supportive way, then sex is not a nonsequitur. It does not have to be forced. It becomes just one more way of expressing mutuality, support, and caring. Ask yourself if you are creating an environment of giving and receiving and of trust and relaxation.

In most situations and circumstances, what culminates in a healthy sexual interaction at ten-thirty on a Tuesday night might well have begun bright and early the previous Monday morning, when the two of you shared a hug that lasted just a beat longer than normal, or a kiss on the cheek, then shared a laugh sometime during the day and some casual cuddling on Monday night. Through these simple acts of caring and kindness, both partners were becoming conscious of and open to a more intimate exchange, the momentum of which began building the day before. In this situation, the sexual interaction is now the perfectly natural extension of two people who are living a pattern of caring, trusting, and comforting each other. What's more, the sexual interaction and the physical and emotional closeness that took place on that Tuesday night becomes the springboard for more thoughts and more appreciative behaviors that will bridge into the next, seemingly spontaneous, sexual interaction.

What I am talking about here is a rhythm or a pattern of sexual interaction. I hope you can see how insensitivity, inattention, and hostility make sexual intimacy highly illogical and rather unnatural. It's often been joked that sex is the most fun you can have without laughing. It may also be the most communicating you can do without speaking. You would not expect the following verbal exchange: "I hate you and everything you stand for, you've ruined my life, you no good rat bastard—and by the way, I love you dearly."

That just doesn't flow; it just doesn't fit together. That is exactly how illogical it is for you to be rude and insensitive all day and then expect to cuddle up at night. The two just don't fit together. Bottom line: if you want a rhythmic pattern of sexual intimacy, then create a relational pattern that reflects the same intimate emotions.

QUESTION: But, Dr. Phil, what if we are past that and everything between me and my partner does seem to be flowing consistently. Yet we still have either ceased to have sexual relations, or we do so only very sporadically. What's up with that?

That can happen. Oftentimes, problems occur originally for one reason and then continue or persist for a completely different set of reasons. You may well have gotten out of the pattern or habit because you are having problems, or in the later stages of pregnancy, or simply went through a very physically demanding time where one or both of you was uncommonly tired. There are times when one or both partners become distracted and allow sexual interaction to slide down the priority scale. These couples have gotten out of the sexual habit and allowed a number of competing activities and circumstances to rob them of this very special, intimate exchange.

Now, some of you might be asking, "Well, if everything else is in place—meaning trust, caring, and mutual support—then why would a pattern of sexual interaction matter?" It matters because the intimacy that comes from sexual interaction takes the relationship to a completely different level. As I said, intimate sexual interactions are a unique and powerful way of communicating, and can run much deeper than anything you can say in words. You may have many close and intimate friends in your life—people for whom you care, support, and verbally share important thoughts and feelings. But intimate sexual interaction is unique to your one primary relationship. Take that away and you rob the relationship of that uniqueness. Sex is that one special thing that you and only your partner share.

Bottom line: if you've gotten distracted and don't think about having sex, that too is habitual. To overcome this, you must consciously commit to putting it back into your life. And don't just think about it—do it. Thinking about it—having good intentions yet falling into bed too tired at night and deciding to put it off until tomorrow—will cause problems. So do it! Forget about the dishes, forget about the television, forget about the kids, don't worry about waking up the plants, just do it.

QUESTION: Well, that brings up another question, Dr. Phil. I can commit to doing it, but frankly, I don't think I'm doing it right. I don't think my partner is satisfied, and I'm not always satisfied. Maybe that's why one or both of us isn't so motivated. So what should I do?

Just as in every other area of human functioning, there are differences between men and women with regard to sex. Women, for instance, have long said, "Men are always ready and raring to go. It's all they think about; they would jump in bed at the drop of a hat." This generalization of men is completely wrong. Well, okay, it's sort of wrong. There are broad differences among men with regard to their sexual appetites. Factors such as personality, age, physical health, prior experience, and upbringing can influence their sexual patterns and preferences greatly. However, it is true that men in general have a shorter arousal cycle than do women. That fact is neither good nor bad; it just is.

But there is a problem that can emerge between a couple as a direct result of the differences in the arousal cycle. Because men are more quickly aroused than women, they are likely to become amorous and initiate sex in very short order. Women can and do become just as aroused; it just takes a little longer. Sometimes, because he doesn't understand the science of the human body, a man thinks a woman is failing to respond to him—and he's upset. Or a woman gets upset because she thinks she is not respond-

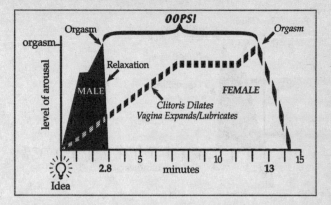

Fig. 1   Male/*Female* Sexual Arousal Pattern

ing quickly enough. The partners don't seem to be in sync. By the time the female begins to become aroused, the male may have concluded that there is a lack of interest, perhaps even decided that he has been rejected, and so withdraws.

This seeming incompatibility of arousal patterns can affect the sexual relationship, not only in the interactions prior to intercourse, but also during the actual act of sexual intercourse itself. Look at Figure 1, the physical response chart. Note that there is a timeline across the bottom of the chart divided into minutes. The male's response curve is the solid line, and the female response curve is the dotted line. Isn't it interesting that the male's sexual cycle starting at the contemplation of sex through erection, orgasm, and loss of erection lasts an average of 2.8 minutes? His response curve is almost vertical: rising up and dropping straight down very quickly. (You can insert your own joke right here if you'd like.)

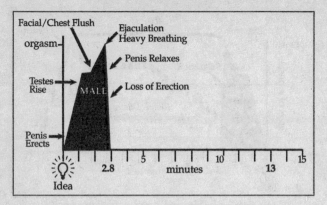

Fig. 2   Male Sexual Arousal Pattern

Contrast this to the female's response curve, which builds more gradually and then plateaus at around seven minutes. The entire cycle lasts approximately thirteen minutes. The problem is that clitoral dilation and vaginal lubrication usually do not occur until several minutes after the male's cycle is completed. Therefore, only twenty to thirty percent of women climax during intercourse, largely because "Mr. Quick on the trigger" is long gone before her physiology has a chance to gear up.

Clearly, you can do the math as well as I can. If the male's cycle lasts 2.8 minutes and the female's cycle lasts thirteen minutes, then we have about a ten-minute gap in compatibility here. Women, underline this portion for your partner. This ten-minute gap between the peak in the male cycle and peak in the female cycle is what foreplay is all about. Guys, "Brace yourself, darling" is not foreplay, even if you are from Texas and it takes you ten minutes to say it.

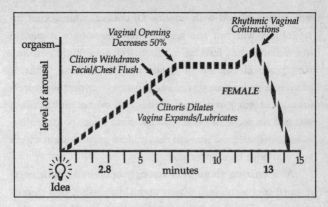

Fig. 3   *Female* Sexual Arousal Pattern

For something to qualify as foreplay, it has to be arousing. By the way, that means arousing for her. Remember part of our formula: a good relationship means the needs of the two people involved are met. That is true of the sexual relationship as well.

In the area of sexuality, just as in every other area of human functioning, knowledge is power. Use this knowledge to make your sexual relationship more compatible and rewarding for you and your partner as well. So that you more fully understand the physiology behind male and female responses during sexual intercourse, I have included Figures 2 and 3 for a more detailed breakdown of the male and female response patterns respectively. Study these so you will understand how your partner's body works. By understanding the behavioral, emotional, and physical aspects of sexuality, I suspect you will generate better results.

The bottom line to a good sexual relationship is to have

sex, regularly and with quality. Of course, your sexual interactions will run the gamut from passionate romantic lovemaking that lasts all night to the seemingly perfunctory physical release of unadorned intercourse. That is okay, just as long as you're sensitive to your partner's preferences at any given time. By being sensitive and flexible, you will do some of both, and also find many points in between. Oftentimes, you will find middle ground upon which you can both be comfortable.

As a parting thought, I strongly encourage both partners to overcome inhibitions about discussing this important part of their relationship. You can greatly help your sexual relationship in general and your partner in particular if you communicate to him or her what your thoughts, feelings, and preferences are. Even though it may seem awkward at first, push ahead and have a good and open discussion. It is even okay to giggle and be embarrassed as long as you have the discussion. And remember, if you want a good sexual relationship, you have to do it instead of thinking about it.

QUESTION: Dr. Phil, you've told me that it's okay to argue, that it's fine to be confrontational when necessary—but that I must do it without being cruel or vicious or humiliating. That's a tough chore. Are there any good rules for fighting with your partner?

As I said earlier, whether you have arguments is not what determines the long-term success or failure of your relationship. It's how you argue and more important, it's how you end it. Disagreements and the arguments associated with those disagreements are inevitable. They can be okay and in fact constructive if done properly. Before we get to the rules, understand a primary requirement: maintain control. Because it is okay to argue within a relationship does not mean that you have license to be childish, abusive, or immature. It means that if you have legitimate feelings, you are entitled to give a reasonable voice to those feelings. To do this in a constructive way means that you have to require certain things of yourself that you may not have required in the past. A good place to start in exercising that control is not to take yourself so damn seriously. In the give-and-take of a relationship, self-righteousness is seldom appropriate and is typically unjustified. Have your disagreements, but lighten up and recognize that every irritation does not call for a federal indictment or the weeping of angels.

So here are some specific rules of engagement. Follow them and you might just find that your differences of opinion can actually lead to some constructive changes in your relationship.

RULE ONE: TAKE IT PRIVATE AND KEEP IT PRIVATE.

If there are children involved in your relationship, whether you are married or not, do not fight in front of your children. I repeat, do not fight in front of your children. To do so is nothing short of child abuse. To fight in front of your children can and will scar them emotionally, all because you don't have the self-control to contain yourself until you and your partner can take it private. Fighting in front of children will scar them emotionally to the point that it changes who they are.

Children look to their parents as their solid and safe base of operations. When they are subjected to open hostility and fighting between the two people that they rely on for their personal security and safety, that base is shaken to its absolute core. They begin to experience insecurity and have fears about the disintegration of their family unit. They often blame themselves for the argument, whatever its content, and take on the burden of both of the partners' pain. Moreover, the children are typically not around for the reconciliation. Therefore, they get the exposure of all of the trials and tribulations without the benefit of any of the peacemaking. It shakes them to the core and erodes their self-esteem and confidence in their own social situations. In particularly volatile homes children are afraid even to bring their friends home for fear they will be embarrassed by the open and uncontrolled hostilities. If you are going to have disagreements, and you are, don't make your innocent children pick up the tab.

RULE TWO: KEEP IT RELEVANT.

If you and your partner just have to have it out over some particular problem or subject matter, you need to put hard boundaries down around the subject matter. Specifically, if you are going to have a fight about one partner's mother, then require yourself to stay with that specific subject matter. In other words, if fifteen minutes into the disagreement you are now talking about the other partner's mother or one of your "idiot" in-laws, you have gotten outside the boundary lines.

So often fights deteriorate into a free-for-all, so much so that it becomes totally inefficient and no progress is made and nothing gets resolved. Ask yourself and your partner, "What are we fighting about?" and when you get the answer, stay with it. You may even have to say to your partner, "We are getting off the subject here. We said we were fighting about your mother. Let's stay with that. We can talk about other things some other time, but let's stay on the subject." Stay on the subject or you will be having this fight again, because you will not get said what it is you feel you need to say.

A common distraction that will take you outside the boundaries is spawned by defensiveness and personalization. It's easy to start out with a "Hey, you want a piece of me, just come and get it" attitude. But when comments start to sting or get a little too close to home, it's not nearly as much fun. If you can't stand the heat, don't get in the kitchen. If you do get in the kitchen, stay the course.

RULE THREE: KEEP IT REAL.

As I alluded to earlier, it is real easy to be an "emotional chicken." Because most disagreements do in fact boil down to some type of perceived acceptance or rejection of one partner or the other, it can seem much safer and easier to pick some meaningless symptom to fight about rather than mustering the courage to deal with the underlying issue. For example, it is much easier to attack your partner for spending too much time with friends or watching television than it is to broach the real issue, which is "I feel rejected because you choose to spend free time with someone other than me." Resolve that if you are going to go through the pain and energy of an overt disagreement, you are at least going to deal with what really is at issue. This of course requires that you become honest enough with yourself to get in touch with what really matters.

There is nothing more foolish and inefficient than to go to all of the trouble of having the fight and never really address the issue. Get real about what is bothering you, or you will come away from the exchange feeling even more frustrated. Here's a hint: remember that anger is nothing more than a symptom of an underlying hurt, fear, or frustration. If what you are arguing about is anger-driven, one of you has not gotten real about what is truly going on. Challenge yourself to have the courage to give your true feelings a voice.

RULE FOUR: AVOID CHARACTER ASSASSINATION.

Hiding behind substitute benign topics is only one of the ways to play it safe and avoid what is really at issue. Another safe but equally destructive strategy is to attack your partner personally. You must remain focused on the issue rather than deteriorate to the point of attacking your partner's worth and self-esteem. If your tone becomes vicious or sarcastic and your focus becomes the criticism of your partner as a person, at the expense of the issue, you will predictably invoke defensive and retaliatory responses. There are many things in a relationship about which reasonable folks can differ. Your partner is not wrong because he or she doesn't agree with you. Your partner has not ceased to be worthy of being treated with dignity and respect because of some conduct with which you take issue. I know you have heard your own parents tell you that it is your behavior they are angry about, not you. It's true—and it should be true in your relationship. Even if you do not like the conduct of your partner, refuse to allow yourself to deteriorate to the point of attacking him or her personally.

Comments that begin with the following phrases should be absolutely taboo:

> Well, what about you . . .
> Well, I suppose you think you . . .
> You make me sick with your holier-than-thou . . .
> What makes you think you are so . . .

RULE FIVE: REMAIN TASK-ORIENTED.

Know what you want going into the disagreement or fight. Do not allow yourself to become circular and argumentative with your partner because you don't have a goal in mind. If you are going through the pain and turmoil of an argument, at least know where the finish line is in your own mind. Decide what it is that you want, because it may be more readily attainable than you think. The problem is often that people do not know where they are trying to get, and therefore may not recognize when they have achieved their goal. Know what you want so you recognize it when you have it.

If you get what you want, accept it. You may not be through being angry yet, but if what you want, for example, is an apology and you get it, then accept it. Don't just keep railing on and dog-piling your partner because they gave you what you wanted too quickly.

RULE SIX: ALLOW FOR YOUR PARTNER TO RETREAT WITH DIGNITY.

How you stop fighting is at least as important as how you fight and what you fight about. If your relationship is built on friendship, at some point in most disagreements one partner will extend an olive branch in an attempt to de-escalate or defuse the hostilities. How you respond to that can determine the outcome of not only that disagreement but your entire relationship as well. By reconnecting through the acceptance of your partner's efforts to de-escalate the problem, you send an important validating message that says, "We are okay here; we can disagree and still be okay."

Incidentally, be careful to recognize when the olive branch is being extended to you. It can take many forms, including apology, humor, partial acknowledgment of your point of view, or a change of subject to something less relevant but emotionally charged. To ensure that you are approaching your disagreements in a win/win scenario, make sure that no matter how right you are, you remain determined to give your partner a face-saving way out of the disagreement. Allow him or her to retreat with dignity. This show of class on your part will be greatly appreciated and endear you in a meaningful and needed way.

This is particularly important whenever you are on the right side of the facts in the disagreement. If your partner is clearly wrong, be merciful, accepting, and gracious. More often than not, since most areas of conflict will never be resolved, you will both just vent for a while and then move on. How you put things back together at the end of a disagreement is unbelievably important. By the message you send or the receptivity you show to your partner's message, you can ensure that both you and your partner survive the dispute with self- esteem and security intact.

RULE SEVEN: BE PROPORTIONAL IN YOUR INTENSITY.

Once again, for God's sakes, lighten up. Every single thing you disagree about is not an earth-shattering event or issue. You do not have to be mad every time you have the right to be. Asserting yourself is an option, not a requirement. Sometimes you can even state your complaint and not call for or require a response. I am not suggesting that you be passive or stuff your feelings, but I am saying that there is virtue in overlooking certain imperfections. Your partner will appreciate it if you let them off when they know you could have made a bigger issue out of it. Stay in control and remain proportional in your emotionality. Don't make a big deal out of everything.

QUESTION: How do I deal with drug and alcohol abuse in my relationship?

Deal breakers! Absolute, drop-dead, zero-tolerance deal breakers. Let me remind you of the obvious: drugs and alcohol are substances that, if abused, create an altered state of consciousness. When you are dealing with a drug- or alcohol-controlled partner, you are dealing with the drug or the alcohol, not with the partner. When someone succumbs to the addictive control of drugs or alcohol, he or she has given up the dignity of conscious choice and is now a passenger on a runaway train that will run right over you if you stand in its way. People addicted to drugs or alcohol are not the people you think they are or the people you want them to be. The addiction changes them and suspends their logic, values, and integrity.

I know that I am being intolerant here—but I intend to

be. I very much want to influence you to draw a line in the sand that says, "I will not live in a relationship with a partner who is addicted to drugs or alcohol." I cannot tell you how many relationships I have seen destroyed in the twenty-five years that I have worked in the field of human behavior. I cannot describe to you how many tears have been shed and years lost by partners who are deluded by the rationales and justifications of drug- or alcohol-addicted partners maintaining that they can handle it or that they don't really have a problem. So many of these relationships were destroyed because the non-addicted partner did not have the courage to draw that line in the sand and say, "I will not live in this toxic hell." So often, had that partner been strong in their resolve, the addicted partner might well have been forced to deal with the self-destructive realities of his or her addiction before they destroyed themselves and their relationship.

If you sincerely believe that your partner is a substance abuser, I recommend that you get immediate professional consultation to confirm your suspicions. If in fact your fears are confirmed, I further recommend that you confront your partner in a loving, caring, but unambiguously firm fashion in which you require him or her to get immediate and ongoing professional help. Persist until your partner goes—and if he or she resists, then that is a deal breaker. You must be prepared to leave your relationship until such a time when your partner can objectively verify to you that the problem is under control and that he or she is in a program of ongoing monitoring and treatment. Your partner must understand with absolute clarity that you will not remain in a relationship with them as long as there is substance abuse. There are no exceptions and there is no wiggle room. Be strong in your resolve. You may well be saving more lives than your own.

Understand that when I say there are no exceptions and there are no mitigating circumstances, I mean none. Lack of funds is no excuse. Nonprofit organizations for drug and alcohol abuse are available and have wonderful programs. State, county, and federally funded programs through community mental health and state mental health and mental retardation outreach clinics all accept patients with fees determined by the ability to pay. **(See the Appendix for addresses and phone numbers of government agencies.)** All of these programs cost much less than what your addicted partner is spending on alcohol or drugs. Most employers have health insurance or employee assistance programs that will also help. The financial dodge is the most common resistance that addicts and alcoholics seek to hide behind—and it is the most absurd one.

I understand that lots of people want to be forgiving of an abuser because of the fact that drug and alcohol abuse may be genetically predisposed and is a "disease" that should be treated with care and passion. As a professional with years of experience in the field of behavioral medicine, I strongly suspect that I can make that argument as well if not better than most. It does not matter. Why someone destroys your life doesn't change the fact that it's destroyed. The fact that alcoholism might be a disease does not give you back one scintilla of your life. The fact that it is a disease does not lessen the need for intervention and, in fact, may call for even greater urgency. Every disease, or at least its treatment, involves an element of personal choice. By forcing treatment, you require your partner to exercise that choice. That is a gift.

Love your partner from afar, forgive your partner in your heart, attend your partner's treatment sessions—but don't live with them. You deserve better. When you demand it, you will get it and not a second before.

One final thing: if there are children involved, then underline everything I have just said. If you don't have the courage to protect them, then they are at the mercy of the drug and alcohol abuse. Don't you dare even consider giving in to your trepidation of confronting the situation because you are the only thing that stands between those children and a destroyed life.

QUESTION: What about physical abuse?

As strongly as I feel about drug and alcohol abuse being a deal breaker, I feel even stronger about the unacceptability of physical abuse. Let me tell you straight up: if you are in a relationship with a pattern of physical abuse, you need to get out and get out right now.

There are no justifications, there are no excuses, and there are no apologies that will undo physical abuse to you or your children. I am speaking to men and women alike here. There are a surprising number of battered men in America, although it is clearly a fraction of the number of battered women. Either way, this is a deal breaker of the highest order. Everything I said above with regard to drug and alcohol abuse applies here. I will not repeat it other than to summarize and say that if this is part of your relationship, you don't have a relationship. Emotional abuse and mental abuse are bad enough. But when someone violates your person, they have crossed a line that must be zero-tolerance. If you or your children are being subjected to physical abuse of any sort, you or your partner need to find another place to be right now.

Again, there are no excuses. There are resources available to protect you and your children. Whether it is private funds and family support or governmental agencies, find the resources and protect your life and that of your children. Again, you must remember that children are passengers. They have no ability to fend for themselves in this situation. Do not live one more day with physical abuse. **(Agencies and resources are listed in the Appendix along with the drug- and alcohol-support options.)**

If this is your situation and you heed my advice and take action, be firm in your commitment. If you have lived in this situation for any period of time, you know that it is cyclical. The pattern is typically abuse followed by guilt and promises of no further abuse. Abusers can seem so totally rational outside of the episodes of physical violation. They can seem pathetic, pitiful, and truly sorry. But remember, the best predictor of future behavior is relevant past behavior. One of you needs to get out and stay out until competent, professional help objectively advises you that it is safe to live under the same roof again.

Take me seriously here. The statistics on domestic violence are staggering, and the number of child and spousal murders is escalating at an alarming rate. Don't feel that you are overdramatizing, and as a result underreact. Act immediately and act definitively. Do not listen to excuses and do not blame yourself for provoking your partner. You may well be doing that, and if so, that's dumb, really dumb. But it does not justify physical attacks on you or your children.

QUESTION: How do I deal with mental and emotional illness in the relationship?

The term mental and emotional illness is a common term that I interpret to cover a broad spectrum ranging from harmless quirks or idiosyncrasies on one hand to life-threatening psychoses on the other. Individual quirks and idiosyncrasies, while sometimes inconvenient, are not the stuff of which relationship deterioration is made. A good yardstick that I have recommended to laypeople for years is to ask yourself whether or not the questionable thought or behavioral patterns interfere with functionality. If an individual or couple is continuing to function well—and therefore the questionable behavior is not interfering with his or her quality or enjoyment of life—then it is my opinion that to consider professional intervention may be appropriate but is probably much less urgent.

If, on the other hand, the questionable behavior has risen to the level of interfering with the quality of individual or relational life, then perhaps that behavior is worthy of more focused intervention. The question I recommend asking is: "Is this creating a problem for either or both of us?" If it is, then something needs to be changed. If it is not, my attitude is "Don't fix what ain't broke."

If you have determined that the behavior is more serious than what I have just described, then you must deal with a different set of questions. I will share with you the thought process that I always went through during the years that I worked as a professional psychologist. My first consideration, any time an individual or concerned family member speaking on behalf of another individual presented a problem or complaint, was to determine whether or not the problem or complaint constituted a threat to the individual or others. If I determined that it did pose a threat to the safety of the patient or others, I determined that that patient was a candidate for in-patient, closely supervised care rather than out-patient interim care. I recommend that be your first consideration as well.

I realize that I may be speaking here to a reader concerned about a relational partner or to a reader concerned about his or her own emotional problems. If it is you I am speaking to, do not be arrogant about your ability to handle something that has you scared or in denial. Its severity may in fact be more than you can handle on your own. My advice is, get help. Whether you are dealing with a simple phobia, a measure of depression, or some severely disruptive interference with your thinking and reasoning, get help. Both medication and therapy have proven to be highly effective in managing and/or eliminating even some of the most severe disorders. But physicians and psychologists cannot heal whom they don't see. Do not deny yourself or your relational partner the chance for a happy, well-adjusted life.

Because of the alarming increase in frequency of depression, I feel that I must address it and the frequently associated suicidal ideation. Suicide among all age groups is a major problem in America, as well as in a number of other countries. What most people do not realize is that roughly half of all suicidal deaths are later determined to have been accidental. That is, the deceased did not really intend to die, but in fact was making a suicidal gesture for manipulative reasons or as a desperate cry for help. In those accidental suicides, the victim simply miscalculated the danger of the drugs, gas, or other means of self-destruction, and wound up tragically and unintentionally dead. The other half took their own life and fully intended to do so.

If you or your relational partner is experiencing suicidal thoughts, they must be taken seriously and should involve professional help immediately.

It is a myth that those who talk about suicide don't really do it. Nothing could be further from the truth. If you think it is scary to admit that this kind of problem is a reality in your relationship and you are tempted to slip into denial rather than face the ugly truth, don't do it. Facing professional intervention is nothing compared to the reality of dealing with a suicidal aftermath, whether it is you dealing with a lost partner or a partner dealing with the loss of you.

I became involved in the aftermath of a tragic situation that brought this home clearly to me a number of years ago. An executive for a major company with whom I was consulting in Miami, Florida, presented himself in my Dallas office one Friday morning totally unannounced and clearly distraught. Hal sat down and mechanically related a story of great concern. He told me that his wife, Kim, had been depressed for a number of months but had refused to get professional help. Hal, currently the president of a very large multinational company, was on the short list of candidates to be promoted to chairman of the board. Hal told me that if it came to light that his wife was in some "nut house" (his term, not mine), it would ruin his chances of promotion. He revealed to me that she had frequently been up late at night, wandering through the house, unable to sleep. She had told him on a number of occasions that she felt as though he and the children would be better off if she were dead. He went on to say that he knew that she loved her children dearly and therefore would never do anything "like that." He also took comfort in the belief that people who talk about suicide don't really do it.

After considerable counsel, I convinced Hal that he could not be more wrong. I convinced him that he needed to get his wife to a professional psychologist or psychiatrist in Miami immediately. He said that his wife was taking their two children, girls age nine and seven, to camp that day for a two-week stay. As his mind began to work, he concluded that this would be a perfect time to really focus on Kim's problems and try to get her some help.

With new resolve and conviction, he climbed back aboard his private jet and returned to Miami. Not wanting to waste another minute, he went straight from the airport to his home, arriving there at about four in the afternoon. When he entered the house, music was playing and he could smell a fresh pot of coffee in the kitchen. When he entered the kitchen he saw a note beside the coffeepot. It read: "Hal, I made you a pot of coffee. You need to call 911 and then call Bob and Sharon. Please do not come in the backyard. I love you and the girls. Try not to hate me. Goodbye, Kim."

In complete shock and panic, Hal ran into the backyard and found Kim's body. She had carefully and tightly wrapped her head in a towel, lay down by the side of the house, and shot herself in the temple with a .357 Magnum. She defied every myth of suicide. She talked about it before she did it. She used a gun, which women supposedly do not do. She had no prior attempts, and she had everything in the world to live for. And today Hal and the two girls remain completely devastated.

The moral of the story is clear: if you are dealing with a

serious mental and emotional illness in your relationship, get professional help and get it now.

QUESTION: You have said that both partners either contaminate or contribute to the relationship. What if I have terrible and debilitating baggage that I have brought with me into this relationship? Doesn't that mean that I am a contaminator?

The answer to your question is yes. If you have in some way been emotionally scarred prior to entering this relationship and those scars remain unhealed, you are a contaminator—inadvertent and unintentional, but a contaminator nonetheless. Perhaps you were scarred as a child by sexual molestation, or physical abuse that changed your ability to freely participate in an intimate relationship. Perhaps you were deeply hurt in a prior relationship or marriage and carry pain and fear from that relationship. Perhaps you had a painful and combative relationship with your opposite-sexed parent that makes it difficult for you to relate freely to a relational partner. Whatever the cause, if you have been scarred emotionally, that experience changes who you are and how you relate within your current relationship.

In truth, you cannot give away what you do not have. If you do not have a clean, pure, and unencumbered love in your heart, then you cannot give it away. Don't delude yourself that you can effectively compartmentalize that emotional pain and keep it from infecting your relationship. It takes too much energy to keep it contained. It is constantly there, constantly fighting to bubble out and contaminate your relationship. The very fact that so much of your relational energy must be devoted to containment of your pain changes who you are.

Not a very pretty or hopeful picture, I admit. However, that picture only shows where you are now, not where you can be in this relationship. Denial or suppression of feelings and problems do nothing to help your situation. You cannot help yourself or your relationship by suffering in silence or hiding who and what defines you. You must be willing to take the risk of disclosure in enlisting the aid of those who love and care about you. If, for example, you were raped or sexually abused as a child, and that has understandably affected your feelings of self-worth and your ability to have an intimate relationship with your partner, then you must know that cannot be good for your relationship. By disclosing the problems and challenges you face rather than succumbing to the fear of judgment, you give yourself a chance for success.

The good and bad news is that you are accountable. It's bad news because no one can fix it for you, and good news because that means that you have the accessibility you need to fix the problem. I know that it sounds strange to suggest that people are accountable for what happened to them as a child—so let me be clear. I am not suggesting that child had even one-tenth of one percent of any accountability for what happened during childhood. That child was a victim of a sick and evil force. But as an adult, that grown child has responsibility for what he or she does about the aftermath of those tragic events of childhood. That grown child can now choose to escape from that prison and walk out seeking help and healing. No one can do it for them, but they can do it for themselves. Accountability as a grown person is undeniable.

Do not continue to silently suffer and thereby unintentionally but undeniably contaminate your relationship.

Disclose to those you trust and seek help from those who can render it. You are worth it. Reaching out for that help can be your first step to proving your worth.

QUESTION: What should I do about God in my relationship with my partner?

I believe that I have the responsibility to disclose to you when I am including personal opinion in my writings as opposed to restricting myself to more objective research, observation, or experience. Now is one of those times. While I have substantial experience with the role of God in relationships, I must tell you that I am not totally objective here because I have strong personal feelings on this issue. I do not seek to impose my personal beliefs on you, but I do want to share what I believe is undeniably true.

Each person's relationship with God is and should be very personal. My personal belief is that there is a higher power in this universe, a higher power that I call God. If you do not share my belief, then perhaps you will read this section for general interest. If you do share my belief, in whole or even in small part, then I suspect you will find specific value in this section.

I believe that God has a plan for each and every one of us. I believe his plan is reflected in a number of ways. First and foremost is the fact that we are even here. But beyond that, I believe his plan is reflected in the specific gifts and talents that he bestows on each of us. I believe that he chooses each of us to be strong in certain areas so that we have the opportunity to use those gifts in His service. I also believe very strongly in free will. I believe that we are given the gifts, and it is up to us whether or not we use them in God's service and for the good of those in our lives. I further believe that as part of God's overall plan for our lives, He provides for us a mate, through which He meets a number of our needs and inspires in us certain qualities and talents that are important.

Understand that this says a lot about your relationship with your partner. Because I believe that God knows you, I also believe that special provision is there for you. For that reason I do not believe that you can reject and criticize your mate and at the same time accept God and his will for your life. By rejecting and criticizing your mate, you are basically saying, "God, I know better than you. You gave me the wrong mate with the wrong characteristics. That is not what I need, so I am going to change my partner to be what I think I need instead of being what you think I need." I believe this so strongly that I even recognize that there is divine purpose in your mate's flaws and fallacies. It is your job to find what that divine purpose is, but I believe that your partner may well be weak where you are strong, and have flaws and fallacies that inspire the best of who you are. I believe that these flaws and fallacies can create a situation in which you are needed rather than just convenient.

I also believe that there are profound teachings about relationships in the Bible. I am keenly aware that there are those of you reading this book who do not believe in God, Jesus Christ, or the Bible. That does not mean that there is not value in what I am pointing out. Whether you believe that the Bible is the good book, or you just believe that it is a good book, you have to at least acknowledge that it is profound, and that it is the number one best-seller in the history of mankind. I have already told you that I believe it is "the" good book, so I am going to share with you some specific passages for you to consider and dwell upon. I trust that whether or not you believe, as do I, that these passages are divine in inspiration, I do think you'll agree that they are at least wise counsel.

At the very least, you should know that one of the best descriptions of love—the rare kind of self-transcending love that we should all aspire to—comes from I Corinthians 13:4: "Love is patient, love is kind. It does not envy, it does not boast, it is not proud. It is not rude, it keeps no record of wrongs. Love does not delight in evil but rejoices with the truth. It always protects, always trusts, always hopes, always preserves. Love never fails." Read that again, particularly "Love never fails." The plan is for your relationship to work.

Here are some other examples that might inspire you:

THE BIBLE ON SEX
I Corinthians 7:3–5 (NIV)

The husband should fulfill his marital duty to his wife, and likewise the wife to her husband. The wife's body does not belong to her alone but also to her husband. In the same way, the husband's body does not belong to him alone but also to his wife. Do not deprive each other except by mutual consent and for a time, so that you may devote yourselves to prayer.

THE BIBLE ON LOVE
Ephesians 4:2 (Living Bible)

Be humble and gentle. Be patient with each other. Make allowance for each other's faults because of your love.

THE BIBLE ON THE VALUE OF MAN AND WOMAN
I Corinthians 11:11 (NIV)

In the Lord, however, woman is not independent of man, nor is man independent of woman. For as woman came from man, so also man is born of woman. But everything comes from God.

THE BIBLE ON FORGIVENESS IN A RELATIONSHIP
Colossians 3:12–14 (NIV)

. . . clothe yourselves with compassion, kindness, humility, gentleness, and patience. Bear with each other and forgive whatever grievances you may have against one another. Forgive as the Lord forgave you.

THE BIBLE ON FIGHTING
Ephesians 4:31–32 (NIV)

Get rid of all bitterness, rage, and anger, brawling and slander, along with every form of malice. Be kind and compassionate to one another, forgiving each other, just as in Christ God forgave you.

Just as I have acknowledged your right to share my view or not, you too should allow your partner their own independent personal beliefs about their spirituality. Some partners will be very open and candid about their beliefs, while some will feel that it is highly personal and not to be intruded upon by another. Meet them where they are and respect their point of view. Please know that I also believe that there is a substantial difference between a spiritual person and a religious person. A religious person may be quite spiritual, but a spiritual person may not be at all religious. Everyone has their own way of being, and I'll bet that with the spirit of compassion and acceptance that we have long discussed, you and your partner will find common ground that works for both of you.

I have seen tremendous relational victories claimed in the name of God, and I have seen damage and destruction justified by hypocrites claiming God's endorsement and power. In fact, I have seen just about as much of the latter as I have the former. That is not God's fault; it is ours. I have long said that I love the Lord, it's Christians that I can't stand. I say that only partially tongue in cheek because of the damage and destroyed lives I have witnessed by "Christians" self-righteously judging others and calling it godly. But I have also seen sincerely God-centered relationships withstand all manner of attack and challenge. In fact, an interesting statistic shared by David McLaughlin in his wonderful series entitled *The Role of the Man in the Family* reflects that the divorce rate in America is at a minimum one out of two marriages. But the reported divorce rate among couples that pray together is about one in ten thousand. Pretty impressive statistic, even if you reduce it a thousand-fold.

Personally, I sincerely hope that you have God in your relationship in whatever way works for you. If you do not, that is okay with me; I am confident that your sincere heart and hard work will serve you well.

QUESTION: Is there a point at which you have to admit that it is just not going to work, cut your losses, and walk away?

My answer is yes. If the relationship we are talking about is a marriage, I know that many Christian leaders would disagree. I confess that I am not nearly spiritually mature enough to believe that. Easy examples of when that kind of decision is justified in my mind, and in fact mandated, are found when the relationship is infected with physical abuse or drug and alcohol addiction and the partner refuses to acknowledge the problem or to make a sincere effort to get help. The harder call comes when all of the problems are matters of choice and personality. The harder call comes when both partners seem to want to make the relationship work, but just can't get there. I have two major thoughts that may help you in your decision-making process.

First, do not ever make life-changing decisions in the midst of emotional turmoil. When feelings are running high and language and rhetoric even higher, this is not a time to make decisions that will affect your life and that of your partner and children, if any are involved. Never be in a hurry when making decisions, the consequences of which will be around for a long time.

If you are riding an emotional roller coaster, get on flat ground so you can take a rational and objective look at things before you start making life-changing decisions. Hopefully, the process of this book has flattened out your roller coaster enough to give you a better perspective on where you are.

My second belief about getting out of a relationship is: If you are going to quit, you earn the right to quit. You don't just get mad; you don't just get your feelings hurt and decide to bail out. You earn the right to quit. Until you can look yourself in the eye in the mirror, until you can look your children in the eye and say I did everything I could to save this relationship and it could not be done, then you have not earned the right to quit. Arrogant as it may sound, until you have done everything I outline in this book, then I don't think you have earned the right to quit. You have to go through this process first, and if at the end of that process you can say, "All right, Doc, I did it all and it is not going to work," then you have to make a decision at that point.

I don't think you ever save a relationship by sacrificing yourself. That is not saving; that is simply trading prisoners of war. You may want to nobly say, "I am willing to give myself up for the relationship." But I feel about that like Patton did about war. He said, "I don't want to hear any of this crap coming in from the battlefield about good men dying for their country." He said, "Let them other sons of bitches die for their country. That is not my idea of victory, trading lives for ground." Similarly, I don't want you going out there and saying, "I will let my spirit die for this relationship." I don't want you to say, "I will give up my hopes, my dreams, my dignity, my purpose, my spirit in order to fold myself into this relationship." That is not victory. One entity may live and another entity dies. That is not progress.

Trust me, if that is your approach, the relationship is not really living. It is just living on the spirit of one part of the relationship. That is a parasitic existence at your expense. You know that that will not work long-term. Work hard to save your relationship. You deserve the effort, but I acknowledge that the day may come when you have a difficult decision to make.

I hope I have covered some of your questions. I knew that no matter how many subjects I included, I would never cover everything because I know how creative you guys can be. I must say, however, that with the tools and concepts you have acquired in working through this book and your ability to tap into your core of consciousness, I believe that you now have the ability to find the answers that you need. When necessary, take a step back from your problems and challenges, and look back through the book and your journal for answers and guidance. Remember that you have within you the answers to every question you have or will ever have. Your task is to tap into that core of consciousness and have the courage to live the truth.

A Personal Letter
from Me to You

To My Women Readers,

I conclude this book with a candid and personal letter from my heart to yours. Like the magician that lets you see behind the curtain, I want to tell you a few honest but seldom acknowledged truths about life and relationships from at least one male's perspective. I'm not saying that what I'm going to tell you in any way makes the conduct okay or desirable, or that it necessarily represents the profile or viewpoint of all males, but I do think my makeup and evolution over the years has been pretty typical and probably reflects what you are dealing with.

First: Speaking personally and to blow the whistle on my brethren, *we men don't get it!* We want to get it and we sometimes think we get it, but we don't. It doesn't matter why we don't, so I won't give you some victim story about how we've been programmed wrong and why it's not our fault. It doesn't matter why; what matters is that we just don't get it. The really stupid stuff we do and, more important, don't do, comes from ignorance and from what I'm sure would seem to you to be a bizarre set of priorities that we are so welded to that they can dominate and define us.

For example, we oftentimes measure success very narrowly and almost always from a huge financial perspective. We take pride in protecting and providing for our families, and we bear private shame when we feel that we have failed. We can become so tunnel-visioned and obsessed that we forget or ignore that you need so much more. We lose sight of the reality that you need love, support, interest, and caring. This caveman mentality can render us blind to your pain, your loneliness, and your needs. In short, we can be incredibly selfish. Men really do want Betty Crocker in the kitchen and a sex kitten in the bedroom. And we want it all after you get home from work, and all without any expense. We measure you against mom and expect you to put us first, but we haven't a clue how to reciprocate in ways that matter to *you*. Our egos are fragile, and when the world seems to turn hostile, we do our turtle routine, shut down, pull inside ourselves, and aim the brunt of our frustrations at you. We want your help, but we then criticize and nitpick at you if it is offered, especially if you are right.

We may not get it, at least not in the way you wish we would. But that doesn't mean that in our own fumbling, bumbling way that we don't care. We feel, hurt, and need just as urgently and deeply as you do. We act tough and hide our emotions. It may be true that big boys don't cry, but let me assure you, men do. Our tears may be silent and run down the inside rather than the outside of our cheeks, but we do have deep feelings—and deeper needs. When we seek to control by intimidation, it is to hide fear and doubt. When we bluster, it is because of our frustration with ourselves. When we criticize and belittle, it comes from a false sense of superiority, designed to disguise a wounded ego. Please do not be put off by our contradictory "foreign language."

Bottom line: we want and need for you to see through our "macho mask." We need you to reach behind it, take our hands, and press them to the warmth of your heart.

Truth two: I'm not just trying to con you and make you feel better about the future of your relationship when you are dealing with a partner who will not get in the game. You really can make a huge, huge difference in the quality and course of your relationship, even without the active and conscious participation of your male partner.

I am living proof. I have been successfully and happily married for twenty-three years because my wife, Robin, would not have it any other way. Our marriage has at times succeeded not because of but in spite of me. In those twenty-three years I found and tried out every bad habit and insensitivity imaginable, and a few that were unimaginable. The immaturity and insensitivity with which I entered this marriage should have spelled its doom. But she would not permit it. My obsessive, workaholic lifestyle should have created a vast chasm. She would not hear of it. I have committed innumerable acts of idiocy, forgotten key events and commitments, said things I didn't mean and omitted things I did mean, and should have said. There have been times that she had me dead to rights and showed the class and restraint to let it go. She chose not to confront and make issues out of my fallibilities, and chose instead to focus on my better qualities and the values of our family. She has loved me when I was anything but lovable and stood by me when, but for her, I would have been standing totally and at times deservedly alone. She made our marriage and me as her husband a success when it truly would have been easier not to. And she did it without my help and active participation. So can you.

Our marriage is a flesh-and-blood example of the fact that with persistence and caring, one partner can inspire and bring out the best in the other. I have not always been a tuned-in and caring husband, but she has brought out the best in me and I am way, way better at being a partner because of it.

I'm not sure that I deserved the commitment and your mate may not deserve it either, but I'm pretty sure you do. Don't give up on us in general and don't give up on him in particular. Use what you've learned here and become part of the movement to start changing this world, one life and one relationship at a time, beginning with yours.

To My Men Readers,

I'm assuming that this letter is the first thing you're reading in this book. Either way, give me three minutes to talk to you man to man. If your partner has asked you to read this letter, it is because she loves you and cares about your relationship, so don't turn into some hardheaded mouth breather who resists because she thought of it or because you might have to expose yourself emotionally.

I don't know what your particular situation is, but if the lady in your life went to the trouble to get in the car, drive to the store, go inside and pay the money to buy this book, you could be in a lot of trouble, buddy. If you bought this book yourself, good for you. Either way, I want to give you a wake-up call here. This book is not some feminist-mentality witch hunt designed to give her ammunition to fry your ass and blame you for what isn't working in this relationship. And it sure is not some touchy-feely, poetic approach to getting you on a blanket in the park talking about your feelings. There is a plan here. A plan that cuts to the chase, deals with reality, and generates results. You get to focus on what you want and what you think is important right along with what she thinks matters. Here's the kicker: she will not only hear what you have to say, but will actively find out your needs and desires with a serious commitment to not get her feelings hurt.

Now, you can stonewall her. You can continue to blame her for whatever has happened in your relationship. But in the end, that dog won't hunt—and you know it. Is it really worth it to continue trying to get through life ignoring your own gnawing sense of dissatisfaction? Is it worth it to avoid a chance at happiness because you are so proud and because you hate to admit you've got a lot of improvements to make? I know exactly where you are. I've been in that place myself many, many times. But I promise you, you can use this book not only to find out how you went off course in your life and in your relationship, but to find out how to get yourself out of that ditch. And the book will do it without making you feel like a sap. You won't lose your manhood if your read this book. You'll probably rediscover it.

You deserve a peaceful, happy, mutually rewarding relationship that includes fun, support, sex and intimacy, companionship and freedom. Read this book, do the work, and you won't believe how your life will change. I strongly believe you will never have more help or a better chance to put your relationship on track than you do right now.

It's not too late, but it can sure get that way if you fail to take action. I don't want you to blow this. As the old saying goes: "Ain't that always the way, you never know what you got till it's gone."

A FINAL WORD

Well, there you have it: the tools and clarity necessary to create what you want and deserve in your relationship. You've heard me say throughout this book that the best predictor of future behavior is relevant past behavior. That's your big burden; that's your great obstacle at this point in your journey. Your patterns and habits of thinking, feeling, and behaving are still so ingrained as to have become automatic. The flow of life in general, and your lifestyle in particular, will conspire to suck you back into the tired, aloof, and unproductive relationship lifestyle that you have worked so hard to escape. But you now know that you can win if you immerse yourself in all that resides in your core of consciousness. Nurture that reconnection with yourself. Recognize that in the history of this world, there has never been and will never again be another *you*. That is a huge deal, and that means your life and how you manage it is a huge deal. Don't you dare allow yourself to settle for living and loving like some second-class citizen.

Give yourself permission—in fact, demand of yourself—to go forward with hope, optimism, and unbridled passion. Don't be afraid to admit that you want it, and don't be afraid to get excited about having it. Living, loving, and laughing are as healthy and natural as anything you could ever do. I believe it is part of God's plan for this world. The only reason more people don't do it is because we, in our infinite wisdom, decided to "fix" the plan.

Get back to the basics that are set out in this book and

live them with the passion, energy, and excitement that you may not have felt since you were a child. Remember how you used to dance and sing when you were too young to be self-conscious and care what anybody thought? That's the feeling, that's the fearless and undaunted spirit that will light a fire under you, a fire that will surely engulf your partner in the heat of that passion. You have prepared to win. It is time to claim and live the victory.

The U.S. Department of Health and Human Services (HHS) Substance Abuse and Mental Health Services Administration's (SAMHSA) National Drug and Treatment Referral Routing Service provides a toll-free telephone number for alcohol and drug information/treatment referral assistance. The number is: 1-800-662-HELP.

National Domestic Violence Hotline
1-800-799-SAFE (7233)
The National Domestic Violence Hotline is staffed twenty-four hours a day by trained counselors who can provide crisis assistance and information about shelters, legal advocacy, health care centers, and counseling.

For a referral to a psychologist in your area, call 1-800-964-2000. The attendant will use your zip code to locate and connect you with the referral system in your area. If you do not live in the United States or Canada, contact your na-

tional psychological association or local mental health fa-
cility. If you believe you need immediate assistance, please
call your local emergency number or the mental health crisis hotline listed in your local phone book's government
pages.

LOCAL RESOURCES

State Department of Mental Health/Mental Retardation
County Mental Health Center
Local hospital—ask for social services